How to FISH the PACIFIC COAST

A Manual for Salt Water Fishermen

By RAY CANNON

Fish Delineations by Carla Laemmle

Lane Publishing Co. · Menlo Park, California

A Quest for Pleasure

Man's quest for the goal of complete pleasure can be achieved, but is seldom blundered into, and he must remember that the ocean gives up her riches reluctantly. Only the skilled and the alert, who disguise their wisdom behind that mask called "fisherman's luck," are consistently rewarded. And even the angler steeped in the sport who truly feels that he has achieved the ultimate in the art of ocean fishing has yet more to learn than all his experience has taught him.

The purposes of this book are many: To bring the salt-water angler up to date and supply answers to the perplexing questions that beset the beginner; to clarify the confusion of the common names of fishes; to advance the art of ocean angling; to stimulate general interest in the conservation of our mighty ocean resources; to equip the fisherman with "know how" by proposing the most effective size and type of tackle, kinds of bait, and methods of attaching or hooking; to give information on the geographical location of the various species, and the time to look for them.

Readers of this volume will profit from the work of many scientists who gave their valuable time and energy in advising me and in contributing and modernizing the data needed. The author cannot adequately express his obligation to them, particularly Dr. Carl L. Hubbs, of the Scripps Institute of Oceanography, and W.I. Follett, Curator of Fishes, California Academy of Sciences.

I am especially indebted to my teacher, Dr. Boyd W. Walker, University of California, Los Angeles, for research, for the "Description of the Fishes," and for assistance on writing various scientific material. I am grateful to the aquatic biologists of the California Fish and Game Commission, Marine Division: Dr. Frances N. Clark, John E. Fitch, Julius B. McCormick, William Ellis Ripley, Doyle E. Gates, Howard H. McCully, Richard S. Croker, Phil M. Roedel, and W. L. Scofield.

I am also grateful to Don Gooding and Les Hatch, Washington Fish Commission; and to Arbe J. Suomela and F. C. Cleaver, Oregon Fish Commission.

I am indebted to the scores of fishermen who let me in on their secret tricks and who helped test new ideas: Mike Haggar and Gregory Golubeff, specialists in rock fishing; Eddie Urban, albacore; Dr. Yin Kim and Harry Taggart, yellowtail; and experimentalists Don L. Gilman, Paul Fung, Cora Galenti, Key Chang, Pete and Bea Donaldson, and Dick Wotton.

At Ensenada, Baja California, help came from Braulio Maldonado and Gilberto Solis; in British Columbia, it was provided by Hal Denton and Jack (Pintail) Lillington; in Washington, Lew Holcomb; in Oregon, Don Harger, J. F. Flynn, and Ed Neal.

Also of great help were William J. Burke, Mrs. Joseph Laemmle, Louise Youngren, Martha Haggar, Mabelle James, David Chow, and James A. Farnsworth. Valuable assistance was given by numerous sports club officials, tackle dealers, and sport-fishing enterprises.

PHOTOGRAPHERS. Richard Ballarian: 40. Ray Cannon: 72, 88. Richard Dawson: 16. L. O. Gocean: 4. Mike Hayden: 24. Harry Merrick: 12. Jack McDowell: Cover, 1, 58. Darrow Watt: 30.

Tenth Printing January 1976

J. Edward Gough, D. M. D.

Contents

Lay of the Coastland

In length our fishing range extends from the southern tip of Alaska to the Bahia de San Quintin, Baja California. In width it reaches from the meeting place of the salt and fresh waters to the edge of the continental shelf.

❧ BAJA CALIFORNIA ☙

The southernmost point, the bay of San Quintin, and the waters around its offshore island, Isla San Martin, are teeming with sea life. In the early morning light the calm, glazed mirror of the surface is suddenly shattered by the surge of hungry sea creatures beginning another day in the eternal struggle for survival.

Every square foot of these waters contains millions of microscopic vegetable and animal organisms. This mass assemblage, called "the plankton," is nourished and developed by the nitrates, phosphates, and chemical changes in the water. The prevailing afternoon and evening winds of this region plow and churn and upwell the waters of the sea, causing a great concentration of plankton on the surface.

Early morning mist lingers amidst tall pines and driftwood along the Oregon coast. The north shore ranges from forest to rock pile-ups to sand.

At the first break of dawn, small patches of ripples begin to appear. In a matter of seconds, these disturbances extend until they cover acres. They are caused by ANCHOVIES, SARDINES, and other small plankton-feeding fishes skimming the surface for this rich food. As the light increases, silvery flashes appear in the ripples. Then, almost at once, a mound appears and boils; a dozen follow in rapid succession. One erupts, then another, until the entire surface is a mass of explosions, each revealing a great game fish slashing in pursuit of the forage fishes.

Attacked by a school of predators, a whole shoal of ANCHOVIES, whose main defense is in their vastness of numbers, tries to make individual escapes by taking to the air, sometimes leaping two or three feet. Such a commotion signals the beginning of a Neptunal war that approaches total chaos. Helldivers, cormorants, gulls, sea pigeons, and pelicans descend from above, diving down into the milling mixture.

Of all the land animals only man has achieved such a high degree of mass slaughter. "Havoc" and "chaos" could be used to describe the land's comparatively minor disturbances; but in this nether world survival beyond the day hangs barely on the fine line of chance. The appearance of a momentary lull is deceptive, for the rage continues beneath the surface in all its fury. As soon as a calm occurs in one spot, a crashing, splashing storm breaks out in another.

These separate "breaks" often form a pattern and move in one direction. The alert angler dashes in in an attempt to intercept and join the shifting battle. Often,

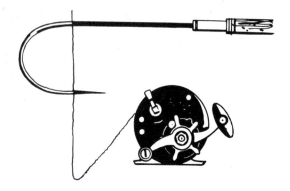

before he makes contact, greater denizens race toward the scene. The PORPOISE, SEA LIONS, and SHARKS catch the game fishes in such a mad frenzy that their presence is ignored. If the angler succeeds in making contact at this point in the frenzied commotion, and if he is a novice or not of a hardy and rugged nature, he is likely to become so panicky that he will wish he had stayed at home and in bed.

These fantastic carnages are very rare in the San Quintin area except in warm and less windy years. They occur quite often in coves and bays southward and throughout the Sea of Cortez (Gulf of California). The prevailing water temperatures are extremely cold in the San Quintin region and on up to Punta Banda. This is due to upwelling from great depths, caused by strong winds pushing the water shoreward. Some fishes occur in northern California and in these cold waters, but not in southern California.

The land at this southern tip of our range is arid and the foliage is of the desert type. But in the protected coves and bays northward along the coast the vegetation and its accompanying animal life thrive. Some forty miles north of the bay, the sandy beaches are abruptly halted by a magnificent, rugged shore line. The submarine rock gardens beneath the tide line are beyond description in their exquisite beauty. Masses of highly colored sea animals attach themselves to the rocks or travel among the varied sea plants that sway to the rhythm of the pulsating waters. Everywhere natural breakwaters jut out to form protected coves, some large enough to allow a fair sized boat to enter and dock. A road leading from Santo Tomas, about twelve miles inland, follows a stream down to this paradise for rock anglers.

At Punta Banda the formation suddenly changes again to massiveness. At spots sheer cliffs plunge from a mountain top to a depth of a hundred feet. At one place the face of a broad bluff tilts backward from the depths.

Enormous sea swells run as high as a hundred feet up the smooth surface, then break out into a crashing spray, a phenomenon so frightening that some cannot endure the sight of it. Deep holes around and between the bluffs are accessible to fishermen and harbor big fish seldom found near shore.

Punta Banda is the northern tip of a mountain forming a sturdy six-mile-long peninsula, which together with its small Isle of Todos Santos, protects Bahia de Todos Santos and the port town of Ensenada. This beautiful bay provides some fine WHITE SEABASS, YELLOWTAIL, and KELP BASS fishing. Quite a few of the species found here are seldom taken north of the locality.

Ensenada and the enchanting little resort places along the beach have kept abreast of the times in supplying facilities to fit the angler's needs. He may fish fifty feet from the door of his *cabaña* or go out to the deep sea in pursuit of the MARLIN and TUNAS.

Warm, sandy beaches, here and there broken by rocky formations, extend for seventy miles from Ensenada to the border. These surfs are calmed and somewhat protected by kelp fields. Surf casters' heaven is this area, and nine months of the year they explore and fish it. The reluctant CORBINA and king size SURFPERCH are fair game here. Skiffs with guides are available at every cove.

A few miles seaward, out beyond the first series of kelp beds, the ocean floor arches up again into a chain of submerged plateaus projecting above the surface at the north and displaying a row of peaks known as Los Coronados Islands. The territory around these islands and the shallow banks of the plateau are the foraging fields of great schools of big-game fishes.

Large numbers of private and party boats from San Diego and Point Loma fish these rich grounds, and seldom are the fishermen disappointed. Taking limits are to be expected. The number of big YELLOWTAIL encountered around these islands seems inexhaustible. Thousands are taken out annually without any apparent reduction in their numbers. Migrating BARRACUDA and BONITO are abundant near the banks. ALBACORE and BLUEFIN TUNA linger in more distant feeding grounds. But the most consistent and popular fish on all beaches in this whole region is the BARRED PERCH.

∾ SOUTHERN CALIFORNIA ∾

Anglers around the San Diego Bay area are easily able to find greatly diversified fishing here. There are at least a hundred excellent fishing spots in the bay and probably half as many more of them out along the open shore.

A dozen little towns lie along the coast and most of them have piers, party boats and barges for the convenience of anglers who wish to fish the kelp beds and off-shore banks. Boats from Oceanside and San Clemente fish from Dana Point to Catalina Island.

Along the shoreline of the colorful town of Laguna Beach, the Pacific waters have carved stone bluffs which resemble a massive Chinese garden, the gentle curves graduating into deep coves. Each is isolated from its neighbor by a colonnaded wall exhibiting some of the sea's finest handiwork. A few feet below the water's edge are flat footings for the lush sea plants. This rocky coast line, starting at Dana Point and ending at Balboa Bay, was one of southern California's best rock fishing areas—but pollution and overfishing depleted it.

There is hardly a place on earth where ocean angling is more popular than the expanse between Balboa Bay and Point Dume. Nearly every known style of salt-water fishing is practiced and every type of sea-going vessel employed. Six-foot kayaks and million-dollar yachts put out in quest of adventure that only fishing can supply. Hundreds of chartered and regularly scheduled boats land, and an even greater number of privately owned craft sail from the various harbors in the pre-dawn hours.

Great and small, the crafts venture to kelp beds, coves, and off-shore banks, or to Santa Catalina Island. Some go on to San Clemente Island and, when the ALBACORE come in, fish on the fourteen-mile bank and the shelves that radiate from Catalina and Santa Barbara Islands.

Fishing in this part of southern California is by no means confined to boats. On the beaches, the rocky shores, breakwaters, docks, piers, and barges, thousands of anglers seek the pleasure and prize of the sport. Few confine their quest to any single species. Even the "albacore special" boats turn about to find other fish when the TUNAS prove scarce.

NORTH OF POINT CONCEPTION

Fishes limited in their movements to the warm currents are plentiful as far north as Point Dume, but are scarcer north of Point Conception. Between these points anglers practice the art in the same manner as southward. Scheduled and charter-boat owners have developed live-bait facilities at Port Hueneme, Ventura, and Santa Barbara. The boats cross Santa Barbara Channel to fish around the islands, principally Santa Cruz.

North of Point Conception a change takes place: the shore water becomes cooler. Because of this temperature change, the Point is somewhat of a dividing line between a number of warm water species and those that frequent the cooler currents. But the species' food preference may affect its range limit even more than the temperature. The Point is thus not an abrupt dividing line. Many of the fishes common in one section are merely less plentiful in the other, or in some instances, they are rare.

The Morro Bay area has developed into an angler's Mecca since pioneering Virg Moores introduced live bait there some years ago. In addition to the vast numbers of LINGCOD and ROCKFISH, especially the abundant BLUE ROCKFISH, that rise to the surface for live bait, ALBACORE and SALMON have been added to party boat catches seasonally. The delightful bay abounds in HALIBUT, JACK-SMELT, and other species. The beauty of the wooded State Park and its small port attracts people from all southern California.

Freeways and access roads have opened up this shore area; and its fine rock fishing stretches up the coast and on past San Simeon.

With the exception of the Pismo Beach to Morro Bay section, the coast line between Point Conception and Monterey Bay has had little angling attention, not because of lack of fish but because so few people fish there. Lompoc, Santa Maria, and San Luis Obispo are the only centers of population in this coastal area, and only a few of the residents have recently discovered the thrill of ocean angling. Even fewer are aware of the abundance of fishes along the rocky portions of their coast line.

Some of the fishermen from the villages along the coast follow the methods of their European ancestors, who were the early settlers. They fish the off-shore reefs principally for ROCKFISH, FLATFISH, and LINGCOD, their knowledge of the fishing grounds qualifying them as guides for visiting anglers.

Ocean angling methods differ from one region to another, but there is at least one consistently practiced from Monterey Bay all the way up the coast to the northern end of our range: Slow trolling, a method used extensively in the pursuit of SALMON. The trolling speed is about three knots, one fourth the speed used south of Point Conception. Also different is the fishing depth, the trolling being done below thirty feet for the CHINOOK SALMON.

Monterey was a fishing center long before the arrival of the white man. Indians came from far away to troll-fish the bay in light flimsy canoes. The later settlers learned quickly from the Indians, but had to await the coming of the Chinese to learn methods of curing and processing their catches. New arrivals from Europe joined to establish a commercial fishery that continues today after a history packed with dramatic and thrilling incidents.

As we follow the coastland to the north, its nature changes from flat or rolling country covered with sage brush or scrub oak to heavily wooded areas, some even covered with the giant Redwood.

The town of Santa Cruz has become famous as a place to fish. The natives were among the first to discover that the SALMON is but one of many ocean game fishes. Nearly every village up to Point Arena has followed the progressive spirit of Santa Cruz in establishing facilities for the many new fishermen in the region.

⤐ SAN FRANCISCO BAY AREA ⤏

Further north, the San Francisco Bay area seems unlimited in fishing scope and richness. About twelve per cent of the million licensed anglers in the State of California fish this area. Among the many fishes found here, the STRIPED BASS commands top attention. This prolific import has continued to increase, and if the food supply is not destroyed by contamination will go on reproducing in such numbers as to keep the present horde of fishermen happy. However, anglers' organizations, aware of the danger, are advocating programs designed to stimulate fishing interest in species other than STRIPED BASS, SALMON and TROUT by promoting derbies and contests. Their success with such worthy endeavors should be widely supported.

The spinning and fly casting craze has had some influence in the glorifying of the SHAD and other fishes so plentiful in the bay. SHARK derbies have met with mixed enthusiasm in this area. But a well-publicized SHARK tournament for youngsters under good guidance should prove a whale of a success. The Bay could do well with fewer of these predators. Make sure all meat will be put to good use.

Party boats and other facilities in the Bay Area have been improved considerably in the past few years. Boat operators seem to have developed a lot of scientific "know how." If their aptness for finding fish is not based on knowledge, then they are masters of clairvoyance or black magic, for they really make contact. Fishing in these well-populated waters is "as you like it." There are so many species so widely distributed that there's plenty of elbow room for everybody. There is space for casting, lunching or sprawling, and you can fish any style you like within the bounds of good sportsmanship and the state laws.

In good weather, for most of the year, boats sail out to engage the sea-going SALMON, mostly within twelve miles of shore, or on out to the Farallon Islands, in late June and July. Live bait and improved tackle and tech-

niques have added much to the success and pleasure of these trips.

San Pablo and San Francisco Bays form a vast expanse of salt and brackish waters which serve many purposes in the lives of the anadromous fishes (those which go up a river from the sea to spawn). A few of these species remain in the brackish water for some time, as if to become acclimatized before ascending the streams to deposit their eggs.

The big future problem for SALMON and other species is water contamination. The vast quantities of ever-increasing pollutants have heretofore been pushed out to sea after being diluted with cleaner water. These will eventually pile up, making the bays fish-killing cesspools, unless they are halted before the dams divert the great flow. Every person in the Bay area should be enlisted in a crash program to eliminate every source of these poisons, *now!*

The most damaging bay pollutants at present are several industrial wastes, sprays for vegetation, and household detergents. Many of these deadly materials become fixed in solids and settle into massive deposits.

If non-poisonous detergents or soaps were used domestically and the solids partially removed, household sewage dumped into the open ocean would actually benefit fish and sea life. In the basic food supply of the Salton Sea is a vast quantity of pile worms, *Neanthes sp.* They thrive on kitchen and human refuse and are in turn a favored food for a great many fish species. However, large deposits of solids from these sources may have some adverse effect, especially in bays where the currents are not strong enough to transport them out to sea.

⤐ NORTHERN CALIFORNIA ⤏

State Highway 1, which follows the coast line northward, swings inland through San Francisco to cross the Golden Gate Bridge, then turns westward to the north of Sausalito and is enveloped in the Muir Woods as the road strikes the coast again. From this point to Fort Bragg are found magnificent expanses of wilderness, wisely preserved by the State as public parks. The jutting, curving shore line with its string of protective coves and rugged stone formations leaves little for the rock angler to desire; the water is loaded with fish.

Shallow-water ROCKFISH are abundant; so are SURF-PERCHES, SCULPINS, and GREENLINGS, with plenty of shellfish for bait. There are any number of bays and inlets suitable for launching an outboard, and most of the beach towns (five to ten miles apart) are well equipped with many different types of small craft for rent.

About thirty miles above Fort Bragg the road cuts inland to join U. S. Highway 101 which winds through miles of gigantic redwoods then hits the coast again near Eureka. Bay fishing in this area is excellent. CHINOOK SALMON, in company with SILVERS, is taken in the shallow water just outside the Humboldt Bay entrance. The runs follow the appearance of big ANCHOVY schools.

The STARRY FLOUNDER and the large BLACK ROCK-FISH *(Sebastodes melanops),* often called BLACK BASS, BLACK SNAPPER, and SEA BASS are quite plentiful in the bay. Half a dozen other FLATFISHES and ROCKFISHES frequent the backwaters and coves. SHAD, JACKSMELT, and SCULPINS are fished here with spinner and light tackle. All manner of boats are available for almost any type of fishing.

In half a dozen state parks between Eureka and Crescent City the prolific wild life of the land comes right down to the edge of the sea. Remote from the crowded centers of population, these immense, wooded territories are havens of refuge for the vacationer who craves escape from the city. He can pitch a tent or park a trailer beside a brook of clear, cool water; he can gather wild berries; and best of all, he can fish to his heart's content. A couple of hours of rock fishing on the incoming and high tides will net him more than enough of the most appetizing food a camper could wish for. In addition to the very abundant GREENLINGS and SEAPERCHES, he can find FRINGEHEADS and eel-like fishes among the submerged rocks covered with sea vegetation.

❧ *OREGON SHORELINE* ❧

One of the most astonishingly beautiful four hundred mile stretches in the United States is the section of Highway 101 where it hugs the shore line of the entire coast of Oregon.

There are more than a dozen major streams between the mouths of the Smith (at the southern border) and the Coos Rivers. Most of them attract the anadromous fishes—STEELHEAD, CUTTHROAT, SHAD, SALMON, and STRIPED BASS. Around the mouths of these streams a horde of sea forms congregate. Crabs and clams may be taken to supplement the fish diet. Rocky promontories that gradually submerge to form reefs are the habitat of GREENLINGS, FRINGEHEADS, SCULPINS, and shallow-water ROCKFISHES.

These rugged spots are too rough on gear for the commercial fisherman. The general lack of information on this area is due to the limited interest of the commer-cial man in fishing such rugged spots, the quantity of the commercial catch being the usual yardstick for measuring the abundance of fish. The native over-emphasis on SAL-MON fishing and the undeveloped technique of rock angling stem from the native's desire to catch a "whop-per" or nothing. He uses a hook and bait (or lure) so big that it keeps small-mouthed and wary fishes at safe distances. Old timers who have fished the rocky ledges of other areas are amazed at the number of GREENLING that can be taken here on No. 2 hooks with mussel bait and at the number of shallow-water ROCKFISHES taken on strips of GREENLING.

Small boats for bay and inlet waters are available at most of the towns and settlements; larger craft for trolling at Gold Beach, Port Orford, and Bandon. Practically every village has its quota of cottages, motels, and other conveniences for the comfort of the angler.

The city of Coos Bay is proud of its thriving sport fishing. From the dock, just a block from the main thoroughfare, a fleet of some of the finest trolling boats carries party loads and scheduled anglers to the calm waters of the bay for STRIPED BASS, and then out to sea for SALMON. Small rental and privately owned craft have blossomed out in response to salt-water angling enthusiasm. All types of trolling, casting, and light tackle can be seen in use. Fly casting into a school of SHAD is a popular development. Every part of this expansive bay has its specialized habitat for one or more species, and there are many kinds of fishes occupying these waters. People in this area, which includes North Bend, Empire, and Charleston, are hospitable; and this friendliness exists all along the Oregon coast.

Winchester Bay and the mouth of the noted SALMON run, the Umpqua River, where the human population multiplies by fifty-to-one during the fishing season, are well prepared with boats, great and small, to accommodate the ever increasing number of anglers. Wherever a stream empties into the salt water on this coast line STEELHEAD, CUTTHROAT, and a number of other species abound. Wherever clusters of mussels and sea vegetation are found there is an abundance of many kinds of fishes. The lay of the land eliminates the hazard of relying on chance in finding fish. If the wind is too strong for ocean fishing, there are nearly always lakes in the low hills that lie along the coast line. These quiet bodies of clear water are usually loaded with excellent food fishes.

Like most of the bays to the north, the Depoe and Yaquina are crowded with the BLACK ROCKFISH, which has all the qualities required: game, big, and a fine food fish easily taken on strip bait or lure.

Thousands of Portland's citizens find Tillamook Bay their ideal recreational area. These bountiful waters leave little to be desired for an outing. With few exceptions, all of the northern species of fish and shellfish abound in and around the bay. The mile-long rock jetty at Bar View provides some of the best rock fishing on the coast.

Towns and settlements along the bay are well equipped to supply the angler's requirements for whatever kind of fishing he may prefer. Despite the many different species available, SALMON is over-glorified here as elsewhere. This is not to suggest that the noble creature be shunned as a wonderful game fish but only an effort to bring attention to other fine fishes in these waters.

About eleven miles north of the beautiful vacation town of Seaside, Highway 101 cuts across to Astoria, renowned as the first American settlement on the Pacific coast and noted for its SALMON fishing and canning industry.

The far reaching tributaries of the enormous Columbia River find their sources in the snow-covered mountains; their plunging waters cradle the young SALMON and TROUT and supply the oxygen and rich food necessary for their survival. Over the years, man's demand and progress have threatened the existence of these noble game fishes. But if the artificially created spawning grounds prove successful, Oregon and Washington can again provide a great SALMON sport fishery in and around the mouth of the Columbia River. The brackish and salt water in the lower reaches of this prolific stream produces enough fighting, predatory fishes to keep many fishermen busy for the next century.

⌒✣ WASHINGTON ✣⌒

Thousands of miles of shore line encompass the inland sea of Washington and British Columbia, and thousands more form the island borders. Great variety can be found in the surroundings of these sounds and inlets, from gentle, sandy beaches to the primitive, timbered wilderness, from the soft, quiet waters of the coves to the tempestuous surge of the breakers. These vast expanses contain such a variety and number of sea inhabitants that they are beyond the conception of modern scientists. Some have suggested that there is enough nutriment in the plankton of these waters to feed the people of the whole continent.

Long before the white man came, the native Indians held a profound reverence for these waters and believed that the Great Spirit sent the fishes up from the depths as blessings for all who lived according to the faith. Present day rituals performed by a few of the tribes are based on this ancient belief. Dam builders have been plagued by the Indians when their work has interfered with the fishing rights held sacred by these tribes.

These immense bodies of water remain a wilderness to the average Washington angler. He has not yet explored the tremendous resources, but seems quite content to limit his pursuits to a couple of species of SALMON and TROUT when all about him there are numbers and species of fishes he has never imagined. Many of these excellent fishes inhabit such rugged, rocky places that their capture by commercial fishermen has proven unprofitable. As in Oregon, an estimate of their numbers has not been attempted. Several near-shore species also escaped the commercial nets and are therefore not included in the reports. Here too the SALMON and TROUT are over-emphasized while other fine species are ignored or labeled with such ignominious names as "rough fish" or "scrap fish."

Some purists may think it the height of sportsmanship to spend all day trying to hook a SALMON with a dry fly, but the principles of salt-water angling differ greatly from the ethical aspects of fresh-water fishing; new techniques must be applied. Each species responds to different kinds of baits and lures; to develop methods of tempting them requires patience and skill, and herein lies the art of the dynamic sport of ocean angling.

The visiting angler will find a new word to add to his vocabulary: "mooching"—a word applied to the old practice of halting every twenty or thirty feet while deep trolling. The procedure is quite effective for SALMON, since, following each stop, it brings the bait or lure into motion on an upward angle. "Spin-fishing" as practiced here is done from a stationary or drifting boat. The angler casts out and retrieves after the sinker has reached the desired depth. The words "spin" or "spinner" refer to a revolving lure, or more particularly to a strip of herring or other fish hooked in such a manner as to allow it to turn over slowly. The light rod and spinning reel are very popular, but not always used in this type of angling. While these two methods are the most prevalent, there are almost as many styles of fishing in this region as in all the other coastal areas combined.

The rugged ocean front and the beautiful bays along it are similar to the Oregon coast both in scenic beauty and abundance of fish. The growth of an exciting ALBACORE sport fishery is in the process of development on the off-shore banks. Out there too are a score of deep-water forms. Among them are the "BARNDOOR" (PACIFIC) HALIBUT, the yard-long (PACIFIC) COD, the 150-pound GIANT SKILFISH, huge SHARKS, and some of the larger members of the ROCKFISH family.

Along the rocky places of the ocean shore line, as well as in the inlets, are many game fishes. GREENLINGS (three species) are especially numerous. Abundant also are the SCULPINS (three species), LINGCOD, and shallow-water ROCKFISHES (five species). In addition there are half a dozen eel-like forms and other highly prized food fishes. Thousands of ideal spots are frequented by the great schools and crowds of fishes throughout the waterways of Washington.

No lack of transportation to the fishing grounds exists for nowhere else within our range are there so many boats per capita. When owners of this great fleet are alerted to the possibilities awaiting them, Washington will become one of the most exciting sections for salt-water angling in the Pacific.

Here too, the introduction of live bait promises to revolutionize the whole fishing procedure, not only on party boats but especially on private craft. Another boom in small boat construction and rebuilding has been started to accommodate live-bait tanks and the conversion to inboard-outboard motors. Very small boats are being fitted out with the new, portable bait-tanks. Improved tackle, from rod butt to terminal, and knowledge of techniques in their use have added much pleasure and efficiency to angling pursuits, all of which are opening up new angling arenas. Some considered to be almost barren have become highly productive when live bait is tried.

The forage and bait fish resources here, as all along the Pacific Coast, are threatened by the encroachments of pollution, dams, and overfishing. The human population increase and swelling interest in salt-water angling demand scientific studies and wise management.

❧ BRITISH COLUMBIA ❧

Vancouver Island, British Columbia, may appear as a small finger of off-shore land on the map, but in reality it is larger than the states of Massachusetts, Rhode Island, and Delaware combined. It is 282 miles long and averages fifty to sixty miles in width. Although it lies north of the 48th parallel (which runs near Paris, France), its winters are warmed by the mild Japanese current, yet kept cool in summer by a prevailing westerly wind. The atmosphere of the prosperous city of Victoria is essentially British. No other Canadian city has a milder climate; average annual rainfall is less than twenty-seven inches.

The island's outer coast line, especially the northern two hundred miles of it, is broken by inlets that penetrate far into the land. Some resemble the awesome fjords of Norway, while others are bounded by gentle forested slopes.

Some of the fishing grounds among them are truly

off the beaten track and can be reached only by boat or plane. Still others are yet to be explored by anglers. Those that have been have proven fabulous. Good highways are gradually being extended up both coasts.

The world famed Campbell River with its more than twenty motels has been equalled in popularity by such places as Comox and Cowichan.

A fairly seaworthy craft can sail up the Northwest Passages. If the search is for dramatic adventure, this voyage will supply it. Twisting whirling riptides and eddies surge through narrow, cliff-bound passages. Eagles, bears, and a few scattered tribes of Indians did almost all of the fishing along these waterways a few years ago. Here the SALMON and TROUT nearly choked the streams and some say that the great sea fishes died of old age in those days.

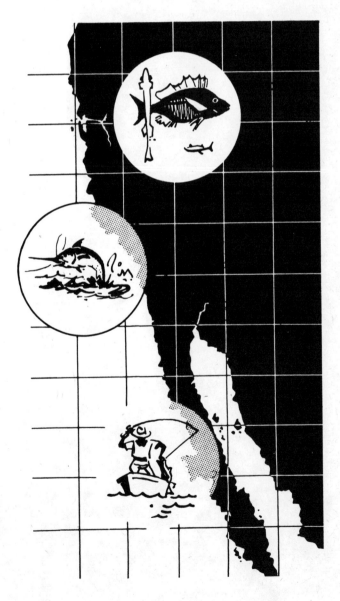

The Angler's Stake in the Future

The ocean and all that is in it, at least that part of it that extends from the low tide line out to the far edge of the continental shelf, belongs to you. No matter whether the title is claimed by the State or Federal Government, you have the final word in the management of the ocean's resources.

Since the ocean's resources are the personal property of every person in the nation, they should be protected by the government accordingly. The license fee paid by anglers and commercial fishermen gives them no special interest, since no governmental agency has been authorized by the owners of this property to grant any interests. It is therefore good horse sense for anyone harvesting these resources to be mindful of this and not abuse the limited privilege allowed.

The absolute necessity for outdoor recreation for the well-being of our citizenry is no longer theory; scientific facts have proven it. Now, with the rapidly diminishing wilderness and recreational areas, we must give profound thought to the ocean and must guard against destructions

A lone fisherman surveys the sea, regretful of the setting sun. The rich bounty of the ocean is the personal property of everyone in the nation.

of the main incentive that provides fishing recreation in it. We must regulate or halt every fish-depleting force or agency.

The greatest error in commercial fishing is in harvesting a species without reducing its natural predators. The second greatest is in failing to protect the food supply of that species. These important factors are controllable.

Once ocean fish population is reduced below the consistent predator demand, its chances of regaining former abundance is very slim indeed, if not impossible.

ᖷ CHAIN OF DEPENDENCY ᖷ

The food chain or supply was established by the processes of evolution and functioned in what appeared to be perfect balance until modern man started to work on it. The history of the fisheries of the Atlantic Coast gives a vivid picture of just how much damage can be done by breaking some of the links in the chain.

Suppose, for instance, that the vast ANCHOVY populations were destroyed. The whole area of the Pacific Coast could be seriously disturbed by breaking such a major link. And there is every reason to believe that this could happen. It is not necessary for man to capture the last member of a species to wipe it out. When depleted below a certain level, the species' natural enemies could possibly reduce it to total extinction.

The case of the passenger pigeon will serve as an example. According to our grandparents there was such an abundance of them that during the seasonal migrations the vast cloud-like flocks would completely block out the sun's rays. A few years of catching them for commercial purposes and the destruction of their feeding and nesting places reduced their numbers to a point where hawks, eagles, and other enemies eliminated the species.

Maintenance of the food supply is not merely a subject allied to conservation, it is the key to it which has not been given the attention it merits. The investigation of food supply should rate first place in marine studies; there is very little information on the subject at present. While we applaud the sincere efforts of the various commissions in establishing regulations and measures for the protection of our ocean fishes, we believe that every known or even suspected source of food supply should be firmly guarded, and that every move suspected of contributing to its reduction be halted until the scientists have made thorough studies.

ANCHOVY

Just after the fast decline of the SARDINE population, the ANCHOVY also appeared to become scarcer, due perhaps to the switch of predators to it. However, with the almost complete disappearance of the SARDINE, the ANCHOVY has regained something of its former numbers but continues to fluctuate up and down precariously.

Granting permits to net ANCHOVY for reduction to fertilizer and other purposes could be disastrous. But angling organizations must keep alert and aware of these threats in order to educate the public on the importance of the species.

There are so many enemies preying upon the ANCHOVY wherever it moves that there is grave danger of complete destruction if its numbers are reduced below the unknown safety level. Chaos seems a possibility if one considers what would happen if the ANCHOVY were reduced to extinction. The hungry hordes would turn on and hunt down the young of all the other fishes. Gambling commercially with this species is a dangerous risk.

KELP

Scientific knowledge up to the present suggests that man can do more to increase ocean fish populations by extending and maintaining KELP beds than by any other known method of control.

Proof of this was shown quite clearly in an elaborate Kelp Study program carried out by scientists of Scripps Institute of Oceanography, La Jolla, California, and sponsored by the California Fish and Game Commission. The author served on the Commission's Committee throughout the five-year study. Among the facts learned were:

KELP provides vast quantities of dozens of food items in the diet of game fish, from larval stage to adult; it provides protection for young and small forage fish from predators (this especially in the canopy of long, floating branches); it provides a haven for eggs that would otherwise be washed ashore, for food for organisms eaten by fish, and for many grazing fishes.

KELP's importance as a general habitat for fish was noted when plants set out were immediately occupied, especially by KELP BASS, indicating that more beds or extensions of old fields would serve to increase fish populations accordingly.

New strains of this plant have been discovered. One of them, off South America, grows in much deeper water than does the California variety. If adaptable to our coastal shelf, it could be transplanted in vast, new areas.

Another strain, which flourishes in warm as well as cool water, grows off Baja California. It could replace our local beds that seem to die out in especially warm-water years. Plants from it, transplanted off Southern California, flourished until destroyed by grazers.

However, Dr. Wheeler North, Director of Research of the Kelp Study, found a method of controlling grazers, thus giving every reason to believe that imported KELP strains will flourish if a large quantity is set out and kept under control until reproduction begins and the new plants establish themselves. The great ichthyologist, Dr. Carl Hubbs, overall head of the Study, concurs in this, as do other scientists concerned.

Unless transplanting, or some less harmful method of harvesting, is inaugurated, the rapidly growing demand for more and more recreational fishing will halt all KELP cutting—this, in a sudden explosion of indignation by an exploded human population. People will discount all of the old claims: that fish have no business to transact in the KELP beds, and that removing the important bulk of the plant is not damaging to fish life.

Another related study shows that our beaches are rapidly being eroded, the sand being dumped into deep, canyon-like trenches. Due to dams halting the free flow of streams, little or no sand is transported to the shores. Vast KELP beds would reduce the force of wave action, thereby delaying the final erosion for many years to come instead of the predicted thirty years.

⚮ GOVERNMENTAL REGULATION ⚮

The various bureaus and commissions of fisheries of California, Oregon, Washington, and British Columbia have, with the assistance of State and Dominion universities, conducted elaborate and splendid scientific studies. Their findings have been made available to the state legislative bodies. But too many people who can do something are too busy with the local economy, taxes, campaign funds, and legal clients to study scientific documents, especially when they deal only with the people's happiness. To some, happiness is not a commodity from which dollars can be obtained. One day, perhaps, these persons will realize that the lack of it can be very expensive.

Crash campaigns should be waged, not only to protect our dwindling natural recreational resources but to expand them by every means: buying islands and shore lines and access to them; constructing piers and marinas and small boat ports and havens; planting KELP fields; halting pollution of streams, bays, and backwaters; building natural spawning grounds for anadromous fishes; setting aside parts or the whole of our continental shelf as a recreational area.

If ever there was a reason to protect the CROAKERS and the STRIPED and KELP BASS, then there is now a far greater reason to take several other species off the commercial list. Fish that are vital to anglers and are of little importance in the commercial catch should be declared game fish and strictly prohibited in the market.

⚮ SPORT FISHING VERSUS COMMERCIAL FISHING ⚮

In regulating commercial fishing we already have enough scientific facts to warrant rigid management. In cases where a fish population is suspected of being reduced, commercializing it should be halted until research proves it has regained its former abundance, plus a surplus.

The present management of our ocean fisheries is a farce, its bag-limits ridiculous. There is a total lack of wisdom shown in holding angler daily-bag-limits down to two-to-ten fish, while allowing commercials to capture whole schools, and as often as they can. If a species has been depleted to the point where the small angler-bag-limit is necessary, then where is the logic in unlimited commercial hauls?

The realistic argument in favor of local commercial fishing is that it helps to keep favorable balances in fish populations.

Most all fishes are carnivorous predators, but when balances are maintained, good purposes are served. For example, the author has observed MACKEREL riding herd on a school of ANCHOVY without molesting any but the weak and non-conformist. By keeping the diseased or deformed members cleaned out, natural selective breeding-up of the stock is maintained. Also, when an individual ANCHOVY dashes out of the school for a morsel of food it is gobbled up, thus maintaining conformity in preserving a tight and single-minded school. This is necessary in forage fish, whose main defense is in their vast numbers. When over-abundant, however, MACKEREL, BONITO, or others may decimate whole forage fish schools.

There is much evidence suggesting that SHARKS and HAKE should be greatly reduced. In this, commercials could perform an important service to the angler and general public. The Russian boats now netting HAKE may be doing us a favor.

One of the most important findings made by scientist Dr. Elbert H. Ahlstrom was that young HAKE, in countless numbers, raid the spawning grounds of the SARDINE and ANCHOVY and may well be the vital limiting factor in the return of the SARDINE to its former abundance.

To survive, an ocean fish must reproduce in quantities to satisfy the natural predator demand, plus a spawning stock and plus enough surplus to guard against unusual disaster.

⚮ SALMON ⚮

Except for restocking the streams, CHINOOK and SILVER SALMON hatcheries have proven inadequate and not nearly as economical as artificial spawning and brooding grounds would be, if developed on a grand scale. These expensive grounds would require enormous sums initially, but if they were thoroughly and scientifically planned, the productivity of young SALMON, held back and protected from disease and predation until ready to enter brackish or salt water, they would soon compensate for all invested.

Large dams not only interfere with migration, they halt the transportation of rich silts and fertilizing chemicals that lodge in stream recesses and deep holes, thereby stimulating the growth of the young SALMON's basic food supply. Such a food supply would also have to be grown artificially.

The author is convinced that if 10 percent of the energy spent on other studies and efforts to save the SALMON were centered on created and controlled spawning areas, far more fish would be produced. This opinion is based on scientific studies and experimentation already done and proven.

Pier and Dock Fishing

There is very little, if any, real luck in fishing. We could say that the angler is sometimes fortunate in being at a certain place at the right time, and with the favored bait and know-how when fish occur. But all these can be calculated and remembered. These considerations can be applied when a seemingly lucky novice catches many fish on one side of the boat, while the experienced, astute angler gets nothing on the other.

Fishing techniques are not difficult to learn. They are more or less mechanical. But to become an astute angler, the art must be developed by practice and by alert and thoughtful experimentation. Even more important is a delicate and sensitive touch in working the bait, in responding to strikes, in setting the hook, and in playing the fish.

All that has been learned or may be gained from this volume will be of benefit, but new methods and combinations of old techniques should be employed in unfamiliar areas or in untried seasons. Then there are day-to-day or even hourly changes in fish behavior, brought on by a temporary, over-abundant food supply—or lack of it—tides, currents, and other turbulences, that must be met with new ideas.

Piers and docks are a natural place for beginning anglers to become initiated. There is always someone around to give advice or lend a helping hand.

These are but a few of the reasons why the art and techniques of angling ever evolve and become more refined. With these changes, new and improved tackle is introduced which, in turn, develops more refinement in skill.

One year after the first edition of this volume was published, most Pacific Coast anglers switched from long-shank to the small, short-shank hooks recommended. Then down went the hook sizes, smaller and smaller.

Spinning tackle and monofilament suddenly became popular and brought on some revolutionary changes; cat-gut leaders were discarded in favor of tying the hook directly onto the mono line, making the casting of small baits and lures easier and causing a boom in the lure business.

All of these advances experienced a setback during the over-warm years, when fish became so plentiful in California they could be caught in the old, primitive style. But in the following cool-water years, anglers were forced to return to the later meticulous methods. We can now expect a continuing decrease in hook, line, and rod sizes; improvements in glass rods; Dacron lines; even greater perfections in the spinning reel; and lures that will attract far more fish than ever.

All of this means that we will have to hustle to keep hep and be ready to learn a whole set of new tricks from year to year, ever trying to improve our angling art and technique.

If you have the soul of an artist and can see and feel the rustic charm of old wooden structures that have long

withstood the lash of time and tide, you will at once recognize something of the hypnotic spell that compels addicts of pier fishing to return again and again, day after day, to the same old spot. Fish or no fish, rain or shine, you will see them, happy, cheerful, and contented, ensnared in the mesh of a magnetic net of their own mental creation.

Here is a place for the beginner to wet his line. It isn't necessary for him to buy a lot of fancy tackle to start with—everything can be rented on the pier or nearby. Also, the greenhorn can rest assured that his mistakes will be overlooked by fellow anglers. If he feels inclined to ask questions, he'll find instructors by the score who will lean over backwards in supplying information. When he gets a hookup, he'll have a like number of coaches. He only has to yell, "Net!" and some helpful neighbor will obligingly drop everything, rush for the net, and lift the catch safely upon the deck—maybe.

The old mussel-covered pilings attract an abundance of fish and they can be taken. There are numerous piers along the Pacific Coast where live bait is available. It is advisable, nevertheless, to take along a few shrimp and some fresh fish, such as mackerel, herring, or sardine which make excellent bait when cut into long, narrow, minnow-like strips. Mussels, small clams, and marine worms can also be used to catch the smaller fishes. Angle-worms or other baits that are highly intriguing to fresh-water fish will not interest the salt-water forms.

The angler who frequents piers sometimes carries a bait container, usually a two or three-gallon plastic kitchen bucket or a special minnow bucket which has a perforated lid, and a gunnysack which he hopes to fill, or at least not take home dry and empty. He prefers a wooden or plastic tackle box. The ordinary metal tool box rusts too quickly. He carries extra loaded reels; a dozen or more sinkers of different weights, from small twist-ons to heavy eight-ounce safety anchors; a couple of snag lines made up with a dozen or more small, plated triple hooks; a couple of dozen hooks of varying sizes, some on "Sevalon" leaders; a few lures, such as small feathers and chrome-plated and white spoons; a sharp knife; a wire cutter; pliers; a few lock swivels; a hook hone; a large pier screw hook to hold the rod; and most important, a lot of optimism.

The time, tide, and weather conditions are given the same careful consideration as for surf and rock fishing. The early morning incoming tide brings with it the fish that are apt to be more active in their search for food. Moreover, the pier angler is fortunate in that he will get a crack at them coming and going. Most shallow-water species are tide followers.

The technique of pier fishing differs greatly from that of any other phase of angling, particularly in casting. Since the overhead method is forbidden on piers frequented by a great many people, the under cast is used. Here is the method: Hold the rod straight down; reel up until the sinker is within three or four feet from rod tip; throw free-wheeling release; start sinker swinging. (Under most piers there are pipes, wires, or cross-beams. If the swing is too forceful, it is apt to foul in them.) Start the casting swing slowly, increasing the force until the rod comes up to an angle just short of forty-five degrees before releasing the thumb pressure on the spool, yet holding a slight pressure on side of spool as in over-casting. To avoid backlash, exert heavy pressure as the momentum begins to slacken. Accuracy in casting is essential, as the lane between other anglers' lines is sometimes very narrow.

Most pier fishermen like a long, flexible rod, principally for the casting value, for keeping the fish from circling the piling.

The weight of the sinker used is determined by the force of the drifting current. It should, however, be kept as light as possible. With sizable live bait, sinkers and swivels are seldom used.

With a spinning outfit, small baits and lures can be cast a greater distance, but if the rod is very flexible, preventing the fish from circling the piling is not easy.

❧ MORE PIERS FOR JUVENILES ❧

Most everyone, except juvenile delinquents, crooks, and hypocrites, talks and preaches against juvenile delinquency and sin, but serious attempts to provide healthy and happy diversions for the young are ridiculously overlooked. Why is this so, when it is so commonly believed that "there is never a juvenile delinquent behind a fishing rod"?

If ever there were values in providing wholesome recreational opportunity for the public, then certainly building piers for angling should rate among the most urgent solutions. Not only do they keep youngsters gainfully occupied, but, more important, they provide satisfaction with life in a complex civilization. The immense pleasure to our aging citizenry should also be included in the potential values.

Can we think of a more gratifying inducement for a recreational area than fishing? Where localities, counties, and states are reluctant to finance pier construction, bonds could be issued and redeemed by token admissions and concessions.

Organizations interested in any phase of the welfare of the young could find very few other ways of using their energies more profitably or rewardingly than by taking groups of kids for a day's fishing. Very little propaganda or urging would be necessary to get children to go all-out for such a fishing project, and once they get the feel of it they will appreciate the privilege.

In the construction of fishing piers, many facilities could be installed to add convenience and attractiveness, such as several live-bait tanks; flushing, fish-cleaning tables; charcoal broilers; smoked fish ovens; several rest rooms; tackle lockers—all facilities being in the center of the pier. A bit of good engineering could no doubt add numerous features that would be advantageous.

Chumming around piers on a large scale often attracts quantities of fish, but some study is needed to estimate the amount and kind of chum most effective.

Since the early printings of this book, several angling piers have been built and old ones made safe for youngsters' finest game.

❧❀ CALIFORNIA HALIBUT ❀❧

HALIBUT is the big "take home pay" for pier fishermen and is a difficult fish to catch when not very hungry or excited. The HALIBUT lies flat on the bottom and observes the goings-on. If he sees a live ANCHOVY, small QUEENFISH or a reasonable facsimile that seems to be in trouble, he may venture an investigation if too much effort is not required. He will flip up and jostle his prey; and if it seems stunned by his blow, taste it gingerly. If favorable, he may do a little munching until he is sure he has killed it. He is then likely to make a run while holding the morsel by the tail, before swallowing it.

These shenanigans are understood by the experienced and patient angler, for each move is telegraphed through the taut line to his sensitive rod. When he feels the time is right, the fisherman slowly lifts his rod until he recognizes by the weight that the fish has taken the whole bait. Then begins a very careful contest. The HALIBUT may submit without a fight at first, or he may make a terrific run. The angler must be alert to this uncertainty and ready to give line, carefully guarding against too much slack. Star drag is set at very light tension.

A HALIBUT once hooked must never be given a loose line, or he will in all probability dislodge the hook or tear it out. Because of the thin, weak membrane of his mouth, this fish must never be yanked or given enough freedom to allow him to jerk the line. A taut line at all times is the rule. Because of this mouth weakness, it is wise to use a net or gaff to lift him to the pier. While waiting for the net to be lowered, the fish must be played cautiously. Many a big one is lost at this stage. Never lift his head above the water and always be ready, with the reel in free wheeling, for a run. Some anglers keep the HALIBUT going around in small circles until the net is a foot or so under water, then maneuver him into it.

It is important in fishing for HALIBUT to locate his hideout. The angler casts a heavy sinker out. Then, by lifting his rod slowly, reeling in as he lowers it again and repeating this procedure, he can feel the sinker sliding down the shelf into a depression. He repeats this prospecting until he finds the deepest hole, then proceeds to fish it.

The bait is cast out just past the hole and slowly pulled down the slope. If the bait is very lively, the angler will then allow it to run for a few minutes and await developments. If, however, the bait is listless or dead, he continues to pull it with short jumps. But the moment he feels a slight tug or strike, he quickly pays line, giving the fish time to work it over.

A small No. 4 to 2 short-shank hook is used when the HALIBUT is finicky, for he will quickly let go if he feels the metal touch his mouth. When excited and gulping everything in sight, he can also be taken on a variety of lures. STRIPBAIT (see Fig. 2) often proves to be much more effective.

On rare occasions a number of HALIBUT will chase a school of ANCHOVIES or other forage fishes to the surface. At first sight of the jumping ANCHOVIES, the angler will quickly get to work with his lure. He casts out past

the school and retrieves with short, pumping motions, not through the middle of the swirling mass, but to one side to avoid scattering them.

🕊 STARRY FLOUNDER 🕊

This FLOUNDER is the most abundant FLATFISH to be found around docks and piers between Point Conception and Alaska. It is a very palatable food fish, and is much sought after by anglers of all ages. It is not only captured along the ocean and bay shores, but for a considerable distance up streams. It is in this respect a rarity among FLATFISHES.

Like many other members of this family it favors a sandy bottom in which to cover itself. It has a somewhat keener sense of sight than the others. The eyes project well above the eye sockets and roll around. Each seems to get its own "eyeful." This wide range vision may account for the FLOUNDER's boldness in taking the bait.

While the STARRY FLOUNDER attains a length of three feet, those taken from piers and docks average about one foot, or in some areas sixteen inches.

This fish is not too choosy about bait but has preferences according to locality. It may be stripbait in one area, a piece of shellfish in another. In and near the mouth of a stream crawfish, shrimp or other crustacean is preferred. A No. 1 hook is generally advisable but where they are running small, a No. 2 to 4 hook may prove more productive.

🕊 TURBOTS AND SOLES 🕊

Many of these fishes are taken more or less in the same manner, the bait varying according to the abundance of it in the specific locality. Although there are many species entering shallow water, there are seldom more than two or three found in any one locality.

We believe that there is a very wide distribution of small FLATFISHES and that they are far more plentiful than anyone knows. Their habit of cupping to form a vacuum on the bottom makes netting difficult for the commercial fishermen; therefore their presence is not always apparent. Anglers using large live bait have also missed them. Some few species will take very small anchovies (pinheads) if the bait is tail hooked. Stripbait is more effective for the greater number; however, squid, shrimp, and clams are preferred in some localities. Crawfish and ghost shrimp may be added for the species frequenting

backwaters. Most FLATFISHES running above four or five pounds will take fairly large live baits.

Regardless of the type of bait, the technique of hooking the smaller species from a pier follows the same general pattern. The bait is pulled along just above the bottom for ten feet or more, then upward for about eight feet. Strikes are ignored until the fish is hooked.

North of Point Arena immature PACIFIC HALIBUT are also caught from docks and piers in the same manner as other small FLATFISHES.

🕊 TOMMY CROAKER (MISCALLED "TOM COD") 🕊

The angler who restricts his fishing activities to one locality can't imagine how utterly confusing is the mixup of the common names of the fishes. This particular species is a fair example. About half of the old-time fishermen south of Santa Barbara called it "TOM COD." They couldn't have done much worse. They might as well have called it "tom tuna," "tom catfish" or "tom whale"; no name would have been more confusing. Other fishermen, to belittle the name "TOM COD," sarcastically dubbed it "PASADENA TROUT." There definitely is a TOM COD, *Microgadus proximus*. It is a true COD and is properly named. Furthermore it is just about the most abundant fish taken from piers and docks north of San Francisco.

Some attempt was made to popularize the name "KINGFISH," but this one died of ridicule. Anglers apply this name to the big fighting SIERRA, a very popular game fish around Florida and the Bahamas.

Heretofore the TOMMY CROAKER has been called "TOMMY" by about one-third of the fishermen. Therefore the addition of "CROAKER" is the logical step and will no doubt help develop a higher regard for this deserving fish.

No other fish is so maligned as this CROAKER. The malicious treatment given the fine fish by some pier fishermen is shameful. His stealing bait (and often getting himself hooked) when the angler is after larger fish is no excuse for bouncing him on the pier and throwing him back, dead.

It is doubtful if a gourmet could distinguish between this fish and a small YELLOWFIN CROAKER if cooked and served in the same manner. Very few anglers are able, without close examination, to recognize the difference in the appearances of these two fishes.

The TOMMY CROAKER can be taken the year-round on almost any kind of bait kept in motion near the bottom. Strips of mackerel, anchovy or sardine are best.

The small, parasitical, worm-like bodies sometimes

found imbedded in the flesh of this and many other salt-water fishes are not toxic within our range.

The presence of great numbers of FLATFISHES near piers along the southern California coast can in a measure be attributed to the abundance of the young of the TOMMY CROAKER. In addition to being an important forage fish, it is a preferred bait fish for KELP BASS and CALIFORNIA HALIBUT.

❧ TRUE CODS ❧

There are three members of the true COD family within our range that are of interest to anglers. The (WALLEYE) POLLACK is seldom taken by anglers because of its feeding habits. Its principal food consists of the minute animals of the plankton and slightly larger crustaceans.

The big PACIFIC COD is an all-around popular fish and can be taken in water as deep as 100 fathoms as well as at a depth of ten feet. It seems to migrate between these depths at certain times of the year. This cod is very abundant at the extreme northern end of our range. A few are caught from docks and piers half way down the Oregon coast. A bottom feeder usually preferring shrimp, it will readily take a strip of fresh fish or meat of shellfish. To preserve its high quality, the flesh must be kept damp and cool.

The small member of this group, the (PACIFIC) TOM COD competes with the STARRY FLOUNDER for juvenile pier and dock fishing interest in the northern reaches. At Eureka and to the north there is an ever increasing number, especially beyond the straits and sounds of Washington. Although a bottom feeder, the TOM COD will follow the bait to the surface when not overfed. In backwaters and near stream entrances, crawfish and the necks and meat of clams are choice baits. Strips of fresh fish seem more generally preferred otherwise.

❧ QUEENFISH ❧

It is difficult to understand just how this relative of the WHITE SEABASS, CROAKER, and CORBINA ever became so widely miscalled "HERRING." It doesn't resemble any of the members of the HERRING family, Clupeidae. (For characters see the section on fish identification.)

The QUEENFISH is excellent not only as bait for larger fishes, but also as a pan fry for every fish-eating human. The flesh is fine-grained and the flavor delicate. Next to the TOMMY CROAKER, this one is the most constant and can be depended upon ten months out of the year south of Santa Barbara.

When the sea is not too roily and the wind not strong enough to whip up whitecaps, the QUEENFISH will be around to accommodate the angler when larger fish are reluctant, or conspicuous by their absence. This is not to imply that every novice can catch a sackful by scratching his left knuckle and wishing. The QUEENFISH must be seduced with a certain amount of subtlety.

Skill, practice, and proper gear are required in taking a goodly number of the mature QUEENFISH. Rig up two No. 2 hooks on monofilament. Attach these a foot and a half apart on a three-foot leader; a light clamp-on sinker will suffice for weight. Try casting back under the pier where the bait tank overflow drops. An assemblage of big, lazy "QUEENIES" usually congregates there waiting for the half-dead anchovies that are carried down the drain.

Begin by allowing the sinker to go to the bottom; then retrieve until feeding depth is located. Let the bait sink a couple of feet below this point; then retrieve slowly and continue the slow pull regardless of strikes. The QUEENFISH will often nibble the trailing end of the bait before swallowing the whole of it. When fairly certain the fish is hooked, step up the tempo of the pull, but don't yank.

The first choice for bait is a very small, live grunion or anchovy on the top hook and a strip of anchovy or mackerel on the lower one. If no small live bait is available, use the strips on both hooks. These strips are fashioned to resemble small, slender fish about two inches long. The flesh is scraped from the small, tapering end of the slice to give a wiggly tail-like effect when drawn through the water. The hook is inserted through the thick end. (See Fig. 2.)

QUEENFISH have been depleted in some areas due to pollution from poisonous industrial wastes, certain detergents, insecticides, and petroleum. Household and flooding discharges have little or no harmful effect.

❧ YELLOWFIN CROAKER ❧

YELLOWFIN CROAKER are caught from a few piers in late afternoon on an early evening high tide near pilings and among the breakers. Strips of anchovy, mussels, shrimp, and soft-shell sand crabs are good bait, but pile or sand worms are still better.

There is usually enough commotion in the water along the breaker line to move the bait. While the YELLOWFIN is ordinarily a bottom-feeder, it will rise to feed a couple of feet from the surface near the piling. Although scarce for several years, there are signs of a comeback.

❧ (PACIFIC) MACKEREL ❧

Because of the great fluctuation in abundance, this fish should be scientifically managed. In favorable years it could become one of the most popular game fish for pier anglers, as it is along the Atlantic seaboard. Eastern anglers, who pursue it with light tackle, consider its thrusts and tenacity as qualifying attributes of a first-rate game fish.

Around piers the MACKEREL is usually a top feeder. In addition to live bait, fresh-dead and strips of fish, he can also be taken on shiny lures or feathers. When hungry (and he is most of the time), he will take any moving bait. Cut the first MACKEREL caught into strips and prepare it in the same manner as for QUEENFISH bait. Best of all bait is the "strawberry" *(pyloric caeca)*, a mass of small extended sacs attached to the intestines. Cast bait out away from the pier and retrieve with short, jerky motions. If the pier is crowded, the fisherman will have to "horse" a hooked MACKEREL quickly, or there will be a lot of lines to untangle, for this one is all over the place in an instant.

❧ MACKEREL JACK ❧

A member of the JACK family, Carangidae: here is another name that is all mixed up. Fishermen in some California localities have dubbed this JACK a "SPANISH MACKEREL," a name long established for some very large game fish in the family Cybiidae, of which the SIERRA and (MONTEREY) SPANISH MACKEREL are members.

In an attempt to straighten out this muddle, the California Fish and Game Bureau tried "HORSE MACKEREL," but that name was already established in anglers' minds as referring to the giant ATLANTIC TUNA. A few years ago it was changed again. This time to "JACK MACK-EREL," with the idea in mind that it would, when canned, be an acceptable substitute for (PACIFIC) MACK-EREL. This plan succeeded as far as the market was concerned, but the angler was not impressed.

The new Hubbs and Follett name, "MACKEREL JACK," seems to be most appropriate, since the fish does have somewhat of a mackerel-shaped body. The name also carries over a part of the old "moniker."

❧ (CALIFORNIA) BONITO ❧

Since those bygone days when schools of big-game fishes chased SARDINES around piers, the BONITO has become the most exciting fighter the pier angler of southern California is likely to tie into. He hits as if rocket-propelled and is not always choosey about what he strikes. If there happens to be a school of hungry MACKEREL around, the voracious BONITO will literally churn the water trying to beat the MACKEREL to the food. The more agitation, the easier he is to catch. Small anchovies (pinheads) are first choice as bait.

Bonitos seldom come in around the piling, but a fair-sized cast will reach them. The most interesting method we have ever witnessed for stirring a school was used by an old hand at pier fishing. At first sign of the school, he rushed to the bait stall and returned with half a bucket of dead anchovies and began throwing them out as far as he could. In no time the sea gulls began diving for the chum. The fuss and turmoil drove the BONITO into a frenzy; they slashed and snapped at any kind of a lure.

❧ SURFPERCHES ❧

Back along the surf line, the pier fisherman finds an excellent position to watch SURFPERCHES as they follow the tide and feed in very shallow water at high tide. If the water is clear, they may be seen feeding on soft-shell sand crabs, which usually make the best bait. They are also fond of mussels, pieces of shrimp, and very small, soft rock crabs. No. 6 hooks are used. Little skill is necessary in catching them. However, caution is required in bringing them in. Their mouths are soft and the hook will be dislodged if any slack is allowed. The rule for landing them is "easy does it."

WALLEYE SURFPERCH are taken near the piling all along the pier. The large PILEPERCH will take mussel or small stripbait.

❧ SMELTS (SILVERSIDES) ❧

TOPSMELT are caught from southern California piers with a string of very small hooks and small baits of almost any kind. The larger JACKSMELT are a little more standoffish and have to be coaxed. If a handful of chopped pieces of mackerel, anchovies, or mussels is thrown out around the pier as a chum, the JACKSMELT will almost always gather around. Two No. 4 hooks on a long mono leader with a light sinker will do it.

In one locality, the JACKSMELT will pass up every bait except mussels; in another, small strips of mackerel or anchovy will get them. The unpredictable appetites of these fish suggest that the pier fisherman going especially after SMELT should be prepared with enough kinds of baits to be ready to establish a cafeteria for them.

There are times and places between Ensenada and Coos Bay when big JACKSMELT are the most abundant of all fish near docks and piers and can provide some very exciting fishing on lightweight spinning tackle. Very few are needed for a delicious and wholesome meal.

If the fish are kept in a wet sack and in the shade, their delicate flesh will remain firm and sweet.

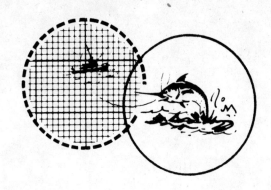

❦ *BARGES* ❦

For many years, large ships, usually very old, have been converted and fitted out as angling barges. They are anchored offshore along the southern California coast, and more recently, in some few bays in the north. More can be expected.

All the good that can be said of pier fishing is multiplied on barges. Here again is a safe and delightful place for the young, the aged, and all between, especially those who prefer more quiet relaxation than is encountered on a cruising boat.

The conveniences include a good galley, tackle store, fish-cleaning facilities, toilets, lots of tables and benches, and the helpful services of a skipper and crew. Some barges have overnight staterooms or bunks. Large shore boats run on a schedule, some every hour from 6:00 or 7:00 A.M. to 4:00 to 6:00 P.M.

Barges anchored behind breakwaters or in protected bays may remain in operation most of the year. Those in exposed waters close and are towed to ports when the winter storm season begins, remaining there until the spring let-up.

The fishing methods are much like those aboard a party boat but with more freedom to move about the large deck, sprawl out, or get exhausted fighting game fish that collect around to get in on the free chum tossed over for the purpose of keeping them close to the hull.

In the south, big schools of BARRACUDA, YELLOW-TAIL, and a lesser number of WHITE SEABASS and KELP and SAND BASS can be expected seasonally. MACKEREL and TOMMY CROAKER seem always to be present. But most consistent of the furious fighting gamesters are BONITO, during their more prolific years. For these and the other large top-feeders, there is one trick all barge anglers should learn. Instead of casting the live bait out, which stuns it, the method of "flying" the bait should be practiced.

Flying is a popular term but is not very descriptive. In practice, a large and alert bait is selected, quickly hooked, dropped to the water and allowed to swim out as far as it will go, with the current, if running. A lightweight mono line with the hook attached directly to it is used, but no sinker or swivel.

For extra exercise, break out the feathers or other whitish lures. Overhead casting is okay, providing great care is taken to avoid hooking a passing fisherman.

Bottom-fishing is about the same as around piers, with the addition of many other species. Some large visiting schools of ROCKFISH, SABLEFISH, and LINGCOD occasionally swarm in.

Night fishing aboard can get highly exciting, and for anglers who are especially interested in SHARK fishing, disappointment is rare. Some species grow to enormous sizes and equal the best of our other game fishes for toughness, tenacity, and tearing up the ocean.

❦ *BONITO* ❦

Barge, pier, and party boat owners have lost fortunes, and anglers tens of thousands of pleasant fishing hours, simply because the fine qualities of the BONITO were not emphasized. This par-excellent member of the SPANISH MACKEREL family not only puts up a strenuous battle but is tops for smoked fish. It is also rated highly for baking and broiling, but is not as delicate as others for frying, unless bled when first caught. This is done easily by cutting the throat terminal.

J. Edward Gough, D. M. D.

Surf Fishing

The aristocrat of ocean fishermen is the surf angler. His pride, prestige, and dignity would be shattered if he were caught fishing on a pier, a boat, or off the rocks. He would no more fish such places than a dry-fly man would use angleworms.

The surf man's field is the soft, clean beach, where the foaming white breakers beat to the rhythm of the sea's pulse and recharge the waters with effervescing oxygen. There is no other type of fishing that seems to have such a magnetic drag on its followers. Such is the lure of the laundered sands.

Some surf fishermen may go out for the inspiring beauty, some for the restfulness, the sun tan, the cure, physical or mental. But when the endeavor of those who go down to the sea after fish is planned and executed correctly, there are fish to be taken.

Like the rock angler, the surf man enjoys dealing with nature single handed. He dislikes being surrounded by man-made contrivances and helpers to give him bait and gaff his fish. His ideas of the sport are exactly opposite to those of the SWORDFISH angler, who fishes from a swivel chair and has almost everything done for him, even to having the boat chase his hooked game fish. The surf angler likes being a "lone sea wolf."

Surf fishing attracts the angler who wishes to contact and contest nature all by himself. Good casting techniques and a tide timetable are essential.

Anyone can develop a sufficient amount of casting technique with a little practice. With a bit of "horse sense" properly applied, he can become a fairly good surf fisherman. To qualify as a surf angler, however, there are things that the beginner must know and know how to use, such as equipment, bait, and when, where and how to get the fish.

The extraordinary length of the surf rod gives the angler many advantages. It gives a high angle to the line, keeping it above the surf wash and the pull of the shallow beach undertow. When the line is allowed to drag on the sand or bottom, light strikes cannot be observed. The length and flexibility of the rod amplify the vibration of the strike when the rod is being held, and is easy to see when the rod is set.

☙ CASTING ❧

It is in casting that the whip and length really count, and the surf angler loves to cast. The physical satisfaction of the heave and the appeased ego when the sinker pulls off line by the hundreds of feet certainly eliminate, temporarily at least, any feeling of inferiority the angler may have.

Before starting the cast, the novice must make sure that the reel spool is in free-wheeling, the left hand grasping the bottom of the butt, the right hand at the reel seat grip with the thumb on the spool. (If you're a southpaw, you're on your own.) The rod is held over the

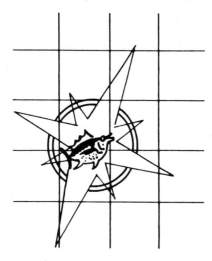

right shoulder; the sinker, suspended three or four feet from rod tip, touches the sand. Some champions stretch out eight or ten feet of line from tip to sinker; but for the beginner, the shorter length is recommended.

The eyes are kept on the spot aimed at. The swing, up and over, begins slowly, increasing until the top of the arch is passed. The rod is brought down to slightly less than a forty-five degree angle or pointed at the sailing sinker, the angle calculated to keep the line playing out straight with the rod. If the line running through the tip-top guide is going out at an off angle, it will reduce the distance and more than likely cut the guide. The amount of thumb pressure to apply must be learned by experience. It should be held at full pressure, then partially released when the rod passes the apex. If released too soon, the result will be a high loop; if too late, the cast will be short. At the release, the thumb shifts to the side of the spool and a very slight pressure is maintained, tightening up as the momentum slackens. And now comes the most ticklish hazard to good casting; if the final pressure is applied either too early or too late, a backlash is almost certain. It is doubtful whether anyone can be taught a sure cure for backlashing. It must be overcome by practice.

For the squidder-type, a conventional reel built for a 250-yard capacity, loading with only 200-yards of Dacron or mono line is advisable, thus leaving room for thumbing the side of the spool when casting instead of forcing the thumb-burning method of thumb-on-line to avoid backlashing and bird's nests. The spinning reel should be kept loaded to full capacity, always with lightweight mono. (See section on tackle.)

In addition to the sand spike for holding the rod, and the creel-type bag instead of the heavy tackle box, some special items are needed for increasingly popular night fishing; i.e., a night lantern, a change of shoes, and dry clothing.

CROAKERS AND (CALIFORNIA) CORBINA

SPOTFIN, YELLOWFIN CROAKER, and the most sought after of all, the highly prized CORBINA, are increasing in numbers, and you may see surf men way down along the sandy shores below the border, all the way to San Quintin Bay after them.

At high tide the CORBINA and SPOTFIN come in fairly close. To determine the distance at which they are feeding, vary the length of the cast until the heavy strikes begin.

The (CALIFORNIA) CORBINA is the most difficult of the surf fishes to hook. On occasion a whole school of them can be seen feeding on soft-shell sand crabs all around the angler's hook, but ignoring his bait completely. Some say that the large-size hooks keep them away; others maintain it is the heavy, short leader. We support both contentions and add that the method of hooking the sand crab has something to do with it. The hook should be inserted up through the tail end with the barb of the hook barely exposed. The bait should not be kept in constant motion, but pulled in very slowly, two or three feet at a time, then allowed to rest for a half minute before the slow retrieve is repeated.

A six-ounce, or less, pyramid or triangle sinker, just heavy enough to hold against the undertow or current, is tied to the end of a four-foot, 10 or 12-pound test monofilament line with a No. 2 to 6 short-shank hook on a 3-foot mono leader, attached one foot above the sinker, for CROAKERS, or a four or five-foot, very lightweight, mono leader for CORBINA.

While the soft-shell sand crab is most often the preferred bait, there are times and conditions when the CORBINA will insist on pile or rock worms or mussel.

When fishing in a bay, or where the water is not overly agitated, the competitive instincts of both the CORBINA and the CROAKER can be aroused by chumming in the following manner: Open about a dozen mussels and, without removing the meat, dump them into a likely hole or depression. This will attract numerous small fry and the resultant commotion will in turn attract the larger game fish. The hook, baited with mussel, is then dropped a few feet down tide from the chum.

The next thing for the beginner to consider is the landing. When a big one is hooked, the angler shouldn't run back away from the water unless the fish makes a run in his direction faster than he can possibly reel in. He keeps the rod up and ready to lower it at the slightest pull of the fish, in order to avoid any sudden jerk. This is no easy matter, for herein lies the surf man's skill. He must work the fish in smoothly to a point where he can time his action with a breaker and use its momentum and extra water to skid the fish to the sand. He then quickly gets to his catch, sticks his fingers through its gills, and takes it back a safe distance before removing the hook.

The surf fishes, like many others, have diverse appetites. While those of one section may crave a juicy morsel of mussel, those of another may dote on soft-shell sand crabs. However, sand worms, pile worms, rock worms, or whatever you choose to call the many species of marine worms, will attract CROAKERS when all other enticements fail. A goodly assortment of the various baits should be obtained and tried out until the CROAKER's fancy has been ascertained.

❧ LEOPARD SHARK ❧

The surf angler will observe that the sandy bottom gradually slants downward, then suddenly drops off. It is at this submerged bank that the young LEOPARDS feed. While waiting for the CORBINA and CROAKER to come in, the surf man will drop his bait out on the bank and let it slide down the steep slope. If the water is clear, he can watch the SHARK snatch it and head for deep water. There are two or three species of young SHARKS that occasionally follow this habit of feeding and all are very good fish. They are taken in the same manner, but are most abundant after sunset and at night. A wide range of baits is acceptable to them. Sand crabs are preferred in this type of locality. In San Quintin Bay where they are super abundant, most any fresh bait is good.

❧ SURFPERCHES ❧

There are a half dozen species of light-colored SURFPERCHES that may be taken in the surf in varying numbers throughout our range. These SURFPERCHES search the shallow waters for the small, soft-shelled crustaceans and will take them when used as bait. However, mussels and sand worms are sometimes even better.

In abundance the BARRED SURFPERCH has superseded all other game fish along southern California beaches. With the decline in numbers of CROAKERS, it grew to an enormous popularity accompanied with annual Surfperch Derbies and publicity exploitation, especially by the Redondo Rod and Gun Club, *Western Outdoor News,* and southern California newspapers. Their success in transferring public interest from the CROAKERS to this SURFPERCH, and getting it removed from the commercial list, should be studied and followed by everyone concerned in wise exploitation of other species.

In most cases, winners of the Derbies made liberal use of chumming with crushed sand crabs, mussels, or whatever, also a fairly new product, "Sugar Mackerel," introduced by the very astute and good sportsmen of Japanese extraction. They also used large No. 1 or 1/0 hooks to avoid small fish.

Although CROAKER and CORBINA are still fairly plentiful south of the Mexican border, it is the BARRED SURFPERCH that attracts the greatest number of anglers to the vast stretches of sandy shores that extend on down past Bahia San Quintin to El Rosario and beyond.

The San Ramon and clam-loaded La Cruz beaches north of San Quintin and the stretches (also full of clams) extending below the Bay are favored for their super-abundance of larger-than-average BARRED SURFPERCH. The soft parts of clams are added to the bait list here.

North of Point Conception the CALICO and most of the whole check list of SURFPERCH become more abundant. Some of these achieve weights of three pounds or more.

❧ FLATFISHES ❧

While SURFPERCHES are the most plentiful of the fishes taken in the surfs of northern California, Oregon, Washington, and British Columbia, there are a great number of other species occurring near the entrances of streams and bays, inlets and estuaries. There are also numerous submerged depressions and steep slopes within casting distance of the sandy beaches that are very productive. The STARRY FLOUNDER and half a dozen other FLATFISHES frequent these places. A four-foot monofilament leader with a No. 2 to 4 hook is recommended when surf fishing for them. Selection of bait varies according to location. A two-inch, fresh stripbait is more generally preferred, but mussel, shrimp, sea worms, or clams are also choice in one section or the other.

The most promising method of making a hookup is by casting out beyond a hole or slope (preferably down current) and retrieving slowly through it. A bait merely dropped on the bottom and left there would almost have to land in the FLATFISH's mouth to get him. A moving bait is more easily seen by all fishes that lie prone on the bottom. At times the FLATFISHES cover themselves with sand with only the mouth and eyes showing.

Three good-sized members of the SCULPIN family and two GREENLINGS are found in the surfs of this northern coast line. Although more often found among the rocks, they do frequent sandy areas, especially near the stream entrances. The TOM COD also frequents this type of locality and may be found in company with the SURF-PERCHES. The young of two or three of the SHARKS are occasionally taken here.

The spawning runs of the SMELTS occur when there is a special size of gravel covering on the beach. They are taken in some places with triangular hand nets and rakes especially constructed for this purpose.

ᦐᦒ STRIPED BASS ᦐᦒ

The art of surf casting reaches a high stage of perfection along the sandy beaches between Monterey Bay, California, and Winchester Bay, Oregon. For it is here that anglers work earnestly to achieve the skill required to take the mighty "STRIPER," the biggest prize in all surfdom.

When the breakers come rolling up on the beach a swift undertow is created. This current plows up the sand worms, crustaceans, and other sand borers and deposits them on the bank at the edge of the drop-off. Here the "STRIPER" tries to intercept them, and here the angler tries to intercept the "STRIPER." Every now and then he does.

When a STRIPED BASS is hooked from a boat, a dock or other structure, he is at a disadvantage, but in the surf he has no such handicaps. When he takes off on a parallel run there's little the angler can do but pay line. The BASS has other advantages; he can cup his tail and get full leverage by using the force of the undertow. Add this pull to the fish's weight and the angler will find that he is the one who is at a disadvantage.

To the art of casting must be added the artistic technique of beaching the STRIPED BASS. To acquire any degree of this skill, the angler must be willing to spend time, use patience and suffer some heartbreaks. The loss of a thirty-pounder just as it is about to be landed has caused many a rugged individual to sit right down and cry—or wish he could. The angler who gets his limit has every right to tell the world, for he has really done something worthy of his self-esteem. Surf casting for the STRIPED BASS is the epitome of sport fishing.

Although various types of lures are successful on occasions, the most effective is a simple rig of one or two, three-foot mono leaders with hook baited with chunk or strip of sardine, anchovy or other fresh fish. The strip should be replaced for each cast. It is the flavor exuding from the fresh strip that really gets the "STRIPER."

The retrieving speed depends on the unseen pull of the undertow. It is therefore necessary to try different speeds until a strike occurs.

Near a bay or stream entrance is usually the most productive place. A sun-up or sun-down high tide is the best time to contact the royal *Roccus saxatilis.*

ᦐᦒ (CALIFORNIA) GRUNION ᦐᦒ

Nearly all out-of-state visitors refuse to go grunioning, thinking it a gag like "snipe hunting" in which the victim is left holding the bag; but the GRUNION are real fish. They come in by the thousands and cavort along the sandy beaches of California.

The GRUNION'S instinct for timing is truly one of the wonders of nature. The first batch of eggs ripen in the female just in time for her to meet that date with a male GRUNION (sometimes two or three). The exact time is when the third or fourth breaker after the crest of the high tide rolls in on those evenings following the first full or new moon after the first of March. The ritual is repeated thereafter on the nights following each succeeding new or full moon.

When a female succeeds in getting one or more males to chase her around in the surf, she waits for the next big swell, then scuttles up on the sandy shore. Here she begins wriggling her tail and speedily digs a hole deep enough to bury herself up to her pectoral fins. She then deposits her eggs while her male companions bend their bodies around hers, discharging the milt which seeps down to fertilize the eggs. This ritual is consummated just in time for all concerned to board the next big breaker and swim back to safety. Since there will be no extremely high tide until the next full or new moon, the eggs remain in the sand to be washed up by the eroding high tide two weeks later. As soon as they are free of the sand, the eggs begin to hatch and the larvae instinctively head for deeper water.

These runs last for four or five nights after each high tide and continue through August, the greatest runs occurring from mid-April until the middle of June. It is unlawful to take GRUNION with anything except bare hands.. At present a fishing license is required for everyone over 16 years of age.

Some surf anglers claim that fishing for CORBINA and CROAKER during a GRUNION run is not so good, but others point out that the chances for a HALIBUT run (in pursuit of the GRUNION) are excellent.

Among the other fishes taken from sandy surfs south of Point Conception are the TOMMY CROAKER, QUEEN-FISH, JACKSMELT, TOPSMELT, STAGHORN SCULPIN, some shallow water SOLES, and an occasional SKATE. (Be cautious when taking a SKATE. Make sure there are two dorsal fins on the tail and not the poisonous spine a STINGRAY would display.)

❧ TRUE SMELTS ❧

Although some members of this family are found south of Point Arena, the great abundances start a few miles north of the Point and continue past the northern end of our range.

Capturing these fishes is rapidly becoming an exciting frolic, very much in the key of GRUNION hunting. At present amateur gatherers are allowed to use dip-nets, squaw-nets and fish-rakes especially designed for the purpose.

The diameter of the round dip-net averages about sixteen inches and is on a ten-foot bamboo handle. The squaw-net is suspended from a triangular-shaped frame. With this very efficient instrument the fisherman can remain in the surf scooping until a load has been accumulated, instead of returning to the beach to dump out his catch after each successful dip. The squaw-net is an unimproved-upon legacy from the Chinook and other Indian tribes. The fish-rake is dragged through the surf, then quickly up onto the beach and is a rather inefficient tool for SMELT.

The most productive period for catching these fishes is an hour or two following a late afternoon high tide. Some experts have developed a technique for catching the SMELTS at night. They locate the school when the fish strike against their legs.

In California and southern Oregon the spawning runs begin in April and last until October. The NIGHT SMELT and SURF SMELT deposit their adhesive eggs on very coarse grains of sand or fine gravel in the very shallow water near the high-tide margin.

The CANDLEFISH (sometimes called EULACHON) is especially abundant in the Columbia River and on to Alaska. It is netted from November to May when it enters streams to spawn.

The (PACIFIC) CAPELIN, an arctic species, is quite abundant in British Columbia but dwindles off in Washington. Its habits are similar to those of the NIGHT SMELT and it is netted after dark. Its beach spawning runs occur during September and continue through October.

All these fishes are very important forage and bait fishes. For various reasons some are showing signs of being depleted, a condition that should be studied.

All members of this family are fine food fishes.

❧ SALMON ❧

Shore casting for SALMON is often possible and profitable from the banks of an estuary, bay or stream entrance, but there are certain qualifying conditions. There should be a deep channel within casting distance where the ebb and flow of the tide creates a strong current. Forage fishes follow these channels, shuttling in and out with the tides. During their in-shore feeding seasons, SALMON meet the forage fishes coming and going.

The CHINOOK, SILVER, and occasionally the SOCKEYE can be taken during their pre-nuptial migrations by shore casting. The technique employed is quite similar to surf casting, the difference being that there are no breakers big enough to help beach the fish. From the banks, the heavy SALMON must be netted or gaffed.

Many anglers fishing these locations prefer much lighter tackle than is used for surf casting. The spin rod and reel are especially adaptable and add laborious struggle to the endeavor. This type of SALMON fishing provides exercise and is not a pursuit in which to practice up on loll fishing. It's cast and retrieve, cast and retrieve, over and over until a hookup is made, then the real strife begins. An outsider would appraise the activity as just a lot of work. Of course he wouldn't understand the glorious self-satisfaction of the beautiful labor.

Shore casters generally prefer to use a strip of very fresh herring or other bait fish, with a flash spoon three or four feet above the baited hook. Others stick to lures, and each seems to have his own special "killer" which may be any one of the hundred different designs. Spin fishermen like to work with spoons and other small lures but often find a crawfish tail or ghost shrimp more to the liking of the SOCKEYE and SILVER. The CHINOOK is more apt to take a very fresh herring, or strip of one, hooked in spinner fashion.

The extra long leader employed elsewhere for SALMON is not practical for shore casting unless the angler has learned to cast with the eight-foot leader laid out on the ground.

For CHINOOK, SILVER and SOCKEYE, the hook sizes are kept below those used in other places.

Although no great strides have been made in developing techniques for taking the CHUM and PINK SALMONS, some success has been met with in the northern regions. We found that rigs should be kept as small as possible: A No. 4 hook on a ten-pound-test leader and a sinker with just enough weight to take the rig down. The bait, just big enough to cover the hook, is meat cut from crawfish tail or ghost shrimp. Salmon eggs are sometimes effective. Reports of these SALMON being taken on bucktail and other flies are well founded.

Rock Fishing

"Modern, civilized man is frustrated, confused, and befuddled," states a noted psychiatrist. "He is a victim of compelling urges that he is unable to define; deep-rooted instincts that have been smothered by the restraints of society. He spends a lifetime quelling the rebellion that constantly surges within him. He pens up all of the primitive emotions acquired when mankind was free and uninhibited, when he dealt with nature in the raw and gave full expression to his feelings. Modern man is rapidly becoming a mouse, the caged dancing kind that's slightly addled."

We met this learned scholar while rock fishing below Ensenada. During the course of the day he not only gave us lessons in the piscatorial art, but gave a wonderful demonstration in "achieving the release from the shackles that bind modern man." The "Doc" put everything into his fishing and roared like a lion every time he got a hookup.

Although his theory may seem a bit deep or far-fetched, there is no question that rock fishing is indeed a primitive sport. If the reader recognizes in himself any of the symptoms suggested in the good doctor's analysis, rock fishing certainly offers plenty of freedom and incentive to let go and blow off the confined steam. All who have followed the sport will agree that every trip is filled with adventure. There is a stimulating physical and mental alertness when reserve energy is suddenly called upon for action.

He who becomes a devotee of the rocks has ample opportunity to give full vent to his feelings, whether it be to fight or play, let loose a turbulent temper or sing praises to Nature. Rock fishing gives him a chance to recapture the ability to thrill.

When fishing from some isolated point, few real men can remain utterly placid with the exhilaration that comes when blood streams are being charged with the pure oxygen of the sea breeze. Where is that paragon of dignity and self-restraint who can remain calm when he feels the heavy tug on the rod, hears the singing reel and the whistling line as it slices through the water? The man who fails to get the full primordial quickening lift with the striving and struggling in trying to land the big fighting fish is a man in a bad way and needs a mental as well as physical going over.

This rugged recreation is not all sweetness and light, however. The best of the "rock hoppers" have their moments of exasperation. A hooked CABEZON scurries under or around a rock, hook, line and sinker—gone! A breaker catches our hero unaware—a soaking! He takes a thoughtless step on wet seaweed and sits—busted britches! Forever he loses the biggest one of the day just as he is about to gaff it. All this is very hard on poor losers, but for the real sportsman, it merely adds zest to the element of

Rock fishermen, like surf anglers, must be wise to the weather and the tides. Rocks usually are the most productive of all fishing grounds.

chance. He strives to correct all of his errors and short-comings, but always allows for new ones. He may be ever so proud of his technique, but knows that many a fish will out-smart him. He has no illusions about achieving perfection in this ancient art.

With all the technical knowledge still to be acquired about this sport, it offers an opportunity for the novice. With a few basic points in mind, he can go down to the rocks and catch a sackful. To avoid complete disappointment he should pay particular attention to a number of factors: height of tide, time of day, weather, moon, wind, location, bait, equipment, and "know-how."

Rock fishing must be considered entirely apart from surf angling; the technique employed, with the exception of casting, is completely different. Also, the various species found over sandy bottoms seldom frequent rocky places and vice versa.

The astute angler knows that he must have good tackle of the proper size and weight, that a windy day is hopeless, that the dark of the moon (or when a bright moon is obliterated by an overcast) is more promising for day fishing, and that an incoming morning tide up to one hour past high tide is always favorable. He selects a day when the tide is low, about one to two hours before daylight. This time gives him an opportunity to gather mussels without getting drenched doing it. He then locates a likely spot, a deep passage between the rocks, some of which may be submerged and hidden when the tide comes in.

If the angler starts fishing before sun-up, he will use shrimp or light-colored bait and cast some distance, know-

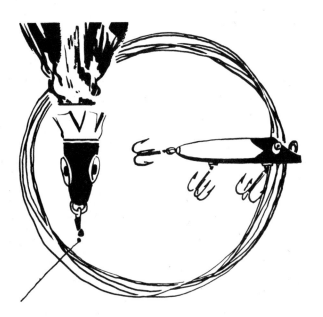

ing that his game will be far out at low tide and will follow it as it comes in. At high tide he may be fishing only ten or twenty feet out, or if the water is deep enough and is accessible, he'll be dropping his line almost straight down.

If he fails to get bites with his various kinds of bait at one place, the angler will not hesitate to move to another. Having once located the feeding spot, he cuts up bait, has extra hooks and sinkers handy, and baits up, using a different kind of bait on each of the two hooks to test the fish's preference. He then makes a short cast or two, keeping his line taut, and waits one or two minutes for a strike (unless the current is carrying his sinker in or to one side), after which he reels in as rapidly as possible. If these short casts prove unprofitable, he will really "send one," showing more patience now, waiting longer for the strike. If, however, mussel is being used for bait, there is no need to wait more than two or three minutes to retrieve, for it loses its "umph" quickly.

When the angler begins to get the first bites, he doesn't strike or yank as in fresh-water fishing. A slow pull and the fish will take a gulp and set the hook himself. Once the hookup is made all the angler's skill is needed. As soon as the rock fish becomes aware of its predicament, it makes a dive for the nearest ledge and gets as far under it as possible. Some smart old LINGCOD or SHEEP-HEAD will try to circle the nearest rock, or foul the line any way he can. It takes a lot of practice to beat rock fish at this game.

The outstanding difference between this type of angling and all others is that the fish, with few exceptions, should not be permitted to run, but must be kept coming in, slowly and smoothly. Due to the tenderness of the mouths of most rock fishes, a sudden jerk would tear the hook free. In very deep water the fish can be played until he starts to sound; then it becomes necessary to "horse" him up. When a big one is hooked, the rhythmic pumping method should be used. Maneuvering the scrapper between the rocks may necessitate a bit of foot work in addition to the full use of the long rod. Never try to drag the fish over an exposed rock. It's safer to chance a little slack and let a breaker or current toss him over or carry him around the ledge. If caught in kelp or seaweed, the fish will often free himself if given enough slack.

Care must be taken when a heavyweight is about to be gaffed or netted. He must not be allowed to be slapped by the breakers against the rocks. Quick action is a "must," once he is within reach.

A landing spot back away from the water's edge should already have been selected, for some of these fighters can stage a pretty fair, dry-land battle, and can with a flip and a flop land back in the water. As soon as possible, get the fish into a wet gunnysack and keep it in the shade.

Some of the more serious students of this "piscolithic art" cut the first few fish open to make a careful study of the food found therein. This often suggests the type of bait most favored. While we were performing such an operation one morning an inquisitive novice, thinking we were dealing in ichthyomancy, asked us, "Getting any messages?"

Chumming is one of the most important moves in the thrill game of rock fishing. By far the best fish attraction is a half-dozen freshly crushed sea urchins thrown out in a folded sheet of paper, so as to keep the chum in one pile. Mussels, clams and almost any other preferred fish foods make good chumming material.

Night fishing among the rocks is just too aggravating for the beginner unless he has previously located a deep hole just off a ledge where casting would be unnecessary. The surface of the hole should be flooded with a bright light. A large flashlight or gasoline lamp will prove adequate.

There is always a special spot which must be located each trip because of the changing currents. The most likely one is apt to be near the tip of a point. One will notice that on the lee side of the point the breakers diminish and the water surrounding the rocks is less agitated, yet restless enough to cause boils and whirlpools that whip up plenty of white water.

Careful attention should also be given to the marine life: Kelp and other vegetation, rock crabs, barnacles, and most important of all, mussels. The number of fish around such a location will vary according to the amount of sea life present.

The observant angler will notice that following three or four high breakers there is a period of less turbulent waters and will make his cast as soon as the last, big swell has passed. This is to avoid the annoyance of having his sinker dragged by the tow of the breaker.

Anglers are sometimes puzzled when fishing near a mass of loose boulders to find the fish suddenly stop biting just before high tide; this is most noticeable when the breakers are heavy. The sudden exodus of the fish is not a mysterious supernatural phenomenon; they are simply frightened away by the boulders crashing against each other when tossed around by the currents. Water amplifies such sounds and acts as a conductor. All fish are very sensitive to underwater sound vibrations, as proven by the effect of dynamiting, when fish are killed at a distance from the actual explosion. It is therefore advisable to avoid these boulder-covered areas during high tide when the breakers become powerful enough to jostle the rocks around.

TO BE KEPT IN MIND

The cast, above all, must be smooth and accurate. Since there is little chance for still fishing, the currents will all too soon foul the line. When trying to free the line, grasp it and pull until something gives. Do not try to force it loose with the rod, as it is not built for that amount of stress.

Retrieving slowly is next to impossible. The motion must be continuous and rapid, the sinker kept well up from the bottom. This can be done best with an especially light disc or spoon sinker.

Keep hooks sharpened.

Try to avoid drawing the line across rocks that protrude from the water.

A deep tide pool can be utilized to keep the catch alive. If it is too deep or tideswept, the catch can be strung on a heavy line ten or twelve feet long and made fast, just in case an unexpected swell should overflow the pool. Some fish can be kept alive for days in this manner.

Equipment: Plenty of extra hooks made up on wire leaders; a dozen disc or oval sinkers; an extra loaded reel; a sliding plastic float; knife, pliers, wire cutter; a mussel pry (tire remover from auto kit, or a sharpened piece of auto spring); a long-handled gaff or hand net; hand towel; a knapsack instead of tackle box; tennis shoes instead of boots, with an extra dry pair. A complete change of clothing is advisable.

RED WATER (GONYAULAZ POLYEDRA)

At times during the early hours the sea is too calm and the water too clear for certain big fish. This does not mean that very muddy water is better. It is definitely not. When the water is red you might just as well leave that section. The so-called "red water" is not just muddy water. It is caused by millions of minute organisms that strike an area like a plague, killing and sickening most of the sea life over which the cloud passes. These little specks of animal life use up all of the oxygen in the water and otherwise contaminate it. Mussels, clams, and other shellfishes become poisonous and if eaten by humans are likely to prove fatal. With the first appearance of "red water" in the summer, the states along the Pacific quarantine mussels and clams as unfit for human consumption.

ᑫᕈ DEEP HOLE FISHING ᑫᕈ

There are many and varied aspects of rock fishing, and each requires a somewhat different method. The most baffling is in fishing a deep hole of fifty to one hundred feet. Small fish are seldom found in these deep waters; therefore the size of the tackle must necessarily be much heavier. Fish inhabiting these depths will take very large hooks and have no fear of heavy wire leaders and swivels.

The difficulty lies in keeping these fish from diving under a ledge on the way up. A high speed triple-multiplying reel is of some help. With a thirty-six-pound-test line and a good strong rod, an artful rock angler can expect to land one out of three. It is aggravating, but when the loss is expected, it becomes nothing more than a hazard of the sport. The most trying operation at this depth is in retrieving when there is no fish on. The beginner will more than likely hook into the ledge every time he pulls in until he learns to retrieve rapidly or finds a rocky point jutting out from which he can flank the ledge. A spoon-shaped sinker should be used here and the point of the hook should be turned in. (See Fig. 1.)

There are numerous deep holes that can be fished along the shore line of northern California, Oregon, Washington, and British Columbia. There are also deep holes between Point Banda and Point San Jose, twelve miles southwest of Santo Tomas. The deep holes at Point Dume and Laguna Beach, California, have been partially filled.

This type of rock fishing is really rugged and requires strength and endurance. The size of the fish and the struggle to bring it up from the depths make it hard work. But if you're after exercise or fish, this is a way to get all you want of both.

The reason for so few devotees of the deep holes is a lack of patience to learn the technique. Since there has been little, if anything, published on the subject, the followers of this pursuit have had to gain their skill by the trial and error method. Once the technique is mastered, however, the deep hole angler is seldom satisfied with any other kind of fishing.

ᑫᕈ OPALEYE ᑫᕈ

From San Lucas on the southernmost tip of Baja California to the north of the Oregon border, the gamy, elusive, yet abundant OPALEYE can be taken. Because of a similarity in shape, this extra-fine fish is erroneously called a "PERCH," but it is far more difficult to catch and is an excellent food fish.

Until a few years ago, ichthyologists classed the OPALEYE as herbivorous. Modern scientists have since discovered that the green and brown, grass-like sea growth and KELP eaten by this fish is often covered with minute animal life (hydroids and byrozoans). They also found that this fish is quite fond of the soft part of rock mussels.

The OPALEYE is recognized by the color of its opalescent blue eyes. The young have one or two whitish or yellowish spots on each side of the back and can be seen darting under rocks and into crevices in the tide pools.

The OPALEYE follows the tide and is taken in the white water churned up by the boils and swirl pools around rocks and near edges of submerged bluffs or perpendicular rock walls. It is sometimes seen, in company with the HALFMOON, over offshore reefs.

The main challenge in the contest with the OPALEYE is to keep him from getting under rocky ledges without being too impatient to bring him in. An abrupt jerk or hard pull may cause the small hook to tear out.

Because of the very small mouth and cautious manner of taking food, the angler finds it necessary to use exceptionally small short-shank hooks, No. 6. Two hooks are often used, both baited with the soft part of mussels, the tough part around the edge of the shell not being used for this fish. Some prefer one hook directly on mono line.

The cast is made just after the last of a series of big breakers has crashed. The line is held taut and reeled up rapidly when the current moves the sinker shoreward. The OPALEYE rarely strikes hard. He surreptitiously nibbles, masticates a bit, and then, if no resistance is felt, he swallows the bait, often without giving the angler so much as an inkling as to his whereabouts. If he succeeds in screening out the hook, he will dive back into his hideout under the rock, wait for the breakers to once again churn the clearing water into a concealing white blanket of foam, and then sneak out for another go at thievery.

When this blue-eyed bandit becomes so careless as to allow himself to be hooked, the angler will feel the jolt in a no uncertain degree, for the OPALEYE certainly can raise a ruckus. The fight he puts up is far beyond his weight. He cups his tail to catch the force of the out-going current, then when the current changes, he suddenly switches and makes a run straight toward the shore. Unless the angler is alert, his fish will be under a rock, an

FIG. 1. *Spoon sinker, turned-in hook avoid snags.*

aggravating contingency that will test the composure of the calmest angler, for he must patiently wait for the fish to make the first move, then quickly bring it about and start the skirmish all over again.

There are times and conditions when the OPALEYE will refuse mussels and can be taken only with the sea grasses, perhaps due to the seasonal abundance of animal organisms on this growth. Some bait shops carry this vegetation for sale. Canned peas have proven a very effective bait.

To secure such baits as moss, grass, or mussels, a sliding bead on a mono looped leader is lowered to cinch the bait which then hangs down over the hook. (See Fig. 15.)

Vegetation will attract the OPALEYE only when it is in motion as when the swirling waters or currents toss it around. Off shore the OPALEYE will take a bit of shrimp, soft clam, or small stripbait.

Netting of the six to eight-inch OPALEYE by small commercial fishermen should be given serious consideration. Tons of these game fishes are taken long before they have had a chance to mature, and to make it worse, are sold in the fish markets as "PERCH." This unwarranted waste is the height of shortsightedness. Given another year's growth, the OPALEYE would increase in size considerably, eventually attaining a weight of seven pounds.

SHEEPSHEAD AND SHEEP-HEAD

The first white American sportsmen to go in for salt-water angling and perhaps the first to take up any kind of sport-fishing were the early aristocrats along the Virginia coast. The sport was called "sheepsheading." Those hardy Americans considered the SHEEPSHEAD, *Archosargus probatocephalus,* an exceptionally game fish. "Sheepsheading" became a popular pursuit up the New England Coast, down along the southern shores, and around the Gulf to New Orleans.

In 1814 Samuel Lathem Mitchill wrote a glowing account of the "sporting exercise of capturing the SHEEPSHEAD by angling," "its fighting ability," and the "high quality of the flesh."

All of the praises sung by those early anglers could be echoed for our West Coast SHEEP-HEAD, *Pimelometopon pulchrum.* Because of the name, fresh-water fishermen condemn this fine fish, confusing it with the sluggish, coarse-fleshed fresh-water DRUM, *Aplodinotus grunniens,* called SHEEPSHEAD, which is found in the Great Lakes, backwaters, streams, and mid-western lakes. There is very little resemblance between the two except that they

both have a head that according to some folks resembles that of a sheep.

The Pacific SHEEP-HEAD excels in many ways as a food fish. For chowder and salads it is superior. When the skin is removed, it compares favorably with any other fish for frying, broiling, or whatever.

Usually found over a rocky bottom in twenty or more feet of water, the SHEEP-HEAD moves in with the tide, coming up to a five or six-foot depth at high tide where he feeds principally on mollusks and crustaceans. His appetite for lobster has gained him the reputation of being a first-class villain for lobster trappers.

For deep water, pieces of white-meated crustaceans such as shrimp with the shell left on, crab, or lobster make the best bait. Near shore, mussels and rock crabs may be added. He will also take clams, live bait, or stripbait.

When fishing for SHEEP-HEAD in particular, the angler should try to locate a channel running back into the rocks where he can stand near the edge and draw the fish in past him, rather than trying to get it over the ledges of a strait formation. Unless the tackle is sturdy enough to "bounce" this one, a long-handled gaff or net is almost a necessity. If none is at hand, a weighty fish can be landed by utilizing the momentum of a breaker to help swing it ashore.

The SHEEP-HEAD is one of the few salt-water fishes that can be struck hard. His mouth is so tough there is little likelihood of the hook tearing out. Subtlety is unnecessary in persuading this fish to take the hook; but from that point on, skill is essential, and quick decisions must be made in maneuvering him. In order to do this efficiently, a good idea of the lay of the land should be held in mind. The hazardous ledges and the gaps and channels between them can be calculated at low tide. With the picture of the formation well remembered, the rock angler with his long rod can then confine the fish's activities to the channels.

The instant the hook is set this tackle wrecker must be kept moving. If he tries to sound, he must be fought without fear of tearing the hook free. When he tries his mad plunges, he must be held for all the tackle will stand and a rhythmic pumping applied. If he should succeed in fouling the line, it is held taut for a moment; then relaxed gradually. Feeling the slack, the fish will try to hunt a better cave—and the struggle is on again.

When the husky male is hooked, he will not only dive under the rocks, but shuttle around them or take a hitch on a clump of kelp. He will cup his tail, shake his head, and make sudden lunges up to the time he is lifted from the water. A wide-awake angler can land him only when he can out-smart him. South of Ensenada this fish attains a weight of thirty pounds or more.

OCEAN-WHITEFISH

The OCEAN-WHITEFISH is about the most difficult game fish a rock angler can hope to land. Possessing a long, roundish streamlined body built for speed, its lightning-like runs often lead the angler to believe he has hooked a YELLOWTAIL or TUNA. It is even more troublesome than a SHEEP-HEAD of equal weight and follows somewhat the same line of defense, heading for the submerged rocks and kelp stalks the moment the hook is felt. If it can be kept from fouling the line for a few minutes, it sometimes rises to the surface, leaping and thrashing. If the water is fairly deep, it can be played for some time, but the moment this blitzer starts to sound, he must be brought about and forced to surface.

When the angler wishes to avoid other bottom-feeding fishes, he slips on a plastic float and attaches his leader six feet above the sinker. The OCEAN-WHITEFISH feeds at about this level. It is most abundant out around the southern California islands and along the rocky shores of Baja California, is often found in company with the SHEEP-HEAD, and has about the same kind of an appetite.

The male has a high, fat forehead.

During winter months the OCEAN-WHITEFISH retreats to deep water, where he is often taken with ROCKFISH.

SEAPERCHES

Wherever there is an abundance of sea life among submerged rocks between Vancouver Island, B.C., and San Quintin Bay, Baja California, and beyond, some members of the family Embiotocidae can be found. The SEAPERCH division of this family numbering a dozen or more, is at once distinguished from the light-colored SURFPERCH by deeper colorations.

While the SEAPERCHES are usually more plentiful and much more daring than other fish frequenting these shallow feeding grounds, they are not taken without an effort. A three-pounder starting off on an angle offers real resistance. They are energetic and as tricky as many of the other rock dwellers, and like them, follow the tides in and out. The young and half grown are the first to come in near the shore and usually remain long after the large individuals have gone back to the deep holes. Some species move out to very deep water during winter months.

The SEAPERCHES are schooling fishes and various species are often found feeding together. When one is caught, you can be sure that others are near, especially where the water is somewhat agitated. Even when the wind and ground swells get rough, some few can be taken in sheltered coves. When the water is very clear and calm, enticing them to come out from under ledges and other coverings is difficult.

A No. 2 to 4 hook on mono line or leader tied about a foot above the sinker, makes up the rig. If hooks catch into the rocks too often the points should be turned in slightly. The small, sharp hook is likely to cut out of the very tender mouth of the SEAPERCH. It is therefore advisable to play these fish gently.

When mussel is used for bait, secure as much of it on the hooks as possible. The soft part will dissolve or scatter and act as a chum.

Often the rock angler will find a sloping, sandy area between jutting ledges. If the water is agitated sufficiently to form a shelf, the angler will drop his mussel or shrimp-baited hook just beyond the shelf and pull it up the slope. A number of the light-colored SURFPERCHES come in with the tide to feed on such a shelf.

HALFMOON

Next to the SEAPERCH the HALFMOON is the most consistent of all the shore-feeding fishes and can be counted on the year-round south of Point Conception.

In the rough waters near a rocky shore the HALFMOON is a bottom-feeder, but out in the calmer waters around kelp beds it strikes the bait nearer the surface.

Mussels and shrimp are the best bait among rocks. Offshore, small strips of fresh anchovy, mackerel or sardine are effective.

KELP BASS AND SAND BASS

Both the SAND BASS and KELP BASS can be taken from shore by rock anglers who have developed a fair amount of accuracy and distance in casting, for they rarely come in close to shore unless there is an extensive kelp covering. The SAND BASS will sometimes venture away from the sea growth, but the KELP BASS prefers the protective refuge the massive vegetation affords him.

When a kelp bed is found within casting distance, the fisherman will locate an opening in it and aim for the middle. He'll allow the bait to sink to the bottom, then slowly pull it up six or seven feet and repeat.

In order to keep the sinker as light as possible, many

anglers use a sliding, plastic float for the extra weight required for casting. Live anchovies, queenfish, or sardine bait is best. If not available, stripbait kept in motion will attract these BASSES. They will also take shrimp, rock crabs, strips of fresh mackerel, or mussels.

❧ CABEZON ☙

CABEZON, the blue-bellied SCULPIN, otherwise called "MARBLE SCULPIN," "BLUE COD," and "BULLHEAD," is found in abundance from Alaska to below San Quintin Bay, among rocks and marine vegetation near shore, but more often near the mouth of streams.

As a food fish, the CABEZON is highly esteemed. Its skin is slick and tough and is usually removed before frying. The flesh has a bluish tinge, becoming white when cooked.

Shrimp is the best bait for CABEZON, but it will readily take mussels, sand worms, sand crabs, small rock crabs, or stripbait. It feeds on the bottom and its strike is hardly felt until the hook has been swallowed. Once it has taken the bait, there is little chance of losing it, since its mouth is exceedingly tough. A No. 1 hook on a ten-inch leader attached a foot above the sinker is customary.

Because of the quality of the meat and the fact that it weighs up to twenty-five pounds, the CABEZON is much sought after. Wherever one is caught, it's a good guess that a dozen more are around. When the rock angler locates the hangout, he is almost sure of a fish feast. But roe of the CABEZON is poisonous.

❧ GREENLINGS ☙

North of Point Conception and on up to the Kodiak Islands of Alaska, members of the GREENLING family can be caught from rocks, especially wherever the vegetation grows close to shore.

An enormous number of these fishes is found along the rocky stretches of the northern California and Oregon coast, and they seem even more plentiful on the northern end of our range.

Even though there is this great abundance, they are not to be taken without skill and effort. Relying on "fisherman's luck" will likely net the "loll fisher" a dry sack. These fishes are cautious and wily and the rock angler must employ his wits to win. Once he gets the knack he can really do business.

First of all he should use two very small hooks on six-inch leaders. The cast should be aimed at a spot where the water boils or swirls around a rock formation and retrieved shortly after the bait strikes bottom. If the fish doesn't take the bait while it is in motion, he is likely to overlook it.

GREENLINGS follow the tide very close to the high tide line and retreat with the turn of the tide. Casting out to reach them at low tide requires a mighty heave.

In some regions this fish is called "SEA TROUT." Anglers accustomed to working the fresh-water TROUT have a difficult time trying to reverse their technique. The art in landing the GREENLING lies in the angler's ability and quick thinking in maneuvering the incoming fish between the rocks.

The boys stationed in the Aleutian Islands and along the Alaskan coast during World War II had some exciting times during the summer months jigging for a cousin of the KELP GREENLING called ATKA MACKEREL which travels in schools of hundreds. The method used was to tie any shiny or white object above whatever hook was available, then cast or toss it into an opening in the kelp and jerk the lure up and down.

❧ GARIBALDI ☙

The beautiful gold fish seen slowly gliding around among the rocks and seaweeds, nibbling small animals, is known as the GARIBALDI, a name given by the early Italian fishermen who may have thought there was a resemblance to their great national hero.

Catching this one by any means is illegal.

❧ STRIPED BASS ☙

The romantic history of the STRIPED BASS started shortly after the first white settlers landed in America. Believing the palefaces a plague, the Indians placed the settlement under quarantine. According to their own stories, these ancestors of ours would have starved to death had the natives placed the rivers, and their enormous numbers of STRIPED BASS out of bounds.

John Smith (the one who got into that mixup with Pocahontas) wrote, "The BASSES so choked the stream that a man could walk across on them, remaining dry shod." By the size of this story, John must have been an angler of the first water.

The settlers learned a lot from the Indians, but almost out-smarted themselves later when they stole the idea of planting a fish with each grain of corn. Result—plenty of corn, but fewer fish to eat.

The STRIPED BASS has made history from New Orleans to the rock-ribbed coast of Maine. On each occasion he was the loser, continuing to diminish until 1879 and 1882 when quantities were taken from New Jersey, hauled across the country, and planted in San Francisco Bay. Only 435 fish survived these trips, but within ten years they multiplied to such an extent that they could be taken commercially.

Then came a time when over-fishing threatened to exterminate the Pacific colony, but action by angling clubs and the California Department of Fish and Game succeeded, in 1935, in getting conservation laws passed, thus halting the commercial activities.

Again the BASS increased, distributing themselves all the way from the Columbia River to San Diego Bay. Today they are rated as one of the foremost game fishes of the Pacific. They are seldom taken south of Point Conception or north of the Columbia River. Nor does the dramatic story of the STRIPED BASS end in 1935. New chapters are being written as the commercial and anglers' associations march to the legislative halls to do battle over the noble creature. Fishermen in the Bay City area for centuries to come will pay tribute to the men and organizations who gave so much in time and effort in establishing and maintaining the STRIPED BASS.

No other fish within our range is taken in so many different ways, in such odd, strange and out-of-the-way places, and under such diversified conditions. Nor is any other fish so sought after by various types of anglers. Little tots with their poles and twine tackle catch the BASS from docks, bridges, and banks. Boats of every description, from small canoes to great yachts, are used in the pursuit. The "STRIPER" is captured along the sandy surfs and rocks from Ventura, California, to Coos Bay, Oregon. He is taken with delicate fly rods or with long, heavy surf calcuttas. Wherever and whenever he is hooked, he is a fighter. Among the rocks the "STRIPER" is a raging demon; for it is here in his natural habitat that he grows to great size, shows the most cunning, and causes grave doubts in the mind of the adept angler as to his ability to cope with him.

There have been numerous volumes published, each with its own idea of capturing the wily STRIPED BASS on the Atlantic Coast. Anglers of northern California have developed their own particular techniques which also show considerable variance.

The popular method employed in taking the BASS from among the rocks differs greatly from the "cast beyond the breakers and retrieve" procedure as practiced by surf anglers. The rock fisherman finds a somewhat protected cove or lee side of a rock jetty where the breakers have spent most of their force. There he will toss out a handful of chopped fish or other sea food. This chum is not intended to interest the "STRIPER," but is utilized as a means of determining whether or not there are any small fry around.

At first the rock angler may have some difficulty in tempting the BASS to come out from his rock lair, but as soon as the ensuing commotion made by the feeding small fry stirs that bargain counter urge in him, he'll venture out to grab his share.

Hooking the BASS among the rocks is one thing, but landing him is something else again. The chances of his escaping are far greater in among the rocks than when hooked in other less hazardous localities. Trying to keep his head up and away from the rocks requires skill, muscle, and agility. The rock angler who can force the big BASS to follow the narrow channels between the rocks and bring him to gaff has accomplished an admirable feat and is worthy of being called a sportsman.

⟿ ROCKFISHES (ROCK COD) ⟿

Sixteen species of ROCKFISHES in the SCORPIONFISH family, *Scorpaenidae*, occur in moderately shallow water. Most of these can be taken from the rocky shore. A few of the half-grown, deep-water species venture into shallow places, seasonally, most often north of Point Conception and south of Point Banda, rarely in southern California.

To these may be added the deep-water ROCKFISHES frequenting the very deep holes that can be fished from shore.

Many anglers would be astonished at the great abundance of these fishes. Some thought to be rare are in reality plentiful. Because of the difficulty in getting to them, estimating their number is nearly impossible. Rock anglers who have developed effective techniques for their capture have discovered some "hot" fishing.

In these shallow rock-bottom areas, ROCKFISHES are very agile and rarely fail to give the angler a worthy tussle. Their aggravating habit of snatching the hooked bait and darting back into a deep hole or under the rocks has caused the whole lot of them to be called "GOPHERS" by oldtime fishermen.

To catch a fair amount of them the rock angler has had to develop a couple of tricks. One of them is to use very short six-inch leaders, the other, to start "hauling" as soon as the strike is suspected.

The various species that make up this lot seem to have different kinds of appetites and to further complicate the bait difficulty, each species may demand a change in menu from one place to another. Mussels seem to be the *pièce de résistance*, however, with shrimp, clams, and stripbait running two, three and four.

If the angler is in a position where he can avoid fouling his line, a No. 1 or 2 hook is preferable; otherwise smaller hooks are advisable.

All of the ROCKFISHES seems highly sensitive to currents and temperatures of the water. While they may be caught in considerable quantity one day, they may seem to have vanished completely the next even though weather and other conditions appear the same.

❧ OTHER SPECIES ❧

Many of the species credited with being strictly deepwater fishes can be taken along the rocky shore line beginning at Point Banda and running for about twenty-five miles down the coast. The water along this stretch is much colder than along the southern California coast and the fish are far more plentiful. This region is a paradise for rugged rock anglers who can take a bit of roughing it.

YELLOWTAIL, BONITO, BARRACUDA and SKIPJACK can be taken from the rocks only when a deep channel runs close to shore and then only on those rare occasions when they go "haywire" chasing a school of small fishes or squids and ignoring the shallowness of the water.

There are many other fine food fishes taken now and then by rock anglers. Among those most frequently caught are the young BLACK SEA BASS, SARGO, SPOTTED BASS, SCULPIN, FRINGEHEADS, SMELT, KELPFISH, MORAYS and a number of other eel-like fishes. Members of the CROAKER family are seldom found among the rocks within our range.

❧ BREAKWATER FISHING ❧

Angling from a breakwater or jetty is for the most part like rock fishing, but the submerged foundation of the breakwater often projects out to such an extent that it becomes an additional hazard. On the ocean side, where fishing is usually more promising, retrieving without hooking into this stone base requires "some doing." The amateur will need a good supply of hooks and sinkers and a temper that can be kept under control; for, until he gets the hang of it, he'll be hung up most of the time and have to run the gamut of aggravations. If he isn't completely unstrung by the time he learns how to keep his hooks clear of the shelf, he is in for some fine fishing.

One of the most successful ways of avoiding the annoying entanglements is by the use of a light sinker and a sliding float. A ten-inch leader is attached a foot above the sinker. When retrieving, the angler reels in as rapidly as possible. This quick action brings the leader up to the float, thus reducing the angle of the incoming line and lifting everything clear of the foundation shelf. Some of the more constant breakwater fishermen have cane rods fifteen feet or more in length which reach out past the ledge. For the beginner, hooks with turned in points are advisable.

The outer end of the breakwater is not necessarily the most productive spot. Being near a clump of kelp or a large colony of mussels will often prove more favorable.

In addition to the fishes found among rocks, the breakwater angler will likely find on the bay side a number of species that occur in bays and backwaters of southern California, such as SOLES, TURBOTS, SHARKS, CROAKERS, SURFPERCHES, SHAD, QUEENFISH and BUTTERFISH. North of Point Conception the jetties and breakwaters yield TOM COD, ROCKFISH, FLOUNDERS, SOLES, TURBOTS, SURFPERCHES and a few of the anadromous fishes.

When breakers begin washing over the top of the wall, it's high time to get back to shore. Many fishermen, not realizing the force of such a wash, have been seriously injured. Tennis shoes with non-skid rubber soles help the angler keep his footing on the uneven rocks.

Breakwaters and jetties with their underwater crevices and cave-like openings between the rocks not only give perfect protection to the small fry against their numerous enemies, but also supply their food to some extent. Ocean vegetation and its accompanying animal life thrive in these protected niches. For the young of the SEAPERCHES and other small fishes, these stone labyrinths are truly retreats of refuge. Without some such protection, their survival would be threatened.

A method of catching wolf eels and other eel-like species in northern reaches is done with a 2 or 3-foot stiff wire from pole to squid-baited hook which is poked back between rocks to make contact. It is called Poke Pole Fishing.

NOTE: Beware of taking small abalone from breakwaters; they are protected by law. For size and limit, see state regulations.

Marine Angling Boats

In 1927 there were about 250 salt-water sportfishing boats operating along the whole coast of California. In 1947, according to official state records, there were still only 286. Those twenty years had shown little change in the make-shift type of boats or in the enthusiasm by the fishermen going out on them. Then something happened.

Hundreds of thousands of people, from Ensenada, Baja California, to Vancouver, British Columbia, developed a sudden and intense interest in ocean angling. With the introduction of live bait, new conveniences, and safety installations on boats throughout the Northwest, an explosive boom in angler interest occurred suddenly.

Some say the original fever broke out in war time when food was scarce and the housewives urged their husbands to go out and prospect for some extra table meat. The sea trip proved so productive they were sent out to repeat it. It was about the third or fourth trip when — wham! The bug bit 'em.

This story is not wholly fictional. The meat problem of those days did add incentive; but the deep and compelling reasons that brought the horde of new anglers to the sea were manifold. Some sought escape from the restraints and confusion that engulfed them. Others were

Anglers try their luck near Catalina Island. A trip on a party boat is an excursion, a voyage to sea, and a try at "bringing home the bacon."

motivated by the desire to recapture some of the joys of youth. Still others were seeking health, freedom, relaxation, emotional excitement, companionship, but most of all — adventure.

These were the desires that drew them down to the sea. And each, according to his temperament, found the object of his quest. Those expecting nothing more than fish, were agreeably surprised to find their own case-hardened defenses against romanticism and adventure cracked.

There is that ocean angler for whom the adventure begins with the first thought of going fishing. At once he starts to dramatize the expected thrills in his imagination. In his daydreams his anticipations become vivid scenes of big-game fish boiling around the boat. He even revels in spending that sleepless night before the trip creating masterpieces of combat between man and fish. Nor is the fervor lessened when he jumps out of bed and dashes to the dock an hour early. There may be little or no fishing advantage gained by sailing on a boat that leaves long before daybreak, but without the nocturnal aspect, our angler would be robbed of that feeling of daring to venture out into the mysterious unseen.

Although filled with suspense and eagerness to get to the fishing grounds, he accepts the half-calm, half-nervous jitters with resignation. He is aboard the boat and on the way. And the high-powered motor purrs as it drives the sleek craft at top speed. He could go below and grab an hour or so of much needed "shut eye." He could join a canasta or some such game that's under way down in the hold. He could find coffee and comedians at the galley counter. But nothing is quite so invigorating as standing up on the bow and feeling the cooling mists against the face. He can peer out into the vast darkness into a world apart and give his imagination free rein. Ghost ships and islands appear and fade as in a mirage.

These pictures of the mind lack substance and need not be defined. But when the curtains of night are drawn and the sun comes up at sea, who can find words, in a language bounded by the land's edge, that will describe human responses to the warmth and glory of nature's daily miracle?

This is the bare beginning of our angler's day. As the fishing grounds come into view, everyone aboard suddenly becomes alert. The whole atmosphere on deck seems charged, as anglers break out tackle and rig up for the fray. No more time for reveries now. Quiet enjoyment is halted.

This is it!

Eager anticipation reaches a high pitch and on up goes the blood pressure as the first contact is made. Unlike most anticipated joys that fall flat when finally achieved, the big fish hookup and the ensuing battle seldom fall short of fulfilling the promise. When the sizeable fish is safely on deck, our hero can relax and give over to that full and enviable feeling—self-satisfaction in one of its highest and most complete forms.

There will be plenty of time during the lulls for our angler to recapture his serenity and again indulge in casual, calm, or inspiring pleasantries.

Down past the glass-like surface he can see a wonder world with such dimensions, perspective, and color as to defy the poets and painters of all time. How can earthlings capture those elusive qualities, when their vision and thinking processes are always halted at the soles of their feet?

ᕤᕗ TYPES OF CRAFT ᕤᕗ

The motor-powered craft engaged in transporting angling passengers to the fishing grounds are of all types and sizes. They may include anything from an outboard-driven dory to a sixty-foot cruiser.

There are two prevailing classes of commercially conducted angling boats in southern California. One group, called "charter boats," is hired by parties. The other, most commonly called "sportfishing boats," books individual fares and runs on daily schedules. This group was formerly called "day boats" or "live bait boats." The latter term is now applied to boats engaged in capturing live bait.

Between Santa Barbara and Eureka, including the San Francisco Bay area, the term "party boats" is quite generally used for scheduled as well as for chartered craft.

Along the coast and sounds of Oregon and Washington, most of the large boats are known as "trollers." Some that spend little or no time trolling are also called "party boats." Small vessels in this region that are rented outright are called "mooching boats" and "spinfishers."

The same names used in Washington and Oregon are followed in British Columbia, with the addition of the term "sport cruisers" for large angling vessels.

In southern California, anyone making an advance reservation can sail out on a sportfishing boat. Each carries a crew of two or three men and from ten to sixty passengers, according to capacity.

The live bait or cut bait furnished is included in the price of the fare. Other accommodations vary. Overnight boats have bunks. Tackle may be rented at the dock or aboard. Galley service is maintained on most all-day boats. Well-trained crews collect and hold stakes for the jackpot, handle the bait, assist with the gaff, and help the angler in many ways.

There are two prevailing systems of arranging positions. One is called the "rotating" system. Each passenger is given a number and color corresponding to a number and color marked on the rail. About once an hour the captain calls for a shift, and everyone moves clockwise to the next section, which is painted a different color.

This method gives every passenger an equal chance at the stern position sometime during the day, regardless of when reservations were made. The other system gives preference of position according to the time reservations are made. Those making reservations first would naturally select positions on the stern of the boat so that when it comes to anchor, the current will be in their favor.

There are times when ground swells or winds make fishing difficult, so fewer fish are taken. It is therefore best to consult the weather bureau before making reservations.

The question whether offshore fishing is better when the moon is full or during the dark of the moon, is still a matter of speculation. There is no doubt that a "dark" is better for shore angling. Many experts insist that the surface-feeding fishes feed at night during the dark of the moon, locating the forage fishes by the phosphorescent light they stir up; consequently they are so well filled that they do not surface during the daylight hours.

With beginners aboard the average boat in a school of YELLOWTAIL, TUNA, or other top-feeding fishes, a dozen strikes to one hookup is not an uncommon happening. This is mainly due to the novice's lack of timing, presence of mind, low resistance to the urge to yank, and setting the hook.

If the beginner has ever watched chickens, he has undoubtedly noticed that when one gets a choice morsel, it starts running, the others giving chase. Likewise, if he will observe a flock of sea gulls, he will see that one will swoop down, snatch a fish, and fly off some distance whether it is being chased or not. Fish have this same selfish instinct and act in a similar manner. The novice who visualizes this picture will be helped greatly in his timing. Like all other rules or ideas of fishing, this one is not infallible. Occasionally a heavy yanker will set the hook in a tough part of the mouth, and if nothing breaks, land his fish, but the odds are very much against him.

Admittedly, yanking is not an easy habit to get rid of, since a lot of us began our piscatorial pursuits by using a bent pin for a hook and found it necessary to jerk the BLUEGILL clear out on the bank or lose it.

Some of these yanking reflexes seem to be deeper rooted. Perhaps they are instincts established when some of our prehistoric ancestors used a barbless, forked bone or a straight one which they tied in the middle. When the fish swallowed it, a yank could cause the sharp bone to straighten out crosswise in its mouth. Watching the barbaric force some fishermen put into striking, one can almost recognize the neolithic man at work.

The angler who gets one hookup after another has no more luck than the fellow who fails; there are good reasons. First of all, he has developed his sense of timing. He keeps in mind the time it takes the fish to do a bit of tasting, take the bait by the tail or middle, make a short run, and finally stop to turn the bait around so that it can be swallowed head first. Having waited for what he feels is a sufficient interval, the angler strikes gently, if at all. Fresh-water anglers, accustomed to striking hard when using the very flexible fly rod, will find that the rigidity of a salt-water rod causes it to react quickly and that there is very little whip in comparison.

Fish have an instinct against swallowing a forage fish tail first. Some of the species used for bait have hard spines that slant backward. If taken in tail first, they would stick in the throat of the swallower.

There are times when game fish will hit the bait head first and start off with a run. Chances are ten to one that the hook will be set by the force of the run; but if the angler should give a yank during the run, either the hook will tear out or the tackle will give way. Just try sticking a sharp hook into a piece of fish and see how easily it slides in past the barb.

The proficient angler has a sensitive touch. He feels the weight his tackle can stand, or better yet, the amount of stress that would likely tear the hook out. He applies just enough pressure to force the fish to exhaust itself.

❧ RHYTHM PUMPING ❧

Ordinary pumping is a method of bringing a large fish forward by pulling the rod up without reeling, then reeling rapidly as the rod is lowered for the next pull. The latest rhythm pumping technique follows a similar pattern, but instead of the long, simple upward pull, three to five short strokes are employed. Rhythm pumping is also used to turn a big fish or to halt one that is about to take out line to the danger point or head for rocks.

The premise of rhythmic halting pumping is based on the assumption that a fish can make little progress when it tries to swim rapidly with its mouth open. What's more important, it will soon become weakened by suffocation if unable to open and close its mouth freely. To get oxygen, water must flow freely through its gills. The short, lifting strokes prevent the fish from closing its mouth. When the mouth is open the gills remain closed, and the fish cannot force oxygen-laden water through them. The rhythm must be maintained in smooth-pressure lifts, not jerks.

Timing the length of the strokes is not easy to master. Patience and practice are essential. If the stroke is too slow or too long, the fish will have a chance to open and close its mouth. The effect is also lessened if it is too short or too quick. If the fish continues sulking or going out, the timing is off, but if it starts a ruckus or gives in, the rhythm is working and the pressure and timing are okay.

The number of strokes required to bring the rod to the maximum height depends upon the resistance of the fish, or on how rapidly it can be brought in. Four or five strokes to complete the upward swing for, let's say, a cooperative twenty-pound YELLOWTAIL or ALBACORE, will give somewhat of a vague idea. The timing of the

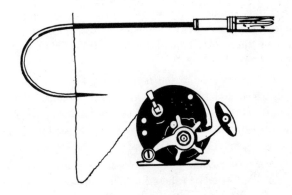

strokes is maintained whether the fish stubbornly resists or permits itself to be easily brought forward.

Even when R. P. is applied, strength and struggle are necessary in bringing a monstrous heavyweight to gaff. Much less pressure and energy are required, however, to "fetch" a fish of less size when using R. P., as compared to the old method.

Some few anglers have long made use of a system of slow pumping to turn or slow down a fish. Usually the practice was applied erratically without any knowledge of the effect on the fish and, therefore, without understanding the necessity of rhythm and timing. The most successful of those anglers developed a certain amount of instinct, or feeling, for timing, by means of trial and error. This manner of pumping was often referred to as "whipping."

When the angler using R. P. intends to turn or halt a fish that is going away, the spacing and timing of the strokes are done in the same careful rhythm as for bringing the fish forward, the difference being that instead of the chain of continuous strokes upward, a single stroke is repeated. Also, due to the flexibility of the rod, the stroke is somewhat longer.

All too often, the beginner fails to start reeling in quickly enough to keep slack out of the line after the apex of the final stroke. Enough pressure should be maintained to keep the rod bending.

Anglers, having formed a habit of knocking themselves out before tiring the big gamester, will learn that fishing can be done with only as much effort as they wish to put into it, and that they need not hesitate to tackle the biggest of MARLIN or BROADBILL, once they get the gist of this technique.

ALBACORE

A line slices the water with a hissing fizz—a crescendo of screeching, singing reels—a crash as a rod tip is snapped off—groans, gasps, yells. "Hookup!" "Let 'im have it!" "Damn the . . .!" "Blast his hide!" "Hookup!" "ALBACORE!"

Bad men go tame and tame men go mad over the prospects of catching a few ALBACORE. Sounds silly? Just try it. If your blood doesn't churn your brain cells into an extreme state of excitation or insensibility, you can just wrap 'em up and lay 'em away—they're dead.

ALBACORE is the pot of gold at the rainbow's end for small commercial fishermen. When these TUNA start running, every hopped-up jalopy of a sea-going tub makes a dash to the briny gold fields. U.S. commercial boats caught over thirteen million pounds in one year, and a boat load of ALBACORE at the price they get is nothing to sneeze at.

During years when water temperatures are too warm, close in, to suit this "chicken of the sea" tuna, there are an increasing number of large (up to 85 feet) angling boats going out for two or three-day trips. They may sail for 50 or 75 miles before intercepting the migration path, which sometimes widens into a belt of 200 to 300 miles, extending from Guadalupe Island off Baja California to the North Pacific.

There are any number of theories on when, where, and how to contact ALBACORE. We have given each reasonable idea a thorough trial with the result that some have proven fairly reliable, or rather, have worked with good "batting averages." There are a few rules, however, that are almost infallible; yet because of the ALBACORE's very nature and the unpredictable changes in the ocean's currents, even these will appear questionable.

The theory that ALBACORE and other pelagic fishes are more likely to be caught on days preceded by full moonlight nights has some points worth consideration. When nights are dark or overcast, the small forage fishes can readily be located by the luminescence (phosphorescence) they create as they stir the water. On the other hand, the brilliance of moonlight outshines the lesser glow of the disturbed organisms, thereby making the movements of the forage fishes imperceptible, forcing the TUNA to seek their prey during the day.

The argument that many fish are taken in the dark of the moon does not necessarily contradict the bright night theory. Even during dark night periods the forage fishes may be reduced to such insufficient numbers that the ALBACORE would continue searching for food on into the daylight hours.

At times there is such an abundance of food that the TUNA are able to fill the very limited capacity of their stomachs during the first couple of hours after dawn, disappearing to the depths for the balance of the day.

There are a number of signs looked for by boat captains in search of ALBACORE and other TUNA. One of the first is in the behavior of the sea birds, for they can be seen at vast distances. When they are hovering near the surface or diving (termed a "bird-work"), it is an almost certain indication that a school of small fishes has been forced to the surface. Often, however, instead of ALBACORE, the school's pursuers may turn out to be SEALIONS, SHARKS, or PORPOISES. On the less obvious side, when the ocean surface is calm, TUNA schools can sometimes be located by the ripples they churn up.

Leaping BLUEFIN may be a tip-off that a school of competing ALBACORE is muscling in on their "smorgasbord," but more than likely the cavorting BLUEFIN are only trying to shake off some hangers-on or just "horsing around."

Submerged banks in some ocean areas are the habitats of numerous schools of (PACIFIC) SAURIES, which are preyed upon by many game fishes. ALBACORE are often disclosed by the aerial activities of the SAURIES. The small fish can be seen at a distance, as they are capable of jumping two or three feet out of the water. Arching DOLPHINS often lead a skipper to a school. These mammals form a strange association and travel with TUNA, especially with YELLOWFIN.

At a distance the surfacing movements of the KILLER WHALE, *Orca gladiator*, resemble those of the DOLPHIN except that, in comparison, the huge mammal seems to be executing his arcs in slow motion. When a school of these killers appears, TUNA leave the vicinity in panic, as do boat skippers.

Pity the poor fisherman on a day when no signs of feeding game fishes are detected, but the deeper sympathy should go to the captain of a TUNA special. He really suffers, trying as best he can to conceal his agony. Some, it is said, resort to sundry hunches, prayers, or even black magic, and sometimes make contact.

When all other methods fail, the skipper is likely to select a hunch spot out of that big, big ocean and instruct his fares to attach heavy sinkers and prospect at various depths. Now and again, to his own amazement, the passengers begin bringing fish aboard.

One of the largest catches by a sportfishing boat during a recent season was made when the boat engine died and the quick thinking captain, to cover his own embarrassment, gave word for his passengers to start fishing. By the time he had repaired the motor (about two hours later), every passenger had a limit of ALBACORE. This is not a tall one; we were there.

At this point let us consider a few notes for the novice. When taking an "Albacore Special" (a vessel going all out for TUNA or nothing), be selective. Remember, small boats carry fewer passengers—a definite advantage. Check on the captain's rating and the number of the crew. Book through a reputable agency or at the dock. If possible, make a trip to the dock the day before sailing and ask questions—lots of them. How are bait conditions? Number of passengers? How many hours will the captain fish? How far to the fishing grounds?

Once aboard, as the trip starts, get additional information. Will bait be supplied on board? Do the captain and mate fish (if charter boat)? Do all fish caught belong to the passengers? Will the captain stop to fish

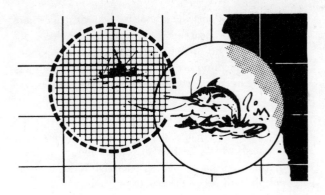

SHARKS? (Good idea especially when few TUNA are found.) Which fish are disqualified for the jackpot? Discuss the use of tackle with the captain. Ask him to test star drag tension, check hooks, line, sinkers, and lures.

Do not call the captain's assistant, often the only crew member, a deck hand or bait boy. His title is "Mate." Making a friend of him at the very beginning will prove helpful. Neither of the crew members are overpaid and a generous bonus for extra services, such as for cleaning fish and helping in other ways, would not be amiss.

An angler about to sail on a scheduled sportfishing or charter boat anticipating ALBACORE should have a number of twist-on sinkers of various weights; sturdy, rapid-retrieve conventional and spinning reels with extra loaded spools (20-pound-test line for beginners); a long sturdy rod with the top three feet very flexible; a range of short-shank hooks in sizes to match baits, which may run from a No. 4 for pinhead anchovy to a No. 1 for a large sardine-size bait. All this is for casting.

For trolling tackle, a sturdy, short trolling rod mounted with Aftco-type-roller guides; a #349 Penn-type reel, loaded with limp, 30 or 40-pound-test Dacron line; heavy keel-sinkers, followed by a swivel and 4-foot-long Sevalon-type, 30-pound-test blue leader.

Two types of lures are needed, one that dives deeply, the other a near-surface runner. Light colors are generally favored, but several should be tried, whether they be feathers, plastic squid, or one of the many hard spoons or jigs. At times, any kind of moving bait will attract.

The one important item ALBACORE anglers are apt to overlook is a supply of hand towels or rags. Cool water, wind, and goo are not recommended for a beautifying hand lotion. Then there is a lengthy list to be made out when going for the over-night voyages. In addition to a change of dry clothing and a sleeping bag (when required), there are several things that make for convenience, such as tape to repair broken guide wrapping, a tool kit, and extra brake lining washers.

Since the boat is not anchored when fishing for ALBACORE, the usually preferred stern positions are of no advantage except that the school is likely to strike there first. A position near the bow gives the angler more freedom to play his fish with less chance of crossing other lines. Let us mention here that tangling lines is the most aggravating hazard in ALBACORE fishing; the astute angler will do everything possible to avoid it.

Nearly everyone aboard becomes over-anxious when a troller yells, "Hookup." All rush for bait at once, and are annoyed when the bait dispenser, ignoring them, calmly continues his chumming, and rightly so. It is his responsibility to entice the school to come near the boat and to keep them around as long as possible. By the use of a second dip-net he will supply the anglers soon enough.

When a fish is hooked on a troll line, other lines are reeled in quickly. Nor is any line let out until the hooked fish is within twenty or thirty feet of the boat and then only by those few on the stern who are able to cast far out. The other anglers hold back until the hooked fish is ready for the gaff. To attract and hold the school, some daring captains will keep the first hooked fish in the water until another hookup is made.

If the troll-hooked fish is lost, the chances are that the school will disappear temporarily. In such a situation, anglers quickly clamp on sinkers in an attempt to intercept the school which might sound to a depth of one or two hundred feet.

When fish are scarce, it is advisable to remain in or return to the position of the first hookup, as the school often circles around for a mile or so, comes back, and can again be contacted. Trail-chumming should be resumed and continued.

There is little advantage gained by the trolling angler from a sport-fishing boat. Chances are usually four to one against his making a catch. If he should be the lucky one, the time required to deck his fish, change over to his light tackle, and get baited up is a handicap in getting to work for the jackpot prize. Fish caught while trolling are seldom qualified for the jackpot.

As soon as the troll-hooked fish is in, or when fish have followed a chum trail and begin feeding near the boat, ALBACORE angling becomes a serious business in which everyone aboard should try to act cooperatively.

Careful attention to the current and drift should be given, so that lines are not crossed by careless casting. Once the bait is out it should be kept in motion by slowly lifting and lowering the rod tip. If ALBACORE are breaking near the vessel they are hungry and will as likely take a moving dead bait as a live one.

The beginner should learn to estimate the tension and strength possibilities of his tackle. Of primary importance is the use and proper adjustment of the star drag, with appropriate thumb pressure to supplement star drag tension. He must know the strength potential of the rod, line, and leader and learn to keep the pulling pressure well below the maximum or breaking point.

Cool calculation is not easy when ALBACORE start boiling, but errors can be costly. The exemplary angler collects his wits and directs his activities accordingly. He is in no haste to be the first to cast out. He surveys the situation and selects the spot at which to aim his cast. He calls "Low bridge," then follows through, keeping his eye on his hook to avoid catching some bobbing fisherman's ear. The reel is kept in free wheeling until the strike is noticed and the fish has made its first short run. Line is then payed out to allow the fish as much freedom as possible. At the end of this run, the spool is thrown into gear and the hook is set with a gentle strike. The fish is then permitted to make his big run and subsequent dashes, with minimum tension on the spool.

If the "CORE" takes off on an angle or parallel dash, the angler quickly follows, keeping his line straight out, although he may have to go completely around the deck. Never at any time is the line allowed to slacken; it is always kept taut. Nor is the fish given any time to rest. The moment the swimming stops, or if the fish sounds, the rhythmic pumping technique is applied and kept up until another drive begins or the "CORE" is brought to gaff.

The moment the fish is within reach of the gaffer, the spool is thrown out of gear with the thumb on the spool flange holding the tension. Free wheeling at this point is important, for if the gaffer misses and another run ensues, the fish is still hooked and can be fought again. It also gives the gaffer more freedom of action in decking the fish.

ALBACORE that appear along our west coast are believed to spawn somewhere in the south seas. Those caught within our range seldom exceed thirty-five pounds, while mature fish found near their natural habitat may exceed eighty pounds and four feet in length. The young, immature fish travel enormous distances, arriving on the banks off the coast of middle Baja California some time in June, then migrating in a wide circle around most of the North Pacific, some going over close to Japan before returning to their southern habitat. This movement pattern changes according to water temperature, the preference being a range of 60 to 65 degrees but seldom below 57 or above 72. Extra-heavy plankton blooms or shortage of forage may keep the schools far out to sea.

During the six favorable years prior to the three-year warm period, ALBACORE were caught on the first full moon after July 1, off or not far below the Coronado Islands, some in southern California. Although far offshore during the warm period, some were taken by commercials throughout January, and as far north as Vancouver.

Following the highly successful example of Virg Moores in establishing live bait facilities and sending his boats out for ALBACORE from Morro Bay, we can expect numerous enterprising operators to follow right on up the Pacific Coast. Heretofore, locating the flexible swimways of the ALBACORE has been difficult, but with modern electronic equipment, radio, and the scientific knowledge gained, locating schools has become much less of a problem. Once facilities are established and properly exploited, there should be plenty of anglers to fill every boat going.

❧ BLUEFIN AND YELLOWFIN TUNA ❧

The size of the TUNA now coming into our waters seems to diminish each season. Many years ago, in the early days of Zane Grey's exploits around Catalina Island, BLUEFIN just short of two hundred pounds were not uncommon. Zane Grey's brother, R. C. Grey, writing of an occasion in 1921, tells of encountering a school three or four miles long, the smallest fish taken weighing well over a hundred pounds. Kite fishing was already in vogue in those days. Nowadays, BLUEFIN TUNA above thirty-five pounds are seldom caught from sport-fishing boats, the average being twelve to fourteen pounds. The few big ones that do show up seem to have developed a wariness about boats and fishing tackle. The angler of today uses a sea-colored, twelve to twenty-pound-test monofilament line with No. 1 hook, at great depths, or No. 6 near surface. For surface fish, the bait is flied out. The hook is set only after the angler is sure it has been deeply swallowed.

The time and pattern of migration followed by the BLUEFIN is very similar to that of the ALBACORE, except that the BLUEFIN's northern trek ends at Point Conception. Few venture beyond the Point. Another noticeable difference is that the BLUEFIN may be found closer to shore. Also they seem to favor the sloping edges of submerged banks, while ALBACORE show little preference.

Small BLUEFIN are by no means scarce; hundreds may be seen in a single day. The problem is not so much in finding them, but rather in persuading them to take the hook. Even enticing a school of them to approach the boat is a rare accomplishment. Due to this reluctance and to the fact that little progress has been made in BLUEFIN angling technique, fishing for this species has become secondary or an added attraction to ALBACORE and YELLOWTAIL angling. A little experimentation is needed to open new possibilities.

During warm years, schools of small YELLOWFIN venture up on the banks to San Clemente Island. The larger fish, up to 300 pounds, occur off Baja California and are super-abundant in the Sea of Cortez. They will take white Compac feathers near the surface and large lures trolled deeply. The young entering our range are more responsive to chumming than BLUEFIN and usually they display much less reluctance in taking the hook.

Of all the TUNAS, or most other fish, the large YELLOWFIN provides the greatest challenge. This is proven by the many above 75 pounds that are hooked, with so few decked. It is the first run of more than an eighth of a mile that does it.

There are occasions when a school of BLUEFIN TUNA will be feeding leisurely without showing themselves. Then suddenly a school of ALBACORE will scoot in among them and start devouring the food. A most spectacular aquatic circus can then be witnessed. The BLUEFIN get panicky, and in their attempt to beat the other fellow to the forage fish, make amazing leaps out of the water. When a hundred or so start performing their "grandes jetées," it is an unforgettable sight.

Most of the time the BLUEFIN seem to jump for the sheer joy of it, acting as if they were playing follow the leader; first one leaps, then another, until a dozen or more have executed the graceful arcs. They also make high leaps and hit broadside, perhaps to try to rid themselves of parasites. It is no wonder that the nickname "LEAPING TUNA" has been popularized as a simile of exaggeration.

When the skipper does succeed in locating a school hungry enough to show some interest in the chum, he follows about the same line of strategy as used for ALBACORE, except for the preliminary use of lures. If the school is made up of lightweights, the angler can handle them as he would the ALBACORE. If his position on the boat is favorable, he will pay the bait out instead of casting.

After a deep school has been located there is a method of chumming it up close to the surface by bending or injuring the bait fish used as chum so they will sink. The response seems quicker when motors are cut off. The splashes made by leaping TUNA make the school easy to locate.

Some anglers contend that for BLUEFIN all live bait is more effective when tail-hooked. When the hook is inserted in the rear half of the body, the bait will remain on or near the surface longer than if hooked through the forepart.

A fifteen-pounder will usually make a first run of a hundred yards or so, and will more than likely do a half dozen more before beginning his bulldog shaking and jerking tactics.

For large BLUEFIN and YELLOWFIN encountered on long voyages aboard the angling ships running down to Guadalupe Island and Cabo San Lucas, moderately heavy tackle with Sevenstrand leaders longer than the fish should be employed. There is little chance of keeping large TUNA from whipping the line in two when a long leader is not used. Out away from shore, blue, plastic-covered leader material seems best.

The beginner will always be fooled by the driving power of the BLUEFIN. A hooked fifteen-pounder will feel like a monster on his line. If he should fail to land it, he should not be blamed too much if he goes beyond the conventional exaggeration allowed in recounting the traditional fish story.

❧ (OCEANIC) SKIPJACK ❧

Toward the end of the ALBACORE season a school of voraciously feeding SKIPJACK now and then appears out of the deep blue to surprise, thrill, and amaze all hands aboard a sportfishing boat. No other large game fish is so eager to cooperate. When hungry, they can be aroused by almost any kind of bait, live or dead—feathers, bone jigs, chrome lures, or spoons. Due perhaps to overfishing, this species is now scarce.

SKIPJACK, as a rule, seldom stray very far away from the school. When one is hooked, a heavy chum will usually produce others. They are taken in the same manner as ALBACORE but range nearer shore.

❧ (CALIFORNIA) BARRACUDA ❧

With the gradually diminishing number of the TUNAS to be found each year, the BARRACUDA gains in popularity. It seems that as long as the enormous population of AN-CHOVIES holds out, the "BARRIES" will be fairly plentiful.

The BARRACUDA is not always as fastidious as the other deep sea fishes except during the early part of the season, when he will snap the bait in half or just chew on it, missing the hook. The wise angler then replaces his single hook with a double job, the first hook three or four inches above the other, the top one holding the bait, the lower one inserted near the tail. (See Fig. 12.)

Since the BARRACUDA has become one of the main-stays for angling boats south of Pt. Conception, anglers going out for other species should be prepared to do battle with a surprise attack by the "BARRIES," not only with the two-hook "booby-trap," but with shorty six-inch Sevalon leaders with No. 2 to 4 short-shank hooks, according to the size of bait. Also in order are ¼ ounce to one-ounce white Compac feathers, the kind that slides up on the leader and away from the mouth full of large, sharp teeth that can soon chew them off.

Retrieving a feather, which has little side-slipping action, as do other lures, requires a special technique. Fast halting movements seem to attract more often, but there are times when a steady retrieve is preferred.

Fishing with light tackle, you can play a BARRIE until pooped only when hooked a good distance from the boat. If hooked close in, he should be horsed (retrieved rapidly).

When using lures, it is customary for anglers to fish from the bow where there is more room and less chance of casting across other lines.

The big "LOG BARRIES" are experienced. They have been around and have developed very conservative ideas. The young yearlings may mill all around the boat, but not so with the crafty old granddaddies. They have a definite complex about boats, and the angler who hopes to contact one of them will have to use a rod with enough spring to send the bait out. A good-sized queenfish, sardine, or whatever other large bait is available will fetch 'em, but only if kept in motion by the angler. As a result of the long, high cast, the bait is stunned tempo-rarily by the smack it gets when dropped to the surface. As soon as it settles into the water, it must be worked to make it appear alive at all. A stripbait will therefore often prove as effective as live bait.

While the BARRACUDA is more often fished on the surface, they occasionally remain at depths down to fifty feet. He strikes hard and makes one long run and a couple of short dashes.

Although the BARRACUDA is a good food fish cooked in various ways, it is the large saddle of roe that is highly prized. When fried, the flavor is not only different from other fish products, but it is loaded with vitamins and other health-giving properties. None of the roe should ever be wasted.

ᕗᕕᕕ (CALIFORNIA) BONITO ᕕᕕᕕ

The BONITO is one of the game fishes that doesn't go out of his way to snub the angler. Nor does he ignore a nice, lively bait, whether it is an ANCHOVY, SARDINE, or SMELT. Without the slightest reservation, he will even strike a chrome lure; and when a ten-pound BONITO strikes, it's no peck. He usually hits on the run without giving the angler the least warning. Often, when the angler is fishing a school of MACKEREL with poise and confidence, he is apt to get a jolt he won't forget. In years favorable to BONITO abundance it should out-rank BARRACUDA in popularity, not only because of its superior fighting ability but because of its great predation pressure on the anchovy population, which is all to the good.

No other fish enjoys a commotion as does the BONITO. Start a rumpus in the water, and he will plow right in. During the ensuing pitch of excitement, he can be taken on any kind of a lure.

The fact that the BONITO is a schooling fish is too often ignored. When one or two fishes are hooked, it is almost a certainty that a school is in the vicinity and can be attracted to the boat by chumming the area. Once a school is contacted, it can be held only for a limited time, but will return again and again at varying intervals. Some floating baits thrown out continuously will keep sea birds splashing around, thus renewing the BONITO's interest.

It is possible to overfeed a school by over-chumming. Once partially filled, a BONITO becomes choosey and the angler will have to change hooks from a No. 1 or 1/0 to a No. 2 or less if he expects to continue getting hookups.

The same recipes for preparing and cooking MACK-EREL may be used for BONITO.

ᕗᕕᕕ (PACIFIC) MACKEREL ᕕᕕᕕ

At last the lowly MACKEREL is about to achieve respectability and be elevated to the status of game fish—at least g.f. second class.

This close relative of the TUNA is no longer to be scoffed at as just a poor fish; for now, thanks to the overfishing by commercials, he has become scarce. His fine qualifications are now being counted and recounted. On the materialistic side, he is saving many an angler from that humiliating predicament of going ashore with a dry sack. As a fighter, the "GREEN STREAK" is daemonic, and capable of tangling more lines than his cousins. According to estimates of nautical engineers, the stream-lined body contour of the MACKEREL is nearly perfect and meets much less water resistance than any of our other game fishes. Last, but not least, this fish has become a choice among vitamin-loaded victuals. Housewives, who once abhorred the aroma of frying MACKEREL, have discovered all sorts of new recipes for cooking and serving this budget-saver. They can smoke, salt, boil, bake, broil, barbecue, steam, or toast it. MACKEREL can be canned, parboiled, or parbaked, then flaked, fried or sauted with sauces. This does not include the Asian preparations such as the delectable Filipino dish of raw MACKEREL with species and nuts, or the Japanese and Chinese chowed MACKEREL with pickled beans and bean curd. Methods of preparation are endless.

The (PACIFIC) MACKEREL occurs in shallow areas during summer and fall months, retreating a mile or so offshore about October 15, then moving on to deeper waters in January, and appearing again in the moderately shallow surfaces in May.

While the distribution of this species extends from Alaska to Cabo San Lucas and back up into the Sea of Cortez, relatively few schools are encountered north of Monterey Bay.

Anglers will find the ravenous schools feeding near the surface during the early morning hours and intermittently throughout the day. They may be brought to the boat and kept around by the new processed chum or ground fish. When no chum is available, casting a strip-bait out and retrieving it rapidly will bring the schools in. When hungry, the MACKEREL will take almost any bait offered. Strips of sardine, mackerel, or anchovy, two inches long, are preferred.

Anglers anticipating a go at big SHARKS, MARLIN, or the giant BLACK SEA BASS would do well to first hook a few MACKEREL, since a large slab from a very fresh MACKEREL serves as a number one bait for these monsters.

Along the East Coast, anglers pay as much as $25.00 per day on sportfishing boats engaged only in the pursuit of MACKEREL.

It is strictly up to the angler to sell the idea to the boat captain, and up to the captain to sell the angler on the merits of the *Pneumatophorus japonicus* as a rated game fish.

❧ KELP BASS ❧

Beginning about the middle of April, sportfishing boats from south of Pt. Conception put out for the KELP beds, which until several years ago were well populated with KELP BASS (erroneously called CALICO BASS and BULL BASS). Without too much effort, a proficient angler could count on getting a limit within an hour or so. Then the KELP cutters, commercial fishermen, too many anglers, somebody, or something, lowered the boom, and this species became so scarce that many boats were forced to give up KELP BASS entirely. Then, in 1953, a law prohibiting the commercial capture seemed to have saved the sport fishery. This came after a highly successful tagging program by the Marine Division of the California Department of Fish and Game. This and the Kelp Study indicate clearly that the KELP BASS population can be greatly increased by regulating KELP cutting and planting new fields of the giant plant.

Populations of fishes that do not spawn in fresh or brackish water are seldom increased by artificial means. While the dumping of old autos and streetcars and the building of other artificial habitats may provide housing for very small numbers and some valuable scientific knowledge, there is little comparison to the vast KELP forests for increasing the KELP BASS and other fish populations.

Since 1953 this BASS has made something of a comeback but has not reached the super-abundance of many years ago. But if profound and honest thought is given the KELP habitat situation and a bit of daring is shown, there is no doubt that an enormous increase could be brought about.

A few years back a boat could simply drop anchor near a large kelp field and start pulling the fish in; but strategy and cunning are required these days. First a long chum line is established next to a kelp area. The anchor is dropped up tide fifty to a hundred feet ahead of an opening between clumps of kelp; line is payed out until the boat is situated so that all hands can cast out

or fish straight down as they choose. Chumming is continued in an effort to bring the fish to the surface.

Although it is difficult even with a long, flexible rod, the angler who can cast with a degree of accuracy will drop a bait out over a clump of kelp. He then slowly lowers and raises the bait until he feels the strike. As soon as the fish hits, he gives line instead of trying to set the hook at once. Like so many other salt-water fishes, BASS often grab the bait by the tail, juggle it around to stun or kill the prey, make a short run, then attempt to swallow it head first. The timing is the most important part of the angler's procedure. If the attempt to bring it in is premature, the fish will not get hooked. If too much time is given, it will likely circle a kelp stalk. In the latter case, the fish will often untangle itself if the angler will keep his line fairly taut, allowing a little slack at intervals. When the BASS refuses to cooperate, try tapping on the rod with a metal object. The sound vibrations telegraphed down the line strike a jarring note which often starts the fish off on a tangent.

When preparing for a boat trip to the kelp beds, make sure you have plenty of hooks on four-foot-long, twenty-pound-test wire leaders, for chances are you will lose a number of them by getting fouled in the kelp. In this event, lift your rod back until you can grasp the line and pull it free with your hands instead of giving your rod and reel the unnecessary punishment. Never try to fish with a kinked leader. The wire leader will often cut the kelp and pull free.

When casting, no sinker is used if the live bait is weighty. If the bait is small, use a clamp-on sinker just heavy enough for casting. The lightness of weight will allow the bait more freedom to run. When fishing straight down, a heavy sinker is used to keep the bait from entangling other fishermen's lines. The large KELP BASS prefer live bait, while the medium pan-fry like stripbait. None should be taken less than the legal 12 inches.

❧ WHITE SEABASS ❧

The drop in the numbers of WHITE SEABASS in the past decade appears disastrous. The cause was obviously overfishing. First, purse seiners wiped out their main food supply, the Southern California SARDINE population, then reduced the big gamefish to an angler catch of less than 4000 pounds for the year 1972. (The few small schools of SARDINE visiting the waters off San Diego come up on tour from the region around Cedros Island.)

There are no hopes for the return of the SARDINE but some authorities believe there is a chance for the recovery of the WHITE SEABASS if Mexico will join us in a moratorium. The possibility of a return to abundance by WHITE SEABASS will appear quite reasonable to Mexico when they check its great increase in the north end of the Sea of Cortez during the last few years.

The WHITE SEABASS is not a bass but a member of the CROAKER family, *Sciaenidae.* Most CROAKER species seldom regain former abundances, but where predators for the young are reduced or absent, they reproduce rapidly, as we have seen in the Salton Sea transplant of CORVINA and BAIRDIELLA CROAKER.

Because of the scarcity of WHITE SEABASS in California waters, we must give close attention to our angling techniques for them.

Being a fighter with a weak mouth, this big fellow is very difficult to bring to gaff and must be played cautiously. If he is hooked among kelp, the contest is no easy matter. After the first long run, thumb pressure is applied for added tension when pulling the rod up. Slowly and gradually the WHITE SEABASS is brought in, but only after he has made a few short runs. During this time the angler forces him to work for every inch he gains by keeping as tight a rein as possible without tearing the hook out.

The two most important points to remember are: Feed out line at the first slight pull and give this fish plenty of time.

Out around the islands, or near large offshore kelp beds south of Point Conception, an occasional large hungry school of WHITE SEABASS may be encountered. The intercepting fishermen often forget all the ethics of the art in their haste to make contact, for the school is apt to depart at a moment's notice. The bait dispenser gets a real workout trying to supply the anglers' demands and to keep the school around by heaving out chum.

Little is actually known of the daily movements of the WHITE SEABASS, but there seems to be a recognizable pattern in his shift from shallow water, shortly after sun-up, out to the slopes or edges of submerged canyons, and his return with the first tide change after nightfall, or on those occasions when food has been scarce. On the deep slopes, stripbait and fresh shrimp will sometimes attract this fish quicker than live bait.

Delicious CABEZON and SAND BASS, both bottom feeders, are also caught on these early kelp cruises. If south of the Baja California border, add the fighting OCEAN-WHITEFISH and four or five species of ROCKFISH.

Many boats fish the kelp beds throughout the spring, summer, and fall, and the clientele is seldom disappointed. During the late summer months, when fishing becomes spotty, a wise captain will shift close to shore, where a dozen or more species of rocky bottom fishes can be taken on stripbait. Or again, he may head for the open ocean in search of BARRACUDA, BONITO, MACKEREL or SKIPJACK.

Our hesitation in suggesting live or freshly caught squid as first-choice bait for WHITE SEABASS and some other species is due to the present uncertainty in finding squid available. Some progress has been made, however, especially around Catalina Island.

The large yoke-hooked bait flied out has proved best in the north end of the Sea of Cortez for WHITE SEABASS. Yoke bait is hooked just ahead of the dorsal fin.

(CALIFORNIA) YELLOWTAIL

About the first of April, the boats at Ensenada and a little later at San Diego start out in pursuit of the elusive YELLOWTAIL, about the toughest customer to handle of all the Pacific Coast game fishes short of the big SHARKS, SWORDFISH, or MARLIN.

YELLOWTAIL are quite unpredictable—here today, gone tomorrow, and back again the next day. One time they will hit anchovies, queenfish, butterfish, or baysmelt; another, nothing but a medium-sized sardine will entice them; and then, on occasions, dozens of them will lazily cruise around the boat refusing any bait whatsoever.

No one as yet seems to have discovered a way to present a bait that will attract a YELLOWTAIL at all times. Often an angler will find himself aboard a boat with "YELLOWS" boiling all around. He may try every known method of hooking the bait, with no success. Suddenly a ravenous school of BARRACUDA shows up and starts milling about and the "YELLOWS" instinctively become alert and begin contesting for their share of chum and bait alike.

You have no doubt read of sportsmen catching a heavyweight with a fly rod. That's all right if you have a fast motor boat and get started early enough in the morning; but from a sportfishing boat, being in a stationary position, the tackle must be more than equal to the occasion. The consensus is that with a long, flexible rod, the angler has a number of advantages. He is able to get more distance in his cast. Because of its sensitivity, the rod helps him in his timing and in keeping the play smooth. The great length helps in keeping the line above other anglers' heads when the hooked fish starts circling the boat. It also serves as a shock absorber when the YELLOWTAIL strikes, which often happens so suddenly that the angler has little time to think, much less act. Fast thinking and speedy action are necessary because these fellows have a habit of hitting the bait when it is being retrieved. Though the angler is holding his rod straight up and ready to relax the tension, he needs the time that split second will give him, even when the star drag is set just tight enough to turn the spool.

The experienced captain of a sportfishing boat knows of certain spots over a bank or around the islands that are especially "hot" for YELLOWTAIL. They usually lie just off rocky shore lines where kelp and other sea life are abundant.

On arriving at his selected location, the captain maneuvers his boat in a series of diminishing circles. The baitsman tosses out live bait on the "in" side about every ten or fifteen feet. As the boat slows down to a stop in the center of the circles, he heaves out a dozen or so with his hand net, then continues tossing one or two at intervals of a couple of seconds.

At first the YELLOWTAIL will hesitate in coming near the boat, and the angler must fly the bait out to make contact. It is very difficult to persuade the not-too-hungry YELLOW to take a hooked bait. Often you will see them grab the chum, boil all around the baited hook, and yet refuse it. They show unbelievable perception in recognizing the difference between the free anchovy (or whatever chum is being used) and hooked bait. Because of this canny instinct, anglers have found that the small, short No. 2 to 6 hook tied directly to mono line is about par for average baits used; they use lesser sizes for small baits. The hook is tied directly to twelve to twenty-pound-test mono line.

For a minute or so after a cast, the angler allows the bait to run (anchovies usually becoming sluggish in a short time). He then begins a series of short pulls and halts as he retrieves.

At the first sign of a strike, the angler gives free line, allowing the fish a chance to make a short run before setting the hook. This is done very warily. The beginner should have his star drag set at a point where the fish will have little work when it makes a run, just barely tight enough to bring it in when the run is over. If the YELLOW-TAIL heads for the kelp, it can be stopped or turned with a rhythmic pumping.

Do not try to "horse" a YELLOWTAIL in when he shows signs of weakening, but keep him coming in with a smooth and gentle pumping movement without giving him a chance to rest. It should be borne in mind that the hook has probably made a slit; if pulled overly hard, the hook is apt to enlarge it, cutting clear. On the other hand, if the tension is relaxed, the fish may "spit" the hook out. (Fishes cannot expectorate in the true sense of the word, but they certainly can put a lot of force into a similar motion.)

When a hooked YELLOWTAIL is running near the boat or being brought in, all anglers nearby quickly reel in. This is not only a rule of courtesy to the successful angler, but a bit of good "horse sense"; for if lines become tangled, everyone involved in the mixup will lose precious time.

Keep your reel in free wheeling and the rod well up and ready to be let down quickly should the "YELLOW" choose to do some fancy flopping as you bring him in to gaff. Stand close to the rail so you can watch.

A YELLOWTAIL is never to be trusted until he is in the sack. Very often, just as he is about to be gaffed, he dashes under the boat, and before the angler can say "scad" his rod is snapped. The fish gets a leverage when the rod comes down across the rail; unless the spool is in free wheeling, something is bound to bust.

Once the "YELLOW" is safely sacked, the angler can afford to take time out for some well-earned refreshments.

Now let's see—a thirty-pound YELLOWTAIL at "caviar prices." Hmmmm, not bad—and then there's that $50.00 jackpot in the offing! Angling does have its angles.

ᏨᎳ SHEEP-HEAD ᏨᎳ

If it is either too early or too late in the season (south of Point Conception) for the big hauls of game fishes, a stratagem used by many a fisherman who is superstitious about going home with an empty sack is to take along a few shrimp. When no one aboard seems able to get a strike, he takes out a large No. 4/0 or 5/0 hook attached to a four-foot leader and baits with half a shrimp, leaving the shell on. He then attaches the leader a foot above the sinker, drops it to the bottom, and works it up and down just enough to keep it moving. Result—SHEEP-HEAD, an excellent food fish.

The habitat of the SHEEP-HEAD is limited however, to rocky places and areas near kelp or other sea-growth.

ᏨᎳ OCEAN-WHITEFISH ᏨᎳ

Out around the islands and off the coast of Baja California, big, fighting OCEAN-WHITEFISH are plentiful. They are "suckers" for shrimp or any other kind of white-meated crustaceans, and usually feed about five or six feet above the bottom.

The OCEAN-WHITEFISH is found over a rocky bottom. His first run is usually in the direction of his favorite submerged ledge. If he succeeds in making it, trying to extract him is almost useless. The angler can restrain the brawler by a series of short pumps. Once the direction is changed, the fish will fight it out near or on the surface. The OCEAN-WHITEFISH is not only a game fish, but an exceptionally fine food fish. In the warm waters between Point Conception and Point Banda these fish are less spirited. South of Point Banda they attain a length of three feet or more and fight like YELLOWTAIL. Shrimp with the shell left on or other crustaceans are the best bait. Same tackle is used as for SHEEP-HEAD.

⤜❦⤛ BONITO SHARK-BLUE ⤜❦⤛ SHARK-SALMON SHARK

The opinion that the BONITO SHARK is a superior game fish is well founded. With the exception of the SWORD-FISH and MARLIN, no other fish within our range can equal his spectacular breaks and leaps when hooked. Although very unpredictable, he can be counted upon to give a splendid account of himself about nine times out of ten. That lazy ten percent will permit themselves to be brought to gaff with practically no resistance. It is not uncommon for a fighting hundred-pounder to break water ten to fifteen times, occasionally clearing the surface completely before giving in. Those feeding near the surface in moderately warm water appear especially agile.

SHARKS are not usually grouped as densely as other schooling fishes but chances are that when one or more is sighted, others can be located in the vicinity.

In addition to the regular chumming materials, BONITO SHARKS will respond to beef blood even in the dry form, but a side sliced from a live mackerel rates first as bait. Because of this SHARK's habit of turning over and over and winding himself up in the line, which he can saw off with his tail, a ten-foot leader is suggested. The moment the SHARK starts this turning, the R. P. treatment should be applied. Unless there are two men to gaff a heavyweight, it is a good idea to break out the "shootin' irons" before trying to deck him.

North of Point Conception, anglers fish the SALMON SHARK in the same manner as the BONITO SHARK, except that a large slice of fresh greenling is used as the number one bait.

The big BLUE SHARK is seen quite frequently in southern waters and is at once recognized by the triangular dorsal fin projecting above the surface. The front edge or line of the dorsal fin of the SALMON and BONITO SHARK curves slightly backward.

While the BLUE SHARK is not as spectacular in battle as the others, his weight and driving power give him a rating among the big-game fishes. All large SHARKS are capable of bruising shins with their powerful tail strokes and should be knocked out as soon as they are brought aboard. It is also advisable to butcher them immediately, cut them into chunks and keep them in cool, damp gunnysacks to preserve the good quality of the meat.

Any of the three of these SHARKS may be found feeding on SAURIES in about the same areas as ALBACORE, also near the mouths of submarine canyons at varying depths down to fifty or sixty fathoms. As food fish they compare favorably to the SWORDFISH (many, including the author, think them superior) and are often sold in the markets under that label. They are excellent as smoked fish.

⤜❦⤛ ROCKFISHES ⤜❦⤛

Here is a family of fishes that is greatly underrated. The species that occur in shallow water are equal to almost any of the bass-shaped fishes in speed, cunning, and fighting ability. Because of the rough tackle-fouling surroundings of the habitat of the very shallow-water species, they are rarely taken by commercial fishermen. Anglers have been tardy in learning techniques to match the tricks of these fishes. So the fish grow old, unmolested.

Some members of this family can be found almost everywhere along our entire range where there is an abundance of sea vegetation and animal life. Unless the boat captain is accustomed to anchoring near shallow rocks, he is not easily persuaded to do so. An old hand will drop the "hook" some distance from the rocky bottom and pay out enough line to drift back over the desired spot.

Many kinds of fresh fish can be utilized for the small, tailored stripbait so effective for these ROCKFISHES. In the northern end of the range greenling, herring, and smelt are good. South of Point Arena, sardine, anchovy, and mackerel are easy to obtain and are the most desirable. The average size hook used is a No. 1 short-shank.

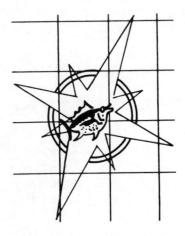

⤸ BLACK ROCKFISH ⤷

Of all the members of this family, this species is the one most available to the average angler. It is also highly rated as a game fish and is regarded as excellent food when cooked in any fashion. Along the Washington and Oregon coasts there are so many of them that they are branded a nuisance by some thoughtless fishermen, yet there is every reason to glorify this splendid fish. He is the one member of the family that rises to take the trolled lure most consistently. He is a big husky that can throw his weight around physically and his runs are truly creditable. A fresh or frozen stripbait is first choice, but he will not quibble over a whole anchovy or herring.

Any type of angling boat fishing north of Point Arena can be employed in harvesting the BLACK ROCKFISH.

⤸ TAMBOR ⤷

Second only to the BLACK ROCKFISH in the angler's catch is this stout contender. The rocky reefs from one end of our range to the other are well stocked with them. Although classed as a deep-water species in California, they can be taken at a moderately shallow depth south of Ensenada and north of Point Arena. Trollers strike them at a depth of eight to ten fathoms off the coasts of Washington and British Columbia.

⤸ BLUE ROCKFISH ⤷

North of Point Conception and south of Punta Banda, Baja California, the BLUE is a very abundant species in moderately shallow water and can be chummed to the surface. Among light tackle enthusiasts, it is rated the best of ROCKFISHES, not only as a game scrapper but as a favored food fish.

⤸ BOCACCIO ⤷

This fish has a great range in depths as well as geography; i.e., from 300 to 165 fathoms, and from Punta Banda to Alaska; also from shore to 300 miles at sea. It is seen in the catches of most all "ROCK-CODDING" boats.

When SALMON, ALBACORE, or STRIPED BASS are not getting attention, boats from Morro Bay northward go out for the "ROCK-CODDING" all summer, but southward the ROCKFISH specials run for the few winter and early spring months only. LINGCOD, FLATFISH, and SHARK are most always included in their catches.

The large drum or ball of line with a half-dozen hooks, once popular for deep-water codding, is rapidly disappearing in favor of the more sporting rod and reel with one to four hooks, according to the depth. The sturdy, short trolling-type of rod mounted with all roller guides is preferred. It need not be especially flexible for the deeper fishing. The #349 Penn-type reel is favored in moderate to very deep places because of its rugged build and fast, 3¼-to-1 retrieving speed. Some oldtimers prefer the larger 6/0.

Whatever kind of reel is used, the line should be kept to a low-pound-test. The larger the size of the line, the more the current will drag. Monofilament seems to meet with less resistance, but because of its elasticity, setting the hook at great depths requires a long stroke. Because of current drift, three hundred to four hundred yards of line are required. In moderately shallow water a twelve-pound-test line will do it, but when heavy sinkers are necessary to get to the bottom, the strength is upped to a twenty to forty-pound-test.

Hook sizes are kept large to avoid catching young ROCKFISH and SANDDABS—up to 4/0 to 6/0 long-shank for big COWS and LINGS. Shorty mono leaders made up on a long, heavier mono are generally used. The sinker should have just enough weight to get to the bottom.

At times, some deep-water species will go for most any kind of a rubbery lure when there is a flavorsome bait on a top hook. A wide variety of fresh baits will get 'em. While bait is preferred in moderately deep-to-shallow water, in the depths most any fresh sea food is acceptable.

One of the most exciting phases of ROCKFISH fishing is in the element of surprise. The angler is never able to guess just which of the fifty-odd species he is likely to bring up. These fishes seem to enjoy congregating. As many as ten or twenty different species may be caught in a single deep hole. Anything from a small STRAWBERRY ROCKFISH to a three-foot RASHER is apt to appear on a multiple-hook rig in one haul.

ROCKFISHES are of many and varied colors. Some of them are very handsome and look like BASS in technicolor; others are weird looking. The average size taken is about fourteen inches, but a three-foot fish is not uncommon. All members of this family are excellent food fish.

ᕱᔕᓄ LINGCOD ᕱᔕᓄ

Wherever there is dockage along the California coast above Santa Barbara, sportfishing boats sail out to the reefs with pay loads and return with contented customers.

There is an ever increasing number of such engaged craft in Oregon, Washington, and British Columbia. When there are few SALMON in prospect, the LINGCOD is the big jackpot fish in this region as it is elsewhere. This is one fish with which the angler can confound those skeptics at home and at the shop. Instead of showing estimates of length with outstretched hands, he can produce a fish in the flesh that's a yard and a half long.

Like the ROCKFISH, the LINGCOD inhabits the rocky reefs and kelp forests, especially where there is a fairly strong current. He by no means limits his travels to the confines of the deep reefs. His is a restless and gypsy-like nature. Tides, temperatures and currents stimulate his wanderlust, but the compelling force is the urge at spawning time. Sometime between December and March, in answer to the call, the trek to very shallow water to deposit the adhesive mass of eggs is responded to.

When not on the prowl, the LINGCOD comes to rest and spends considerable time on his "haunches," represented as pectoral and pelvic fins. It is in this semi-prone position that the angler is more apt to find him. Therefore, to attract the "LING'S" attention, the angler should keep the bait or lure in constant motion and near the bottom.

Bait preference may change from place to place, but a strip cut from a very fresh or live fish caught in the vicinity is usually best.

ᕱᔕᓄ FLATFISHES ᕱᔕᓄ

The pursuit of the northern PACIFIC HALIBUT is gaining in popularity. There are a greater number of rugged individuals taking to the "big tug" sport every year.

Because of the strong currents and the depth of the water out where the heavy "BARNDOORS" are encountered, very sturdy tackle is required; a 16-ounce tip rod; No. 9/0 reel; a 60-pound-test line; No. 8/0 to 10/0 hook; 50-pound-test wire leader, 5 feet long. Sinker weight varies according to the swiftness of the current.

Large herring or other fresh fish of the equivalent size, squid, or large strips of fresh fish kept on ice until ready for use, are favored as bait.

Light tackle is used for the small in-shore PACIFIC HALIBUT.

Beginning in March, south of Point Conception when the winds are not too stiff and live bait can be caught, the boats go out for the CALIFORNIA HALIBUT. If the water has warmed up sufficiently, they go to the kelp beds where HALIBUT fishing can be combined with the search for other species.

Each boat captain has his favorite HALIBUT holes. His plan for the best action is usually to bring his boat crosswise to the current and drift. This gives the passengers on the "off" side a chance to let their lines play out, while those on the other must keep their lines just off the bottom. After one drift the captain repeats the run with the boat reversed, giving the fishermen on the opposite side a chance to let their lines out. If there is any luck in fishing, this drift method allows for it, as there is little chance of using the angling arts. An amateur has the same opportunity as the expert. Quite a few half-day boats specialize in this type of fishing.

Often when bottom fishing south of Point Conception the angler is misled by the freakish chewing custom of discriminating SOLES. They can chew on an anchovy for minutes without giving the angler the slightest hint that his bait is being worked over. Then, when the bait is brought up for inspection he is likely to blame the robbery on crabs. The telltale, sharp teeth marks will give the careful observer the clue. If the culprit is a SOLE, he can be apprehended.

Insert a No. 4 hook in a live bait (pinhead anchovy) about an inch ahead of the base of the caudal fin (see Fig. 11). Then let it down to the bottom, using a sinker as light as the current will allow. Pull up slowly for three or four feet, and let it down again. Repeat this action until a slight tug is felt. Then pay out five or six feet of line, giving the SOLE a chance to take a good gulp. Set with a slight pull.

FLATFISHES taken in the shallow waters are often miscalled HALIBUT. Most abundant of the family is the STARRY FLOUNDER, an excellent food fish which reaches a length of thirty-six inches. The great number taken in shallow water are the small immature fishes. Most of the shallow to moderately shallow-water SOLES and FLOUNDERS show a preference for fresh stripbait and crustaceans.

ᕱᔕᓄ SANDDABS AND SMALL SOLES ᕱᔕᓄ

There are a half dozen small species of the FLATFISHES that require special bait and technique. SANDDABS and a number of small SOLES prefer bits of shrimp, or narrow strips of fresh fish about an inch long. Strips of fresh anchovy, sardine or herring are choice. A strip from the white belly of other fishes with scales removed is very good for SANDDABS.

Two No. 6 hooks on twelve-inch wire leaders are attached a foot apart above a small sinker. The sinker is dropped to the bottom and retrieved slowly. The strikes are ignored as the momentum is maintained. These small fishes sometimes follow the bait eight to ten feet up before gulping it. The instant they are hooked they begin fighting like a fish many times their weight. The trick lies in getting the proper retrieving tempo.

Many years ago small commercial fishermen would string a dozen or so hooks on a barrel hoop, let it down with a rope and lift it slowly in the above manner, often to find it loaded with SANDDABS and small SOLES.

⌒◆⌒ STRIPED BASS ⌒◆⌒

Operators of sportfishing boats, trollers, or party boats in pursuit of the STRIPED BASS have gained considerable knowledge as to the best seasons and most suitable grounds for these schools of fish. During the fall, particularly in September and October, in channels between bodies of backwaters or the bay channels, the STRIPERS are bottom feeders. During May and June they are also found in these localities on their way to the spawning grounds.

It is believed that the STRIPED BASS spends some time in the brackish water between the fresh and salt waters, becoming acclimatized before continuing the migration up into the streams. During the summer the schools scatter. Those remaining in backwaters follow bait fishes and are readily taken around deltas and islands on lures.

There are almost as many sizes and shapes of tackle and baits used for STRIPERS as fishermen going after them, but up to the present the most popular terminal setup has been chunks or strips of frozen sardine or fresh sculpin on hooks up to 6/0 long-shank, buried or hidden in the bait. The rig: a lengthy mono leader with a couple of loops to which the hooks, on shorty leaders, are attached. Now, with the introduction of live bait, we can expect the whole deal to change.

Since burying the hook would quickly kill the bait, and a large, exposed hook would be rejected, we can expect a switch-over to small, short-shank hooks on long, single mono leaders, the hook size varying according to the size of bait employed. (See the section on baits for more details on this.)

This will require more patient and skillful technique, principally in allowing the BASS time to get the small

hook deeper down its throat, as with other large fish taken on live bait.

There is also a possibility that a live-shrimp-bait fishery can be developed for the STRIPER, as on the Atlantic Coast and to a lesser extent in the San Pedro, California harbor. Shrimp is a favored natural food of the STRIPED BASS.

Anglers of San Francisco and Coos Bays have every reason to be concerned with the future of the great STRIPER as well as the SALMON. There is no question that floods of fresh water are required to keep bays from becoming cesspools of poisonous pollution, and as human populations multiply, more and more fresh water will be diverted from streams. Therefore, unless clean spawning grounds, scientifically constructed and maintained, are put into operation soon, the survival of the STRIPED BASS will be in grave doubt. The natural food supply of the young fish, as well as that of the mature bay dwellers, is already being threatened. Here again, the time for action is right now. Any more delays will certainly prove to be drastic.

⌒◆⌒ SALMON ⌒◆⌒

There are no two ways about it, salt-water trolling for SALMON is going to become more and more popular wherever these fish are found. Although the increasing interest is centered on catching these particular fishes, many newcomers to this phase of the sport could be diverted to fishing for other species. It will however require the combined efforts of everyone concerned, from boat captains to state officials. The reason is simply this: There are grave doubts that the SALMON population will be able to withstand the onslaught. We could qualify this statement by adding "for the present"; there is every reason to believe that SALMON can be semi-artificially propagated in great numbers.

There are a lot of very good reasons for the present enthusiasm for ocean trolling that will be discovered by the angler. The most fetching is the yen for adventure. A lot of us go out expecting a quiet, restful day, only to work ourselves into a lather when we strike a school of "LUNKERS." Some of those blessed with restless natures come in feeling as if they had spent a day in the salt mines. But it is they who can enjoy a rest that is seldom experienced by modern mortals.

A trolling day begins when you make a reservation on a regularly scheduled boat taking individual anglers. When your reservation is made, be sure to ask all the questions that apply to this type of fishing. Be sure to wear more than enough clothing; chilling breezes do come up unexpectedly. If susceptible, take along some anti-seasick pills; they really work.

No two schools of SALMON seem to be attracted by the same kind of lure so take along a variety of different patterns and keep changing them. One school will show interest in five-inch spoons, while the next may be frightened away by them.

Baits should be changed often, regardless of whether they retain a good appearance or not. It is believed that a fresh bait leaves a trail of flavor but is soon washed clean of it.

Trolling speeds and fishing depths differ according to the water depth and the speed of the current. The weight of the sinker is determined by these factors. The CHINOOK is usually located some eight to twelve feet above the ocean floor, the SILVER some few feet higher. During those runs when SALMON are following schools of forage fishes they are more apt to be near the surface, even breaking water occasionally.

The breakaway sinker for bottom trolling in deep water (thirty to one hundred or more feet) may weigh as much as two to five pounds, while in shallow or surface fishing, a light six or eight-ounce crescent sinker will suffice. These weights are far heavier than those used on small privately owned craft. All tackle is much heavier when fishing from a regular troller.

Along the Oregon and Washington coasts and to some extent in the straits and sounds, a number of boats are fitted up with outrigger trolling poles. To each of these, four or five lines are attached, each with a heavy sinker. The angler's lines are tied to the sinker with a slipknot. When the fish strikes, his pull unties the knot, leaving the angler's line free of the sinker. This procedure not only saves sinkers, but allows the angler his choice of using light or heavy tackle.

This method of trolling also enforces longer leisure periods, since the nervous angler is restrained from pulling up and lowering and monkeying around. He can't even enjoy the nervous exhaustion gained from gripping the rod with half his might, the other half being expended trying to hold some strength back for the final battle.

Everyone soon learns to relax between hookups. These rest periods seem very short when fishing is up to normal. In retrospect they are remembered as being about like those one-minute rest periods in a prizefight.

Taking the coast line section by section, each consisting of an area which includes from one to four bays or streams, you would find a different set of best trolling rules in each, and rightly so. Each section may have a

SALMON population that has mingled very little with populations from other sectors, and to a degree, developed its own feeding habits. An angler fishing in a locality for the first time should enquire about all minor angling details.

The boats that venture out to the islands or some few miles away from the harbors are manned by certified sea captains who know their navigation and boats. These vessels are well equipped for any eventuality with modern all-safety devices.

By the use of the two-way radio, captains can keep each other informed on fishing conditions and move to join in when one of them strikes a productive area. Since the installation of these instruments, the danger of the greatest hazard to sea-going vessels — a motor breakdown — has been eliminated. Today a tow is assured when a boat needs it.

The safety record of sportfishing vessels is almost unbelievable. The fatality percentage is hundreds of times lower for passengers than when riding in their own cars.

With the development and expansion of live bait on party boats in the SALMON fishery, new techniques will be worked out. Although the methods will differ from those employed elsewhere, some benefits can be gained by studying live-bait usage in catching ALBACORE, YELLOWTAIL, BARRACUDA, and other southern forms.

Some live-bait boats have adopted the manner of trolling until a fish is caught, then halting the boat to drift or move with the current or against the wind so all anglers aboard can fish with a minimum-weight sinker.

When a school is discovered in moderately shallow water, chumming is used.

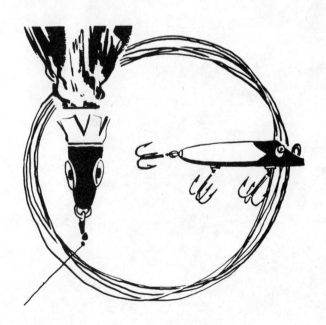

Fishing from Small Craft

Fishing from privately owned boats of lesser size than yachts seems destined to become the most popular form of outdooring yet discovered by man, and with our inland lakes and streams becoming over-crowded, the big interest is shifting to salt water, where there is ample room for the millions yet to come.

New safety measures and innovations for comfort and better fishing have accelerated the shift and added confidence to the adventure. This whole deal of going down to sea in little ships provides real and unequaled adventure and is as safe and pleasant as the amount of thought and planning put into it.

New small craft harbors and launching facilities for trailered boats are being constructed, but not quite rapidly enough to meet the demand. As soon as officialdom catches on and comes to realize the vast trend, we can expect that numerous small havens between ports will be built, thus adding greatly to the safety.

Several years cruising the Sea of Cortez (Gulf of California) in 16 to 30-foot cruisers have given the author an immense appreciation of this means of the pursuit of happiness. It has surpassed, by far, all other

Small fishing craft heads into harbor for its tie-up after a productive day. Privately owned boats provide a maximum of comfort for the salt-water fisherman.

recreational outlets, not only for the relaxation, enjoyment, excitement, and leisure time well spent, but for the health and mental stimulation. We have also learned there can be a lot of aggravation and danger when going for a voyage without wise planning and that every detail should be checked and double-checked well in advance of a trip. The essentials are given in details in numerous publications by the Coast Guard and boating organizations. Small-craft navigation should be studied and observed, courses charted, rules and regulations and courtesies of the sea carefully followed. Above all, in the planning and executing of every necessary step, don't forget to have fun.

First, select a boat that will provide the maximum comfort in rough water — a seaworthy hull that can take it and ride chop-wave-action without pounding. While multiple keel or flatish bottoms are excellent for smooth inland or backwaters, they are apt to lift up and crash down when heading into wind on a rough surface. They are also more apt to flip, if caught broadside to the face of a large wave.

An airtight cabin, at least on the forepart of the craft, is essential in waters that may roughen. One that houses the helmsman and instruments provides additional safety. This should leave plenty of clear deck for fishing and space for a built-in live-bait well or portable tank.

If long, offshore voyages are anticipated, trolling outriggers can serve an extra purpose as mast poles for rigging up an emergency sail, just in case of motor failure.

There has been a noticeable increase in inboard-sterndrive motors, especially for lengthy cruises. As engineering refinements are installed, we can expect this type of power to become even more popular. The advantages over the conventional inboard are: easier to launch and to beach; less chance of damaging prop and drive shaft; easier fishing over shallow reefs and bottoms. Compared with the high-powered outboard, the sterndrive has a longer range and is less trouble to keep in repair at sea.

Do not underestimate the value and importance of safety equipment and keeping them in good order and easy to get at, no matter how many times you have gone out without having needed them. There are always spare parts, tools, and repair kits for everything from radio to hull, to be remembered in the planning. Every article needed for these and for fishing tackle, food, and first aid should be listed and checked before sailing, then carefully stashed aboard so they will be handy.

There are many individual items that should also be noted, such as a sea anchor, flares and distress horns, extra line and anchor, wiring, full extra gas tank, a gunnysack to keep fish fresh, a night light, and a copy of this book to identify fish. Be sure to take extra fishing tackle, in case of loss or damage, including everything from hooks to fishing belt, lures, leaders, sinkers, swivels, lines, rods, reels, tape to repair damaged guide wrappings, gaff, knife, hook hone, pliers, lots of extra hand towels or rags, and a couple of dip nets.

Among the many useful gimmicks, gizmos, and conveniences is one that is highly recommended: a collapsible fish-cleaning shelf attached to the upper rail. Gaffed, netted, or "bounced" fish can be brought directly onto this shelf, clobbered and bled, then dropped into a gunnysack hung nearby — all this without getting blood and goo on deck.

There is a lot to be learned by the beginner that cannot be obtained from any publication or instructor. For this, experience, keen observation, and good memory are the only reliable sources. For instance, the principle of quartering up and down large waves can be learned from others, but putting it into practice requires a special feeling for the force of the water and the boat's responses to it. This is something like driving a car for the first time around a sharp turn, but more so because of the wave power. Hitting a wave head-on will retard speed and likely result in a timber-shaking smack. If the craft is held too far in, the wave may flip it. But once the feel is mastered, the skipper can dare cruising through a rough sea without fear.

There are quiet, sheltered coves all along the Pacific Coast where a small boat may be launched without fear of its being capsized by rough breakers. If the cove has a protective growth of kelp, the water should be especially calm and the operation in and out of it an easy affair. The lee side of a point, promontory or jetty is safe enough, as long as the wind is consistent; but the small boat operator should not allow a shift in the direction of the wind to go unheeded. Keen navigation is necessary in landing through high breakers.

While the commercial marine-angling boats must be taken out where large schools of fish can be found to satisfy the cash customers, the operator of a small, privately owned craft can go wherever he likes. This freedom gives him many advantages. He can prospect for a variety of fishes, follow the tides in and out, and fish close to shore as well as in the deep waters. He can follow narrow paths through kelp beds without fear of fouling his propeller. He can come and go, anchor or drift. He can indulge in whatever kind of fishing pleases his fancy, whether it be trolling, mooching, spin fishing, casting or just loll fishing.

The outstanding advantage of fishing from a small boat is the maneuverability when engaging heavyweights in combat. The angler can dare tackle the quarter-ton BLACK SEA BASS, the huge sixty-pound GROUPERS south of the border, and the monstrous PACIFIC HALIBUT of the north. He can challenge the giant SHARK, SWORDFISH or MARLIN and land a larger percentage than by any other means. There are any number of highly esteemed species that are waiting to be hooked in the channels and reefs just off-shore by the boatsman with an urge to explore.

Cruising is one thing, but the fishing has another set of do's and don'ts. Sunburn, often received in the excitement of fishing, can be painful or cause serious injury. No part of the body should be exposed for long, and a good head of hair is not always sufficient protection. Many who thought so and were not accustomed to wearing hats have been struck down with an illness commonly called sunstroke. Even when shaded, nose and lips should be coated with zinc oxide or other similar medication.

Special, non-skid yachting shoes will provide a good safety measure on a slick deck. Effective pills for sea-sickness can now be obtained. Going without liquids and eating dry toast or crackers will help. It is a good idea to keep a wire cutter handy just in case a hook gets into someone's flesh past the barb. The hook should not be pulled back out, but pushed around until the point comes out past the barb, then cut off.

Although a companion is not absolutely essential to the small-boat fisherman, there are so many reasons for taking one along that it should be considered a "must." First is the matter of personal security; even if the angler could qualify as a champion swimmer, a weather prophet, and a tough old salt, he would still be handicapped if caught in a sudden squall without a helper. Teamwork is needed to launch and land the craft and to operate it when a big fish is hooked.

The skill of the operator is almost as important as that of the angler. He must think and act quickly and be ever ready to maneuver into any position. He must anticipate the time when the angler's line will pay out to the danger point and maneuver accordingly. He should keep the craft going at a slight angle in order to be able to reverse his course whenever the fish makes a run in the direction of the boat. Those almost unbelievable stories about catching enormous game fish with button thread line and a delicate fly rod are not just tall fish tales, but the accomplishment of the feat must be largely accredited to the boatsman working in perfect coordination with the angler.

The small-boat fisherman will do well to follow his tide table and remember that the shore fishes shift with the tide, with some seeking very deep water at the low tide, then moving in close to shore at high tide. When one pursues these tide followers, an isolated clump of kelp out in fairly deep water should be found and made use of as an anchor by making fast to it. If the tide is low and no strikes are forthcoming, move out and repeat the process elsewhere. As the tide starts rising, move shoreward.

Very often the small-craft angler will find himself in a school of bait fishes. With a string of tiny, triple hooks he can snag as many as he requires. Small QUEEN-FISH are easily caught by snagging and make excellent bait. SARDINES and HERRING can be snagged when they come in close to shore to feed just at daybreak. Often they are so thick they can be scooped up with a long-handled dip net. Small SCULPIN and TOMMY CROAKER, also very good baits, can be caught by baiting the triple hooks with bits of mackerel, herring or other fish. The baited hooks are then dropped to the bottom and lifted slowly. Both SCULPIN and TOMMY CROAKER are usually found over sandy bottoms.

The private craft owner would do well to study all other phases of ocean fishing given in this volume since he can, with some slight adaptations, catch most of the species mentioned. For example, in the section on "OPAL-EYE," the same type of gear and bait could be employed for this species, but instead of seeking it at high tide as from the rocky shore, the angler aboard a boat would prospect the submerged rocks some distance offshore at low tide, or at an intermediate distance at mid-tide. The same procedure could be applied to a great number of tide-following species such as CABEZON, SHEEP-HEAD, GREENLINGS, KELP FISH, HALFMOON, SEAPERCH, and an additional number of ROCKFISHES.

To avoid losing anchors, drop anchor up current some distance from the rocks and pay out enough line to drift back over them.

While most of this chapter is for boats above 15 feet, the information can be almost as important when applied to outboard skiffs, which must remain closer to land for safety. They have several advantages over the large cruisers, chiefly in launching and getting ashore on almost any beach, providing the operator has gained experience in riding large waves in and out. Much of it is of equal value to yachts and sailboats.

Whatever the size of the craft, teen-age interest is generally easy to stimulate if the fishing phase of boating is stressed. One of the most encouraging turns in the psychological behavior of youngsters was noted during the first big boom in boating back in the 1950s. The drop in juvenile delinquency among boating-fishing enthusiasts was surprising. If records had been kept of their gain in health, the results, no doubt, would have been astonishing.

While adventure and love of the sea add zest to the popularity, sailing out with some definite goal in mind is the motivating attraction for the greater majority. That place, that goal they like to set a course for, is the fishing grounds. For it is in good fishing that they find complete compensation for the time, effort and energy spent in acquiring and in bringing a boat to water.

The small-craft fisherman has an advantage denied all other anglers. He can slide his boat into shallow inlets and backwaters and catch quite a few game fish that cannot always be taken from the banks. There are a number of TURBOTS and other FLATFISHES that can be caught by slowly moving the bait a foot above or along the bottom.

There are also CROAKER holes in the sandy bottom of bays, where the tide ebbs and flows. The CROAKERS wait in these depressions, watching the moving sand for food. If the hole has been chummed an hour or so before high tide, they will take pieces of mussel, shrimp, clams, and soft-shell sand crabs and sand worms.

⤜⊶ BAIT AND ITS MAINTENANCE ⊷⤛

Chumming is really not considered bad sportsmanship in brackish or salt water, nor is it illegal, as is sometimes the case in fresh water. Too many small-craft men forget the importance of chumming. In bays and among rocks mussels or crushed sea urchins are most effective. Ground mackerel or other fresh fish make good chum.

Fresh-Dead Bait

Many owners of small craft which have no facilities for keeping live bait still believe that pelagic fishes can be taken from such a boat only by trolling.

Extensive experiments have been conducted recently in determining the value of fresh-dead bait for chumming, as well as for hook bait. In a surprising number of instances it proved quite successful, but only when the bait was carefully selected and kept in perfect condition. Bait for this purpose should be procured directly from the seiner while still alive.

To maintain a high quality of freshness, the bait must not be kept in water, nor on the other hand, be allowed to dry out. A simple contrivance, such as a wire-mesh wastepaper basket lined with burlap which is kept damp, will serve as a container. The live bait is scooped directly into this basket, then covered with a wet gunny-sack. Water is thrown over it from time to time.

The reason for the open work and porous material of the container is to permit as much aeration and rapid evaporation as possible. Evaporation is the secret of preserving freshness. The container should be kept shaded and cool. If extremely warm weather is anticipated, light icing may be necessary.

When bait is to be kept for more than one day's outing it should be frozen. The quicker it can be taken from the seiner to the freezer, the better. Small quantities can be frozen in an ordinary home freezer by filling the ice-cube tray space or other freezing compartments with the bait. If frozen promptly, it should retain a good measure of its effectiveness indefinitely.

The chemical guanine occurs in the slime that covers live fish. Soon after death it dissolves and washes off. This is the substance that seems to be most attractive to predator fishes. Preserving it on bait fish is therefore of great importance.

Live Bait

For the most part, anglers south of Point Conception depend upon the NORTHERN ANCHOVY, *Engraulis mor-*

dax, as the mainstay of live-bait supply. Two other species and three sub-species of the family Engraulidae are used to a lesser degree.

QUEENFISH, TOMMY CROAKER, BUTTERFISH, TOP-SMELT, and GRUNION are substituted when ANCHOVY and SARDINE are scarce. These bait fishes are sometimes found in company with ANCHOVIES and SARDINES and often comprise a small portion of the bait catch. Each species is a preferred food of one or more kind of game fish. As live-bait fisheries develop in the northern States and in British Columbia, HERRING and members of the true SMELT family will be added.

In areas where there are no commercial live-bait enterprises, a do-it-yourself method can usually be worked out. On a recent survey aboard a 27-foot cruiser studying live-bait conditions in the Cortez, the author was able to catch bait with very little effort. A black, circular, five-foot (diameter) King Neptune Net was suspended from an outrigger trolling pole, with a bright light over it, the net three feet under the water, the light three feet above the surface. Sets were made just after dark, but were found to be more successful a couple of hours before daybreak. To attract large bait fish, we kept the rig and light out for an hour or more. We found that the plankton-eaters in the ANCHOVY-HERRING groups were not interested in ground-up chum, but that a number of carnivores could be attracted over the net by sprinklings of it.

A bait tank must have a good flow of clean water, but diffused or spread so it will not create a current that will disturb the bait. The drain pipe valve opening should be large enough to allow dead bait to pass without clogging, but screened so live bait cannot escape through it.

On a small craft the weight of the water limits the size of the tank and should therefore be well calculated. More often than not the amount of water being pumped into the tank is insufficient. For reasons of safety a constant flow should be maintained, and to avoid vibration the pump should be powered by an electric motor.

To keep the tank interior spotless, free from fungus and free of scales, it should be thoroughly scrubbed as soon as it is emptied. The bait tank is not to be filled near the dock nor in a shallow place, but out where the water is free from oil, scum or silt.

Before the fishing trip starts, it is wise to check the water pump and electric light suspended over the tank, which is kept burning until broad daylight. The light is necessary to settle bait fish and to keep them milling quietly.

Bait taken directly from the seiner's net will prove far more sturdy than that taken from his receiver. It is purchased by the "scoop," the seiner's dip net, which for lack of standardization varies from two to four quarts.

The number of "scoops" to be taken is limited by the amount of water flowing into the tank as well as by the size of the tank. Over-loading is always poor economy, since it tends to multiply the mortality rate due to insufficient oxygen supply and disturbance injuries sustained by over-crowding.

Bait fishes will usually "mill" counter-clockwise, but it is advisable to make sure of the direction before dipping for the bait. Using the dip net must be done with extreme caution. To avoid disturbing the bait fishes, the dip net should be held just below the surface and moved slightly clockwise (facing the mill) to net them.

Everyone aboard should be warned not to shove the dip net deep among the bait fishes or move it rapidly in pursuit of them.

Bait that is to be kept alive for more than a single day's cruise should be given a survival test by anchoring the boat out in deep water for a couple of hours, or until the bait settles and begins to mill steadily. If the bait fishes continue to thrash around and show signs of dying, a new load is necessary.

Beginning with the first evening after the bait is obtained, it should be fed twice daily. Fresh fish, scaled or skinned, then ground until fine, will serve as the main diet, with cooked oatmeal as a supplement.

Chumming

Elsewhere in this volume various methods of chumming for individual shallow-water species have been described. The concern here is applying the practice for top-feeding fishes of the open sea.

The three most successful types of chum are live bait, fresh-dead bait, and a new processed compound consisting of ground anchovy, fish oil and chemicals, often used in conjunction with the fresh-dead or live bait. In all cases the bait is dropped overboard, forming what is termed a "chum-line."

There are two purposes for open ocean chumming. One is to divert an observed school of fish from its course and entice it to follow the boat. (See "ALBACORE" in the section on marine angling boats.) Because of the short run required after the boat has crossed the course of the school, this chumming activity is termed a "short chum line." The second purpose is to bring fish to the surface when no signs of a school can otherwise be located. Chumming in this case may extend for more than a quarter of a mile; therefore the term "long chum line"

is applied. This line is started in a promising area by cutting the boat speed to eight knots, more or less (according to species anticipated), letting out trolling lines, and dropping one bait fish (live or fresh-dead) every fifty feet. (These distances are maintained whether or not the processed chum is added.)

When fish are seen breaking in the chummed wake, or a hookup on a troll line occurs during the long chum line, speed is cut to a minimum, allowing the boat to come to a halt gradually enough to keep the hookup line taut. Chumming is increased, at point of break or hookup, to one every two or three seconds and continued.

If chum is composed of live bait, two or three dozen may be thrown out as the boat comes to a stop. These bait fishes will dash out, but quickly return to the protective safety of the hull. A large quantity of dead bait will probably drift away, sidetracking the big fish.

When no fish appear during the full course of the run, the boat is brought about to form a circle. As it begins this end of the run maneuver, the rate of chumming is increased as at the above mentioned point of hookup and follows the same pattern for some time after the boat stops.

The short chum line extends on a slight angle from the path of a running school or from an area where some signs of feeding fish are observed, for a distance of about one to two hundred yards, or until hookup is secured. Chumming in the short chum line begins with one bait fish being thrown out every two or three seconds and follows the same method and time as when fish are first observed in the long chum line.

To restrain live baits from leaving the wake of a moving boat, some form of injury is usually inflicted. ANCHOVIES and other small bait fishes may be handicapped by squeezing the gills. Crippling small live baits is not necessary at the end of a run. On the other hand, regardless of when SARDINES and HERRING are used for chum, their speed should always be retarded. This is effected by the removal of an eye or the tail fin. Experienced boatsmen can effectively slow them down by bending them. Squeezing is not recommended.

Very small ANCHOVIES (PINHEADS) make a very good chum bait, but should be distributed differently. Where one large ANCHOVY would be thrown out, four or five "PINHEADS" are dropped overboard.

Birds following and diving for bait in the chum line excite pelagic fishes and are to be discouraged only when they begin taking a majority of the baits or working too near the stern.

The private craft helmsman unaccustomed to this type of fishing should give close attention to activities astern. In the event of a hookup on a troll line, speed is cut to assist the trolling angler in bringing the hookup fish to the stern as soon as possible, yet the boat speed is never reduced so rapidly as to allow slack in the angler's line. Some captains of sportfishing boats prefer bringing the boat about into a semi-circle to avoid tangling the hookup line with other troll lines.

⌘ SALMON ⌘

Of all the burning desires for personal possession, none seems to exceed the ambition to own a boat, and if the present trend along the Northwest Coast continues, a lot more wishes are going to be granted. Most responsible for awakening this intense interest is the king of TROUTS, the SALMON. Perhaps the same fish inspired the American Indian to create and develop his greatest invention, the canoe. In our time, angling for this fish has been so glorified that some fear has developed that two or three species may be overwhelmed by the sheer number of pursuers. The life story of the SALMON is one of dramatic suspense, with enemies and hardships besetting him from beginning to end.

The CHINOOK SALMON travels miles up rivers, then ascends the tributaries until a suitable spawning area with clear, gentle-running water is found. A depression is made in the gravel which serves as a nest. A week is spent in the process of spawning. As the eggs are laid and made fertile, they are carefully covered with the gravel, for water fowl and TROUT are waiting to gobble up any that are exposed. For a few days more the mates stand guard, fighting off intruders; then at last, having fulfilled their destiny, they drift with its current.

The eggs, laid from September to January, take six to eight weeks or longer to hatch if the weather is cold. The young fish after hatching remain covered with gravel for some time before emerging to begin competing for food. Until the spring run-off, or sometimes a year later, the young fry spend their time hunting food and hiding from ducks, terns, and the large, carnivorous fresh-water fishes. Then comes the great adventure down the stream, through churning, hydro-electric plant turbines or over the dams, and if lucky, on past irrigation ditch openings, contaminated waters and all types of obstruction. The survivors swim on and into the brackish waters where they halt the journey to become gradually accustomed to the salt before proceeding to the ocean. In this new world another set of enemies awaits their coming, and again the mysterious instinct serves them; they soon learn the dog-eat-dog law of the sea.

After spending one to five years at sea, the full grown CHINOOK returns and starts toward the very place where its early life was spent. Until man can learn the secret of the animal homing instinct, he will have no idea just how the SALMON is able to return to an exact location. Other theories, such as recognizing the water by its temperatures or the flavor of its chemical compounds, have been disproved. At the University of Washington a few years ago some fingerlings were carried from a classroom tank (where they had been hatched and raised), branded and thrown into the nearby river. Ninety of these same fishes returned, climbed a newly constructed fish ladder and followed a ditch which led toward the class room. The water used in the ditch and ladder was from a different source than the water in which the SALMON had been raised. These facts leave little hope of discovering anything beyond the homing instinct that serves as a directorial guide for the SALMON.

The story of other species is very similar. PINK and CHUM SALMONS seldom go up stream more than a mile, the young going to sea soon after becoming free-swimming. The CHUM returns from sea in three to five years, the PINK at two years of age. SILVER SALMON usually spend the first year, sometimes two years, in fresh water, and mature the third year. The SOCKEYE must find a lake with tributaries in which to spawn. The young migrate from the lake to salt water in one to four years and may mature in from one to eight years, usually in four to six.

At sea the SALMON are accustomed to pouncing upon a school of HERRING, ANCHOVIES, or other small fish, and killing and crippling as many as possible. This carnivorous instinct for slaughter is held over for some time after the pre-nuptial fast has started, and herein lies the SALMON'S vulnerability. Even after entering streams and inlets, any kind of a disturbance creating the illusion of such a massacre stimulates the SALMON to mad action. It is the smart angler who has a ruse or two which he calculates will inflame the killer impulse and start the otherwise passive fish to slashing.

⌘ CHINOOK SALMON ⌘

White men started ocean trolling for SALMON back in the 1860's, but the sportsman's interest was not greatly aroused until about 1947. By 1952 more than 325 sportfishing boats were registered for SALMON fishing out of the San Francisco Bay region. Today this rapidly developing phase of the sport extends from Santa Barbara to Alaska. South of Point Arena about ninety-nine percent of the catch is CHINOOK SALMON, the balance, SILVER. CHUM and SOCKEYE are rarely taken in this area.

Considerable progress has been made by party boats, and now by privately owned craft, in locating open ocean schools. Clues are given by diving birds, depth-finding instruments, jumping forage fish, and boiling rip-tides. But the old method of trolling eight to twelve feet from the bottom in a likely area is still in practice. Expert navigators have feeding banks charted and can return to them.

Deep trolling seems more effective on a zig zag angle up current. Because of the lightweight sinker employed by anglers, the trolling speed must necessarily be slow (two to four knots). In open ocean fishing out of San Francisco Bay, the popular two to three-pound sinker made of cast iron is attached to a "release" which allows the sinker to fall free at the first good strike, giving the angler a chance to fight the fish without the hindrance of the extra weight. North of this area a preference is shown for the crescent-shaped, streamlined lead sinker because it meets with less water resistance and can be kept at a low weight.

Although light tackle can be used when live bait and its special technique are employed, the troller still requires sturdy, medium-weight rods, reels, lines, and terminal rigs; plus 30-pound test monofilament or Dacron line, 9 to 12-foot mono leaders of 20-pound test, and No. 6/0 hooks. Then Penn #349 reel, a development from the old Mariner, is a favorite type of reel for its retrieve speed and sturdiness. Since the introduction of their multiple-speed 6/0, it has also gained in popularity, especially for very deep-water trolling. Equipment and methods for live-bait angling on small craft are similar to those on party boats.

Several gimmicks for holding fresh baits more securely are on the market. In some, the hook is concealed; others have the hook dangling about three inches after the bait.

Trolling anglers carry a great assortment of lures. A large flash revolving lure attached above the leader to attract the fish's attention is sometimes productive, regardless of whether a bait or other lure is used on the hook end of the leader. Experimentation is necessary to determine the size and kind of the hook-bearing lure. Fish in different sections have various preferences. This may also be said of choice of baits. While a fresh strip-bait would prove effective in one area, a whole sardine or herring might be best in another.

Time and the elements seem to have little effect on deep sea trolling. Winds however may effect current changes and fish are quite susceptible to the undertow, perhaps because of the movement of the forage food rather than the change in water temperature.

Angling for the CHINOOK in inlets and backwaters from a privately owned craft is practiced in numerous ways, all of which differ considerably from open ocean methods. Spin fishing, mooching, still fishing and drifting are distinct styles, and in each a different technique is employed.

Although in salt water the CHINOOK customarily follows the deep channels, it will venture up around the shallow bars into shallow backwaters and stream entrances. It is during these occasions that light tackle methods are most productive.

SILVER SALMON

Beginning at Humboldt Bay the SILVER SALMON gradually increases in number in proportion to the CHINOOK. When the two are located in the same waters the SILVER will be found some feet above the CHINOOK, except when a school of forage fish attracts both species to the surface, or when they rise in response to a chum.

Mooching

In all the inlet areas north of Coos Bay and everywhere in the vast expanses of the protected waters that extend from Olympia, Washington, to the north end of Vancouver Island, the odd application of the vagabond's expression "mooching" is heard. Some few years back it was hurled at the fisherman who was considered too lazy to work for his food, but of late the word has gained respectibility. Anglers who have discovered the highly productive principles involved in this type of fishing now proudly call themselves "old moochers." Their pride is based on the fact that they are the fishermen most consistent in bringing in limits of SALMON as well as other fish.

Out of the "drifting with the tide method," in which the fisherman just trusted to luck, has come a technique of considerable importance. SALMON are not the only fish that seem unable to resist a bait or lure taking off from the bottom on an angle upward. In the Cortez (Gulf of California) we tried unsuccessfully every other known method in an attempt to hook several elusive and

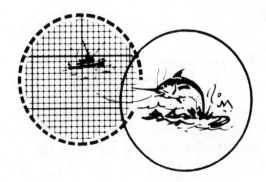

reluctant bottom species (even the natives were unable to catch them), but when we applied this slanting upward retrieve, we loaded the boat.

There is no trick to it. The angler lowers his rig to the fishing depth, then jogs the boat ahead in separated starts and halts, advancing about ten to fifteen feet at each move. The halt period is calculated to give the sinker time to drop to the maximum depth; the forward movement brings it up on the desired slant. The trick is to learn the effective tempo of the upward "heist." The crescent-shaped sinker is kept as light as possible. The rod, in the light bracket, nine to twelve feet long, is set close at hand. The star drag tension is tightened barely enough to hold, or if the click will hold against the pull, the spool is left in free wheeling.

If the hook is kept sharp enough, it is unnecessary to set it. The hook size recommended is far below that used aboard a sport troller. A No. 1 is sufficient for large fish.

Mooching baits for both SILVER and SOCKEYE differ with each locality, but the general methods of cutting them are similar. The stripbait is double hooked so that it will bend enough to make it revolve slowly. (See Fig. 4.) Other baits are hooked in the usual manner.

Spin Fishing

A method of fishing from a still or drifting boat of any size—spinning, or strip casting, as it is sometimes called in Washington and British Columbia—was practiced long before spinning tackle was introduced. It was called spin fishing, no doubt, because the popular bait of the period was hooked so it would revolve rapidly.

The present-day popularity got its big momentum when anglers took to working with the spinning reel, glass rod, and monofilament line. It is now the sporting thing to do. Mono lines have gone down from 20- to 15- or even 12-pound test, or to match the size of the SALMON, especially when live bait is used. No flasher or dodger is used with live bait, and no sinker if the bait sounds. Otherwise, the small sinker is followed by a 12-foot mono leader to allow the bait to swim around freely. Hook sizes are getting smaller. Some prefer trebles when fish are small. The hardy bait is cast out or flied (allowed to swim out).

With strip-bait or white lures, a flasher or dodger blade that is not very erratic is kept at least three feet ahead of the bait. Use large blades for CHINOOK, smaller for the SILVER.

The advent of spinning tackle was the direct cause of vast numbers of fresh-water anglers deserting their grounds for the briny open spaces. This was fortunate for everyone concerned with freshwater fishing.

The SOCKEYE SALMON (BLUEBACK) is a light spinning-tackle fish, because small baits must be cast. The sinker is one ounce or less, with a very small hook when bait is used. The best baits for the SOCKEYE are the spinner and worm, crawfish, or ghost shrimp tails. Lures are kept small for this one. In some localities, especially in brackish water, a fly on the order of a bucktail will often get more attention than baits.

Although little technique has been developed for taking the CHUM and PINK SALMON in salt water, they are at times attracted to a small piece of crustacean meat on a very small hook, No. 4 or less. Salmon egg clusters and small stripbaits will sometimes be taken when these fishes are really hungry. Just before starting on their upstream spawning runs they will occasionally strike small spinning-lures.

ROCKFISHES (SHALLOW WATER)

There are sixteen species of ROCKFISHES out where the bottom is rocky and the water fairly shallow, and forty more out in the moderate to deep water.

Once the private craft angler learns to locate and hook the shallow-water ROCKFISH, he can almost be sure of having plenty of meat to take home. The fish may be taken on almost any kind of bait. The natives along the coast of Baja California, when fishing over a rocky bottom, use the soft part of abalone when lobster is not available. Rock crabs and sand crabs are good bait for the shallow-water species. Shrimp, mussels, and clams may be used, but strips of fresh fish are best.

No other fish can be found so consistently throughout the year.

Assisted by a team of anglers we prospected, investigated and kept after this group of fishes at intervals over a period of years. As a result we believe that we have discovered an unsuspected abundance of them extending the whole length of our range.

Wherever there are submerged, food-bearing rocks, from Alaska to Cape San Lucas, some species of this family can be taken. This does not mean that they remain in a single area throughout the day. They follow the tide in and out and can be contacted somewhere on the reefs between the shallow shore line and deep water.

Traveling with the tide, they follow a narrow set course, as land animals would follow a path. The trails vary from twenty to fifty feet apart, branching off and spreading out near shore.

Because of their rugged habitat and refusal to respond to conventional technique, commercial fishermen seldom take them in quantity.

There is a definite knack in hooking these fish. While one may be caught by still fishing, a dozen can be taken when the bait is kept in motion. The bait should not just be yanked up and down but rather moved upward from the bottom with a gradually increasing tempo to eight or ten feet before repeating.

❧ BLACK SEA BASS ❧

Fighting the enormous BLACK SEA BASS requires stamina with endurance enough to go for many minutes at a time without a breathing spell. The battle is not as erratic as it is with the TUNA and SPEARFISH. It's more like trying to hold a mule that has just made up its mind to go back home for lunch. Unless you have the build of a Samson, it is advisable to wear a complete harness. You'd better have it on when the "BIG BLACK" hits. Fishing this one is a two-man job, no matter how small the boat.

The angler works on the bow, giving the operator full freedom for maneuvering the craft which must be kept going at an angle toward the fish. He endeavors always to anticipate the direction of the turn or shift that the fish is likely to make.

The B. S. BASS is occasionally found in thirty to fifty feet (30 to 50 fathoms elsewhere) of water about a hundred feet out from a kelp bed. After the bait is dropped to the bottom, the boat is pulled about fifty yards up-current and anchored. When the scarcely perceptible strike comes, the fisherman pays out around twelve feet of line. When he feels this slack taken up, he sets the hook with force—and war is declared!

The moment the fish finishes his first run he will stop, and if allowed, shake his head from side to side with such force as to cause the angler to question the wisdom of having mixed with such a critter in the first place. The answer is rhythmic pumping—in other words, beat him to it; for if you don't pump him first, he'll pump you.

The taut line rule for all ocean fishing goes double for this one. The makers of fishing lines haven't, as yet, developed one strong enough to stand the strain when a "BIG BLACK" is allowed sufficient slack to throw his full weight against the line in a single, powerful heave—that is, a line small enough to wind up on a reel.

The secret of winning against this fish is to force him to keep his mouth open. The way to do it is to apply rhythmic pumping with plenty of force. The sturdiness of tackle gives the angler a chance to apply as much muscle as he can bolster to the strokes.

Warning: Keep your fingers away from the mouth of this one. Remove the hook only after the BASS has been dead for some time.

The equipment necessary will give the beginner some idea as to the amount of work that is expected of him to catch the average 200-pound BLACK SEA BASS: A heavy trolling rod; a high-speed 6/0 reel loaded with 80-pound-test, limp Dacron line; a 10-foot Sevenstrand leader, 80-pound-test (because of rocks); a hook 12/0 to 14/0.

Best baits: Most any live fish 8 to 14 inches long; a live lobster, harnessed on (these below the Mexican border, where B. S. BASS and lobsters are more plentiful); live mackerel above the border. Next best: Fresh-dead or frozen mackerel or other fish of that size, but when B. S. BASS are especially hungry, they will take a slab of almost any large fish, whether it's fresh or not. Live baits can often be caught in the same area with B. S. BASS.

❧ GROUPERS ❧

Two species of these relatives of the BLACK SEA BASS occur between San Quintin Bay and Point Dume. Around San Quintin Bay both the BROOMTAIL and BAYA GROUPERS are taken on eight to ten-inch stripbait or whole fresh mackerel or other fishes. Heavy tackle is required, since only the very large individuals visit this region.

Just why so few are hooked by anglers north of Ensenada is still puzzling. Divers are able to spear them occasionally in this area and report seeing them in rocky places as far north as Point Dume.

South of San Quintin Bay and in the Sea of Cortez where they are so abundant, smaller individuals will rise to the lure. Stripbait however is more productive.

The name GROUPER is not to be confused with the rockfish BOCACCIO, mistakenly called "GROUPER" or "SALMON GROUPER."

❧ SHARKS ❧

Around the mouth of a stream or just off the entrance of bays and backwaters, when other game fishes become bored searching for the angler's hook, there are always the SHARKS. Winter and summer alike, they are there, but late afternoon and evening is the most appropriate time for a date with one of them.

"Why am I prejudiced against eating SHARK?" Ask yourself that question. Is it because SHARKS eat people, and therefore it would make you sort of a cannibal once removed? Could it be that their beady eyes and fang-like teeth make 'em look so mean that you just hate 'em? Is it their love-life you find objectionable? Whatever it is, forget it! Except for the SWELL SHARK, all are good food fishes; some, like the THRESHER, BONITO, and SALMON SHARK, are highly prized and often sold in the markets under popular fish names and eaten by unsuspecting customers with relish.

Second, some SHARKS admittedly do look bad; but ideas as to how wicked they look are usually formed by cartoonists' caricatures of "loan-sharks," or "card sharks" —none of which are habitants of the Pacific, at least not under the water out past the breakers.

Now about the love life. (You may have something there.) Some of them do get rather intimate in comparison to most other hairless ocean-going vertebrates. Fishes have various individual idiosyncrasies and notions about how and where to do their romancing. The male of one small species down in the South Pacific blows a nest of bubbles on the surface, takes his lady-love thither, and holds her upside down while she lays the eggs in his bubble nest. The SALMON migrate from the ocean to the head of streams for their honeymoon, while EELS, spending most of their lives in streams, find nuptial bliss in the depths of the ocean. But the SHARKS are not so particular. Whenever the water begins to warm up they start lookin' around. The first one of the opposite sex that turns up is "it." The couple wastes no time hunting for a better place for their love nest, or any other kind of a nest. Those that produce eggs just lay them on the broad ocean bottom; those of the TRUE SHARK order give birth to their young.

SHARKS have no complexes, breeding in a more or less cold-blooded sort of way, the female carrying the young twelve months or less before giving birth to the pups (quite correct—pups).

⤲ SOUPFIN ⤲

This species has survived a couple of terrific onslaughts. Twenty years ago quantities were captured solely for the fins which were shipped to China, where they were dried, shredded, and made into that delectable dish "sharkfin soup."

Next came the discovery that this SHARK's liver was a potent source of vitamin A. For a few years it was a bonanza. The gold rush was on. The price shot up to more than $14.00 per pound for the precious liver. The SOUPFIN population took a "beating," but was spared

when vitamin A was synthesized and the price dropped below the profit level.

The best all-around bait for the SOUPFIN, as well as for most SHARKS in shallow water, is the sardine. Runners-up are stripbait and squid. A large strip of fresh mackerel is especially good at a slow troll near top or bottom. If a live sardine is used, cut off the upper lobe of the tail fin to slow down its movements. When angling in the open ocean one whole side of fresh mackerel is the preferred bait. Taking the SOUPFIN in harbors, bays, or backwaters is prohibited in California.

The SOUPFIN gives birth to thirty-five pups more or less.

⤲ (COMMON) THRESHER ⤲

Of all the ornery, mean, aggravating sea-going critters, this takes the prize. He cuts more didos than a bucking bronco. Can you imagine trying to ride a "bronc" with a tail as long as his body and almost as big? That's something like wrestling with a THRESHER. As long as you hold a rein tight enough to keep him going sideways, you can restrain him. But the moment he gets started straight out, he'll bring up that whopping tail of his and beat the line 'til it breaks.

The THRESHER is usually hooked accidentally by anglers in pursuit of other fishes, but few of them can equal his tempestuous flailing exhibition. He churns the water with his big propeller to such an extent that the angler's nerves are not only apt to be shaken, but shattered. Actually, the power, agility, and speed of the THRESHER are over-rated. His sensational carryings-on are really a bluff. If you just keep him going in circles, he will knock himself out soon enough. While it requires no great amount of energy to turn him, the tail must not be allowed near the line. A snappy pumping will bring him about, and his mouth is tough enough to "take it."

Like most of the other SHARKS, he is more in evidence in the late afternoon and early evening.

⤲ DOLPHINFISH ⤲

During warm water years, the fantastic, jumping DOLPHINFISH comes up from the tropics to as far north as Point Conception. No other game fish within our range can equal its aerial acrobatics. The performance may begin the moment the ravenous fish spots the lure and rips the surface getting to it. On light tackle, fifteen to twenty jumps may follow, some of them twelve feet high.

White Compac feathers, Spoofers, or 8-inch ski-bait (see section on bait) trolled at six to ten knots are best. Use live bait after the first one from a school is caught.

〜 SCORPIONFISH 〜

There are two very definite reasons why the less popular name of SCORPIONFISH was selected for this species instead of the more commonly used name "SCULPIN." First, it is not a SCULPIN but a member of the SCORPIONFISH family, *Scorpaenidae*. Second, the name chosen serves as a warning to the angler that the sting received from the fin spines is toxic, the pain often lasting a couple of hours or more. The hook should not be removed until the fish is securely held with a pair of pliers clamped in its jaws. Because the sting may be inflicted after death, it is advisable to fillet the SCORPIONFISH at once.

The flesh is considered by many anglers to be about the most delectable of all of our coastal fishes. It is a bottom feeder and can be taken on a wide variety of baits. It is very abundant around kelp and rocks.

〜 STARRY FLOUNDER 〜

North of Point Conception one of the most constant and abundant fish in the brackish backwaters, sloughs, and in the mouths of the streams, is the STARRY FLOUNDER, often miscalled "ROUGH JACKET." It is easily distinguished from other FLATFISHES found in these waters by the clearly defined stripes on the fins.

While this fish will take many different kinds of baits, it shows preferences according to the locality. In the more open bays, stripbait rates first, but back in sloughs and streams, clams, ghost shrimp, crawfish and salt-water sand worms are effective, each according to the abundance of that particular kind in the area.

The bait seems to attract this FLOUNDER when it is moved in short halting motions along or near the bottom.

〜 TURBOTS 〜

Among the half dozen members of the FLATFISH family to be found in backwaters, are the DIAMOND TURBOT south of Point Conception, and the CURLFIN TURBOT north of the Point. Both species are probably more numerous than most anglers suspect, principally because they are not easily taken. To capture a quantity of them,

a gentle technique is required. First, the angler must determine the type of food the TURBOT is looking for (especially in the backwaters), then use the same for bait.

Two No. 2 hooks, the top one with a large bait, the bottom one with a small bait, seem to prove the most productive. In moving water very small live bait or stripbait is used. In backwaters clams, mussels and worms are suggested for some localities, crabs, crawfish and ghost shrimps for other species.

When CROAKERS and FLATFISHES are scarce in southern California, there are always SMELTS, SURFPERCHES, BUTTERFISHES, and a number of other small but wholesome fishes to be found in bays and backwater. Sometimes an occasional, edible SKATE may be hooked; but a careful inspection should be given to make sure it is a SKATE and not a STINGRAY.

In the northern regions there are SCULPINS, SURFPERCHES, HERRING, HAKE, and POLLACK.

South of San Pedro around back-bay clumps of growing vegetation and in the swift currents of tides shifting through the narrows, the SPOTTED BASS, a close relative of the KELP and SAND BASS, can be taken on a great variety of baits. Small mudsuckers are favored, with anchovies and small stripbait runners-up. Bay clams, mussels, and shrimp are acceptable.

〜 THE SILVER HORDE (SHAD) 〜

A brand new sportfishery is developing from Monterey Bay to the sounds of Washington, and it promises the fly enthusiasts a great new field of activity. There are few fresh-water places across the country that can offer a more exciting couple of hours than when the silver horde comes riding in with the tide and on into the river.

The SHAD is an anadromous fish that enters brackish waters early in spring and begins the spawning trip up stream about June 1, the larger schools in July. Unlike the SALMON, the SHAD may spawn six or seven times before it dies. A single female may contain up to 150,000 eggs. This is an important statistic for two reasons. First, the roe is among the most delicious of the earth's delicacies. Second, it suggests a possibility that the SHAD will continue to increase.

Before entering fresh water the SHAD may be taken on many types of baits, providing they are small and fresh. Hook sizes should be below No. 4. Fly men use a couple of salmon-egg-colored beads above the fly as an added attraction.

The SHAD can be cooked in as many ways as any other fish if kept fresh and cool.

LADYFISH AND BONEFISH

In the backwaters south of Oceanside, California, and on down the Baja California coast, there are a couple of tarpon-like scrappers, the LADYFISH and the BONEFISH, that can be taken occasionally on live bait or stripbait. The LADYFISH, *Elops affinis,* is a close relative of the TARPON, *Megalops atlanticus,* and fights like him. This one favors slightly muddy water near the outlet of a slough or bay and feeds at high tide. Hot summer months are best. One LADYFISH, at least, was caught in the Salton Sea.

The BONEFISH resembles the LADYFISH except for a thicker body and larger bony-looking head. It has similar habits and is caught in the same manner. In addition to small white feathers, LADYFISH will take small crawfish, shrimp with the shell on, razor clams, sand crabs, and stripbait.

MULLET

The beginner is likely to be driven to distraction when early some morning or late in the afternoon he witnesses the spectacle of a school of MULLET acting as if they were about to leave the waters of some back bay to become FLYINGFISH. Again, he may, on looking down when the water is clear, see half a hundred of these long, silvery fishes slowly gliding up on a sand bar to feed. But try as he may with all the known lures and baits, he is rudely ignored.

If you have the patience and wish to gamble, you can try this one: Lay out a line across the feeding grounds with a half dozen No. 10 hooks attached about a foot or so apart, baited with dough balls made of flour, cotton, and banana. Pull away for about a hundred yards and await developments. The MULLET obtains his food by screening the sand, hence the bait must be flat on the bottom. Some claim to have taken this fish on flies in canals extending out from the lower Colorado River.

FISHING BEFORE DAWN

Just why the element of adventure in the drama of fishing is somewhat lessened when the boat leaves dock after daylight is not easily explained. Hundreds of anglers questioned about the subject readily agree that there is some sort of strange inspiration gained by sailing out into the darkness. To whatever height these pre-dawn imaginations may soar, there are material advantages to match. There is the importance of starting early enough to arrive at the fishing grounds when fish are still hungry and before a lot of other boats have milled around and scattered the fish or caused them to sound. In addition to these benefits, there is the exciting incentive to try out the relatively new phase of open ocean night fishing.

Any vessel equipped with a few fairly powerful lights can work fish to the boat by the use of the long chum line, especially when the "luminous signs" have disclosed the presence of fish in the area.

Before daybreak WHITE SEABASS are likely to be feeding in harbor entrances or moving in or out at the change of the night tides. BARRACUDA are quite sensitive to bright lights and will often come close to the boat in pursuit of a couple of dozen live baits which have been thrown out to attract them.

Although the night technique has not yet been perfected for catching YELLOWTAIL and the TUNAS during the pre-dawn period, some success has been met with. In recent experiments a spotlight focused on the wake, in which the new processed chum combined with floating, fresh-dead bait was used, brought schools to the boat, but the fish disappeared after the first two or three hookups.

CHARTER BOATS

The greater number of the southern California charter boats are operated somewhat like the regularly scheduled sportfishing boats, fishing the same waters in pursuit of like type of game fishes. Though they may differ in size and shape, each boat is constructed with a live-bait well and an ample, roomy deck. The charges vary according to capacity. The chartering party has the advantage of being able to dictate the kind of fish it prefers to go after. Small groups can troll for TUNA exclusively if they wish, or go to the kelp beds for BASS when the larger game fishes are not easily located. They can fish for the giant BLACK SEA BASS, run out to the islands or wherever, providing such a trip is agreed upon at the time the craft is engaged.

Wherever there is good dockage along most of the Pacific Coast, boats specially equipped for fishing in each particular locality can be hired. On smaller craft in the north their one or two-man crews are called guides. There are some few MARLIN cruisers and expert crews for hire at San Pedro, Balboa, and San Diego, California. They are outfitted with fighting chairs and other conveniences and equipment for distant voyages in pursuit of MARLIN, BROADBILL, monstrous SHARKS, or whatever. A radio is important, not only for safety but to keep in communication with other skippers who have found the big billfish.

When engaging a boat it is advisable to make sure of every detail: Size of the boat, experience and reputation of the captain, number of the crew, kind and condition of bait, conveniences, and sailing time. An understanding should be arrived at about the actual number of fishing hours guaranteed over and above the time spent waiting for bait, in delays because of engine trouble, or as sometimes happens in an emergency such as towing a disabled craft to port. Unless all these conditions are previously discussed, the charter party is some time or another likely to be disappointed.

Regardless of the kind of fish that is anticipated, it is a good idea to take along ample tackle suitable for various types of fishing, for there are times when the party would be a complete "washout" if one special species were to be depended upon to furnish all the excitement.

SWORDFISH AND STRIPED MARLIN

It is possible to take a SWORDFISH from a sizable, seaworthy motor boat, but it is not practical for the beginner to attempt such an exploit. It would be far more reasonable for him to gain the necessary experience by placing himself in the hands of a seasoned charter boat operator with a vessel especially equipped for the purpose.

Each year new methods for the capture of this fish are evolved, yet there still seems to be a dearth of ideas on how to inveigle it into taking the bait.

The SWORDFISH is sometimes sighted by a lookout on calm, sunny days, floating with fin and tail above the water, or at other times thrashing a school of forage fish. As soon as the big fish is located, the captain maneuvers to a position where he can circle, dragging the bait across in front of it, the usual bait being a small barracuda, mackerel, mullet, or flyingfish. It is then let out and allowed to sink in front of the fish, then slowly pulled away. If this sword-wielding sea warrior hits it, he will need a lot of line. The timing in setting the hook in all billfish angling is of the utmost importance, and very few beginners have the patience to wait out the long countdown.

The novice should start off with extra heavy tackle: for BROADBILL SWORDFISH, a 9/0 reel loaded with 80-pound-test Dacron; a 12-foot Sevalon leader of 80-pound-

test; and a 10/0 hook. He should keep the rod butt in the gimble of the fighting chair throughout the trolling and the contest, instead of fishing from the belt, as some oldtimers prefer.

Some new techniques are developing in fishing the BROADBILL SWORDFISH near the bottom in 20 to 35 fathoms. Heavy tackle and the salmon breakaway sinker (1 to 4 lbs.) are used.

For STRIPED MARLIN a frozen Catalina FLYINGFISH, fresh MULLET, or other bait 10 to 12 inches long is harnessed (see section on bait) so that it will ski on the surface without revolving or coming loose easily—this, when an outrigger pole is used. For MARLIN, the outrigger serves to keep the line high enough that the bait will skip about forty feet behind the stern. The line is attached by a clothespin, barely secure enough to hold against the pull of the bait. When trolling, the reel is set in freewheeling with the click on, to avoid backlash. The star drag is set with barely enough tension to fight the fish but never below the breaking point of the line.

When the outrigger is not used, as when the line runs directly from the fishing rod, ski-bait (a 12-inch slab tailored from a large fish) glides on the surface and seems just as effective as a whole bait-fish.

When the fish strikes, the boat is stopped, and the skipper waits for the angler to make a long count of twenty and give him the "go" signal to plunge ahead to take up all the slack in the line. Only then does the angler set the hook. This timing allows the fish enough time to get the hook down its gullet. If it's merely hooked in the mouth, the hook can be expelled unless a taut line is maintained at all times, whether the fish is jumping or not.

Rhythm pumping will cause the MARLIN to jump and otherwise tire itself out more quickly. This technique, now applied for other game fish, was originally introduced in fishing MARLIN.

A great range of tackle is employed in angling for MARLIN: from a heavy 6/0 reel and equipment for the beginner to light spinning tackle for the record collector. The most efficient and least strenuous is: a #349 Penn-type reel, loaded with 30 to 50-pound-test limp Dacron; no swivel or sinker; a 12-foot blue Sevalon leader; a No. 7/0 to 9/0 Sobey or Mustad hook (see billfish perfect hook in section on tackle).

A fine new incentive has been added to big-game fishing, and most anglers get an extra reward from fishing for science. Instead of being killed and decked, the captured marlin is brought to the boat, tagged, and released. When the fish is caught again the tag is sent to the U.S. Fish and Wildlife Service, La Jolla, California, giving the scientific lab much needed information in managing and conserving the fishery.

How to Use Baits and Tackle

The sensory organs of the animals living under water were necessarily developed very differently from those of the land animals. Long ago people spoke only in terms as applied to land creatures when discussing those of the waters. Consequently when early investigators found no apparent external ear, they assumed the fish was unable to hear. They questioned how a fish could use the very small nasal passages as smelling organs when there was no gas-laden air available to it.

Modern ichthyologists have developed new hypotheses in regard to aquatic life and are making rapid progress in the study. Recent experiments have shed new light on the homing instinct of the SALMON, the importance of the lateral line as a sense organ, the sense of smell and color perception. Some evidence points to the possibility that the marine fishes may have a very keen sense of taste.

In comparison to land animals, fishes are near-sighted and are unable to recognize an object as quickly. They can however, see movements or flashes at a considerable distance not only in front but on a very wide angle which extends well back. It seems quite possible that fishes require a binocular vision of the bait before they can completely recognize it.

Experiments have shown that a great number of the marine species are not color blind. Many of them change their own color to match their surroundings, often in the space of a minute or so. Some of the FLATFISHES are able to change the pattern of the spots on their bodies to match the bottom. In experiments, blindfolded fishes were unable to transform their coloring. An ocean fish however, may not be able to readily recognize color above his own level in the water, as the brightness of the sky would tend to make the higher object appear in silhouette. This, in a way, may explain the defense mechanism of fishes having light-colored bellies to match the overhead brightness.

Fishes have no external ears that carry sound vibrations through funnels to the perceptive brain cells though some sound vibrations are conducted through the bony structure of the head. However, fishes do have a system of organs that seems to be even more sensitive to vibrations made in the water. These organs are made up of tiny canals which are associated with the inner ears. They are composed of a series of pores appearing as slightly raised areas along the sides of most fishes and forming what is called the lateral line (which may be single or multiple and in some species branch out over the head and dorsal surface). A nerve running parallel is connected to the canal at intervals. Perception by means of these

Live bait tanks are the easy way to obtain fish bait. Many barges and most piers all along the Pacific coast provide this handy service.

The large quantity of water that passes through the mouth in comparison to the amount that is taken in and expelled through the very small holes of the nostrils suggests that the sense of taste should have developed to a high degree. In reverse the land animals inhale great quantities of air through nostrils and have therefore a keen smell sense.

There are taste buds on the tongue of a fish. A CATFISH has them on its whiskers and some even on its tail but just how sensitive these organs are is still vague.

ALBACORE is thought to be capable of following a cold trail of forage fish by the odor or taste of guanine left in the small fishes' path. This chemical is shed from the slick body-covering of small fish. The total disappearance of the vast schools of SARDINES off Southern California waters, due to over-fishing, may have caused the ALBACORE to shift their migratory swimway many miles out to sea.

On land, odor is carried in the air in the form of gases which permeate the air for great distances. This gives the land animals the advantage. In the water such rapid distribution of the more or less solids seems unlikely.

organs no doubt equals or surpasses that of land creatures, since air does not act as effectively as water as a sound vibration conductor.

A leaderless school of small fry traveling at a fast clip can be seen doing intricate maneuvers in perfect coordination as if controlled by a mass of intelligence or some electrical hook-up. Furthermore, they do not bump into each other, suggesting that the lateral line may function somewhat like radar, and that the vibrations received cause the muscles of the body to react automatically, compelling the fish to move one way or another, much like our eyelids snapping shut when an object comes too near the eye.

The lateral line may serve the fish in other ways. One of the latest theories is that through it the fish may recognize temperature changes. It may also supersede the sense of touch, acting long before the body of the fish comes in contact with another object.

Since many fishes make sounds, such as those of the CROAKERS and the singing OCEAN MIDSHIPMAN, they are, no doubt, able to communicate with their own kind.

A great number of marine fishes seem capable of receiving sensations by way of the nostrils which connect to small olfactory sacs just under the skin. The sense impulses are transferred from these sacs to the brain cells by connecting nerves. The nostrils do not connect with the mouth or throat as in the land animals. It is known that SHARKS have a very keen sense of smell. Experiments have disclosed their inability to locate food when their nostrils were plugged up with cotton. Most of the species we are concerned with have two sets of nostrils; the water enters the frontal set and is discharged through the rear pair of nostrils.

❧ HOW TO USE STRIPBAIT ❧

Among the prime secrets of ocean fishing is the proper utilization of STRIPBAIT. Cutting a strip from a fish and using it as a substitute for live bait is nothing new, but there is a wrong and a right way of cutting the strip, of presenting, and manipulating it.

Many will be surprised to find that in numerous cases STRIPBAIT is far superior to live bait and in a great number of instances more effective in taking a majority of our popular game fishes. It is a fact that a substantial number of species will reject almost everything but STRIPBAIT, refusing anchovies, sardines, or other live forage fishes.

Heretofore the general term "cut bait" has unfortunately been applied to all forms of pieces of fish. For future clarification a distinction should be made. When sardines, anchovies, or whatever bait fish are simply cut up into chunks, the meat should be termed "CHUNK-BAIT," while fillets tailored into long strips should be called "STRIPBAIT."

The theory that prompted the experimentation which required more than five years of intense trial-and-error work was based on scientific principles and not the usual fisherman's superstitions. Since modern anglers demand the "reasons why," the author deems it appropriate to give some explanations.

The reader of this volume will recall that fishes have a highly developed sense of taste (or smell), which is somewhat equivalent to a bloodhound's sense of smell. It is therefore good reasoning to surmise that schools of game fishes follow and overtake large schools of small forage fishes by the excretions left as a trail in the water. Once the SARDINE, SAURY, ANCHOVY or other forage school is overtaken, the large fishes run amuck, slashing and maiming as many as possible, then, at their leisure, easily pick up the cripples. These injured forage fishes are then located by the flashes of their spasmodic movements and erratic manner of swimming, and too, by the trail of blood left in their wake.

In the predatory fish, this method of feeding has long since been established as instinct. In some fishes such as the SALMON, the instinct to slaughter is still evident long after the nuptial fast has begun.

All of this has a definite bearing on the value of STRIPBAIT, and the angler's understanding of it will help him considerably in giving the required interest to detail in preparation and the manipulation of the bait.

The fisherman who cuts the strip carelessly, hooks it wrong, or just lets it dangle motionless in the water gains nothing from reading this chapter and will net very few fish. Detail is essential to the angler who hopes to reap the full benefit of this technique.

If the fish that is to be cut into bait strips is alive, very fresh-dead, or fresh-frozen, it will exude far more flavor and will therefore leave a better trail than one that is not so fresh. Strips should not be cut too far in advance lest they dry out and seal up the chumming secretions. If the bait is salted, cured, old or dried out, it will fail to arouse the instinctive appetites of the game fishes because it does not establish the familiar trail of a wounded fish.

The size and length of the strip differs according to the species sought, ranging from the half or inch-long piece used for the SANDDAB, HALFMOON, SEAPERCH or SURFPERCH; to the five-inch strip for ALBACORE, BARRACUDA, and YELLOWTAIL; and on up to the ten-inch fillet for BONITO SHARK, BLUE SHARK, and BLACK SEA BASS. In all cases the fillet is designed to create the illusion of a live but injured fish, i.e., tapering from a broad head end to a pointed tail.

Because of the unpredictable appetites of the game fishes it is advisable to have more than one kind of bait fish. While, for example, a strip from a sardine is a generally preferred bait for BARRACUDA, there are times when this fish will more quickly take a slice of anchovy or even mackerel.

For fish feeding in moderately shallow water or near the surface, a small hook is recommended, especially when the fish sought are not overly hungry, although some of the deep-water species seem more apt to ignore the size of the hook. This is not the rule, however, for members of the deep-water FLATFISHES category. For them, except for a couple of species, small hooks are always preferable.

While the method of tailoring and hooking STRIPBAIT is important, the technique of manipulating it is more so. Since it is scientific knowledge that fish have poor vision but are able to respond visually to quick movements and flashes, it is obvious that cut bait should be kept in motion. Herein lies the art of ocean angling.

How fast should the strip be retrieved? How long should each halting motion be to simulate an injured bait fish? These questions must be answered by the angler himself and only after he has practiced with patience and calculation. Since we cannot give elaborate instructions as to tempo required for each of the two hundred odd individual species, the angler will have to base his art on a few examples and his own initiative.

For a majority of the small, bottom-feeding FLATFISHES, the bait is cast out, dragged along near or on the sandy bottom, then pulled upward by rhythmic halting motions of about a foot and a half each. The slow tempo should correspond to the timing of the beat of a grandfather clock. The strokes should not be abrupt or jerky but mere halts to be repeated smoothly. Bites and nibbles are ignored. No sudden jerk is needed to set the hook. At times it may be necessary to retrieve the bait ten or twelve feet up from the bottom before the FLOUNDER or SANDDAB will quit nibbling the tail and grab for the

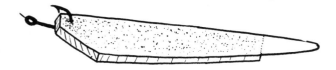

FIG. 2. *Stripbait, made fresh from boned fish flesh.*

Here are some general rules for preparing STRIPBAIT: Remove scales; slice whole side, avoiding bones; split lengthwise into strips of the desired width; cut on an angle so that the head end of the strip will be broad, then taper to a pointed tail end to form the pennant-shaped strip. Insert the hook in the broad end only. (Fig. 2.) The head end of a large strip is cut on an angle. When the hook is inserted near the top of the angle the bait is not so likely to spin.

Meticulous anglers will scrape the flesh, leaving a small section of the skin on the tail end. This flap of skin will wiggle when the bait is pulled through the water, thus adding to the life-like illusion.

All this preparation may seem tedious at first, but with a little practice it can be done with very few strokes of a sharp knife.

SKI-BAIT

This highly effective bait, and the technique for working it, was developed in the Sea of Cortez since this volume was first published. Its popularity there is gaining rapidly, and it will, no doubt, catch on wherever

hooked head end. A few minutes' practice will give the angler the feeding depth and a feeling for the proper tempo and timing.

For shallow-water ROCKFISHES the timing is about the same except that the movements are about half as long as for the FLATFISHES. Since ROCKFISHES are to be found among rocks and kelp, casting out is necessary only when fishing from shore and not at all advisable from aboard a boat. (NOTE: These angling instructions are primarily for the benefit of anglers aboard a vessel.)

For top-feeding game fishes a long cast, long rapid strokes and a fast retrieve are the rule, the speed a little more than half that used in working with a feather for BARRACUDA and ALBACORE. For YELLOWTAIL, the speed should be doubled. There are times when these game fishes will not feed on top, and the bait will have to be allowed to sink before retrieving starts. This will tend to slow down the timing, and correctly so.

(a)

(b)

(c)

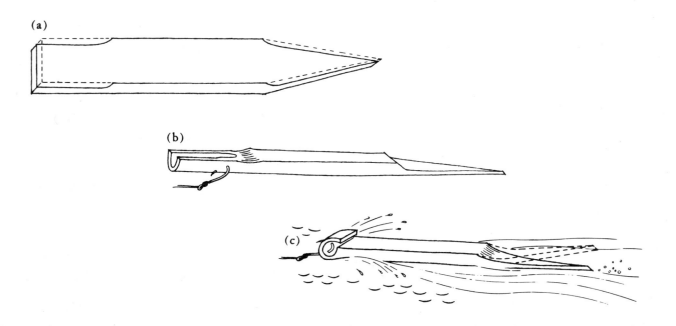

FIG. 3. *Ski-bait, a lively, surface-skipping cut bait. (a) Cut form. (b) Method of hooking. (c) In action.*

FIG. 4. *Spinner bait is double hooked to revolve.*

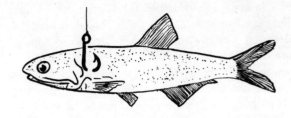

FIG. 6. *Live anchovy bait, hooked under collar bone.*

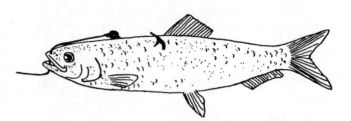

FIG. 5. *Whole-bait spinner can be made from herring.*

FIG. 7. *Pinhead anchovy hooked through mouth and up.*

surface-feeding fish are found. Although tailoring, hooking, and keeping it skiing on the surface may seem complicated on paper, the process becomes easy with a little practice and a sharp knife.

Some fish below the Mexican border have a greater preference for ski-bait than for any other so far tried. DOLPHINFISH and NEEDLEFISH will occasionally leave the water in a series of leaps or come slicing in at first sight of it. PANCAKE POMPANO rarely take any other baits.

MARLIN and SAILFISH will often go for a large ski-bait when nothing else will attract them, especially when it is cut from a freshly caught fish. At times they will tail along behind the favored FLYINGFISH or MULLET for several minutes then leave to grab a ski-bait held back and let out for this purpose.

It has become the standard bait for anglers who like their billfishing from an outboard skiff or when outriggers are not employed.

Other species found feeding on the surface have latched onto this bait, but during such gluttonous binges they are apt to grab almost anything in motion, so we can't be sure it was preferred.

Although absolute perfection is not essential, the design should be followed closely until the knack of cutting and hooking has been learned. Then there are two points that the angler must learn by experiment. First is the thickness of the bait, which must be rigid yet thin enough to be buoyant. The second is the trolling speed required to keep the bait gliding smoothly a good distance back of the boat. Because of changing water conditions, this speed cannot be predetermined. It is designed to

throw up little rooster-tail sprays resembling a small FLYINGFISH about to take off. (See Fig. 3c.)

A slab from the side or belly of a SIERRA, BARRILETE (BLACK SKIPJACK), MACKEREL, or other oily fish is shaped with the ends cut thinner, as in (a) (the thickness according to the size and weight of the bait). The front end is then cupped up so the hook can be inserted through both folds, as in (b). It is then bent back, leaving the bait shaped like a toboggan, as in (c), and ready to ski on the surface. In this drawing the dotted lines indicate the tail flipping up and down.

⤳ SPINNER BAIT ⤳

This bait is used in a somewhat similar fashion to STRIPBAIT, the difference being in the manner of hooking. While the hook is implanted in the STRIPBAIT to keep it from turning over and over, the SPINNER is hooked so it will revolve slowly. If hooked in a manner that would cause it to turn too rapidly the desired action and effect would be lost.

SPINNERS are double-hooked, the hook being inserted through the skin twice, first at the upper point of the head, then a short distance back, as shown in Fig. 4.

The distance between the two insertions is lengthened when the retrieving speed is very slow. Its action can be tested in the surface water before sending it down.

The water soon washes out the flavor exuding from these baits. They should therefore be changed frequently.

A whole herring or other bait fish is preferred for spin fishing by some anglers, principally because it need not be changed quite so often. There are places and conditions when the whole bait fish seems to be more effective, as when SALMON are feeding below the seventy-five foot depth. In a whole-bait SPINNER the hook is inserted up through both jaws, then implanted just below the dorsal fin with the point barely projecting, as in Fig. 5.

This type of hooking is also used extensively for mooching. At times a double-hook rig is more productive, the first hook running up through both jaws, the second across under the dorsal fin.

❧ LIVE BAITS ❧

There are so many kinds of bait that it is almost impossible to set down any single, general rule for utilization that is infallible. Circumstances and conditions will alter any suggested plan of hooking the different baits. We will, however, give a few examples of the more or less accepted methods.

It would always seem logical to hook the bait in the most secure manner possible, but this is not always the case. The size of a LIVE BAIT may have some bearing as to where the hook is to be inserted. Again, the individual feeding habits of the various game fishes should always be considered, and the bait hooked accordingly.

❧ ANCHOVIES ❧

With the ANCHOVY the usual custom is to implant the hook just back of the gill cover and around under the collar bone (see Fig. 6). If the bait is a "PINHEAD" (very small ANCHOVY), the hook should be inserted up through the mouth, coming out just under the eye (Fig. 7).

There are times when the ANCHOVY is hooked through the back under the dorsal fin or near the tail, in order to keep it swimming on the surface (Fig. 8). This method is not recommended for distance casting.

Then, too, some fish are so finicky that they refuse to take an ANCHOVY when it is hooked anywhere about the head.

The ANCHOVY will keep lively a bit longer when the hook is inserted around the clavicle (collar bone). (Fig. 6.) Even when secured in this fashion, the ANCHOVY, being one of the most delicate of the bait fishes, is short lived. It usually becomes so weak after a few minutes that it either must be kept in motion by the angler or replaced.

When game fishes are not very hungry or excited by a school of forage fish or some other intriguing disturbance, they will, as a rule, nibble at a LIVE BAIT, making it necessary to secure it fairly well on the hook. This rule also prevails when the bait is to be cast out.

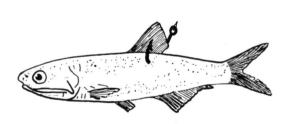

FIG. 8. *Back-hooked anchovy can swim on the surface.*

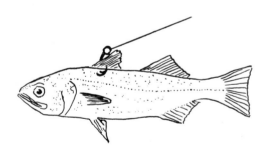

FIG. 10. *Yoke-bait provides more freedom to live bait.*

FIG. 9. *Snout-hooking for sardine and herring baits.*

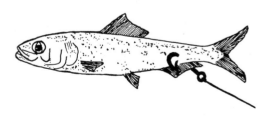

FIG. 11. *Tail-hook large sardines for barracuda.*

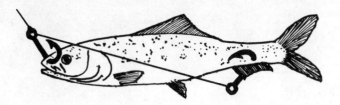

FIG. 12. *Double-hook for barracuda, white seabass.*

FIG. 14. *Snout-hooked mudsucker, for trolling.*

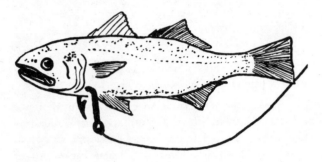

FIG. 13. *Queenfish bait hooked ahead of breastbones.*

❧ YOKE-BAIT ❧

To keep a large LIVE BAIT more active and to give it unrestrained freedom to range over a large area, including greater depths, the YOKE-BAIT will serve best.

BILLFISH and other big gamesters have shown a decided preference for a yoke-hooked live BARRILETE (BLACK) SKIPJACK, BONITO, PACIFIC MACKEREL, or other foot-long baits.

No crippling wound is inflicted when the hook is inserted just under the first few spines of the dorsal fin, as in Fig. 10. It gives the BAIT FISH an easy oxen-yoke pull on the line without tiring it out as rapidly as when hooked otherwise. Many large bait fishes will swim straight out for a 100 yards, then sound, taking the whole length of unweighted line with them.

HERRINGS
❧ AND OTHER LARGE ❧
BAITS

Each species of the small bait fishes has its own particular strong or tough anatomical member from which the hook is less likely to tear. In the ANCHOVY, it is the clavicle; in the SARDINE and HERRING, the snout. (Fig. 9.)

When the SARDINE or HERRING is "flied" (not cast out) and other conditions are favorable, it can be hooked between the anal fin and the lateral line, back near the tail. (Fig. 11.)

When a double-hook rig is used for the tail snapping BARRACUDA or WHITE SEABASS, one hook is inserted through the snout; the other above the anal fin near the tail or through the back under the dorsal fin (Fig. 12.); anglers call it "booby-trap."

❧ QUEENFISH ❧
AND TOMMY CROAKER

The QUEENFISH has two strong pubic bones (breastbones) running from the pelvic fins forward toward the lower jaw. The hook should be inserted just ahead of the base of these fins and only deep enough to encircle the bones. (Fig. 13.)

QUEENFISH will live longer when this procedure is followed, but many anglers prefer the method of hooking them under the second dorsal fin, especially when they are surface fishing and no weight is used.

The TOMMY CROAKER is secured in the same manner as the QUEENFISH, but being tougher, may be hooked in almost any way desired. The same can be said of the BUTTERFISH, at times favorite bait for YELLOWTAIL.

Most deep-bodied bait fish are hindered less when the hook is inserted just under the first spines in the dorsal fin. Several of the game fishes will show less reluctance in taking and swallowing this shoulder-hooked bait than any other, especially the large TUNAS and YELLOWTAIL. For these and others without large, cutting teeth, the hook is tied directly onto the flexible monofilament line for less interference in the swimming of the bait. Hooked in this manner, the flied bait can pull like a yoked oxen and take out a lot of yardage of mono.

This method is especially good for mackerel or other large live bait for MARLIN, BROADBILL, and great SHARKS. By a gentle pull, the bait can be reigned up close to the surface when it sounds to undesirable depths.

ᐁᐤ (LONGJAW) MUDSUCKER ᐁᐤ

All GOBIES, the MUDSUCKER in particular, should be hooked up through the snout. (Fig. 14.)

This small bait fish will remain alive for days if kept covered with seaweed.

Many kinds of bait to be trolled or retrieved as soon as cast are hooked in this manner (Fig. 14), MACKEREL, MULLET, and other live baits included.

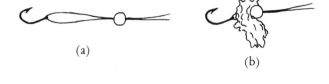

(a)   (b)

FIG. 15. *Leader looped (a); mussel cinched down (b).*

ᐁᐤ CRUSTACEANS AND SQUID ᐁᐤ

In the South Atlantic, SHRIMP has become a very important live bait, but in the Pacific its full potential is yet to be realized. A good start has been made in the San Pedro-Long Beach, California area with the RED ROCK SHRIMP. With it, several seldom-caught game fish species became available and were found to be abundant.

The State and Federal Departments of Fish and Game, having conducted research studies for commercial SHRIMP enterprises, could more profitably develop live SHRIMP and live SQUID fisheries for angling. A failure in the present ANCHOVY population would cause havoc in the salt-water angling if no substitute bait were available.

In the north, other live crustaceans are utilized on a fairly large scale. But the the great abundance of SHRIMP in already known beds all along our coast, little would be necessary to establish live SHRIMP enterprises.

All of this could be said of live SQUID, a bait that has already proven superior to any other kind for some of our best game fishes.

Live SAND CRABS, *Emerita analoga*, have long been exploited in southern California and Baja California, especially for surf fishing. They are very hardy and will remain alive for long periods if kept damp. There seems to be a decline in numbers on beaches that are kept clean of decaying seaweeds, which appear to be the main food supply for this bug as well as for another commonly called the SAND FLEA, an important forage item for small fishes. The soft-shelled SAND CRAB is favored. Larger hooks seem to go unnoticed by fish. This is due to roughness of the shell.

Mexico has numerous warm, backwater sloughs crowded with SHALLOW-WATER SHRIMP and PILE WORMS, *Neanthes* sp., which could be grown artificially in the ocean water warmed and discharged by power plants. Southern California could support such a LIVE BAIT enterprise at almost any of the several shore-side electric plants now.

The double-hook "booby-trap" (Fig. 12) is very efficient when fishing with live SQUID.

Among the most common crustaceans used in the live stage in the north are the GHOST SHRIMP, found on tidal mud flats, and four or more species of CRAWFISH (CRAYFISH), which inhabit fresh-water banks. All of them are useful baits.

GHOST SHRIMP, *Callianassa californiensis*, in some flats in Oregon, could produce more than 1,500 gallons. Commercially they are washed to the surface by water pressure from a hose. CRAWFISH are captured in traps baited with fish and left overnight among the holes of a colony. For some few fish, the tails only are used. This is one of the very few fresh-water or land-side creatures that attracts and continues to attract ocean-going fishes.

The worms you see being used for bait by surf casters are not the ordinary garden variety; they are from the sands, rocks, and timbers flushed by salty tides and are commonly called PILE or BLOOD WORMS. Some CROAKERS and small FLATFISH show a decided preference for BLOOD WORMS.

ᐁᐤ DEAD BAITS ᐁᐤ

A strip, chunk, or bit of almost any kind of a fish caught in sea water will attract a long list of fishes. But there are preferences. An oily fish, such as SARDINE and (PACIFIC) MACKEREL, is favored by some fish over the less oily species.

The soft part of all CLAMS, ABALONE, and SCALLOPS is good, but, in general, the most desirable of the shellfish are the ROCK and BAY MUSSELS.

The bulk of preserved baits is from the deep freeze. If frozen alive, the flavor remains fairly fresh. Less attractive are the canned and salted products. Sugar-cured MACKEREL, makes an excellent chum if nothing else is available.

⟡ MUSSELS ⟡

For shore fishes, MUSSELS are by far the best all-around bait but are the most difficult to keep on. A lot of tricks have been developed that do help somewhat. For one: Four or five pieces of soft MUSSEL are run through by the hook and strung up on the leader. Another: A big gob is secured on the hook and wrapped with fine thread. A very effective way of holding MUSSELS is to rig a short-shank hook on a double-leader with a small glass bead that will slide up and down above the hook (Fig. 15). The MUSSEL is placed between the leaders (a), then when the bead is forced down, the bait is cinched just above the hook (b).

The intestines of ABALONE are also an excellent bait.

The bare point of the hook can then be run through another piece of MUSSEL and the rig is loaded. This is also a simple way to secure moss for OPALEYE bait. Other soft bait such as the soft part of CLAMS, can also be kept on longer with such a gimmick.

⟡ SHRIMP ⟡

Next to MUSSELS, SHRIMP are about the best, general all-purpose shore bait. For fishing among the kelp beds, the shell acts as a protection against the hordes of small SENORITA, SMELTS and the like. Many larger fishes will not hesitate to take shell and all. SHRIMP should be shelled only when small fish are sought, whether among kelp or over rocky bottom.

The small PACIFIC SHRIMP, *Pandalus jordani*, is destined to become one of our important baits. If these SHRIMP are frozen immediately after capture, they will be excellent for the majority of the deep-water forms and no doubt effective for many shallow-water species.

⟡ BAITS SOLD IN MARKETS ⟡

The SHRIMP so often recommended as good bait for a great number of fish should be small and green (un-bleached). Like other fresh bait, SHRIMP should be kept frozen as long as possible. Shelled, cooked, or salted SHRIMP are of little value.

The MACKEREL suggested as an excellent bait, especially when cut into strips, is the (PACIFIC) MACKEREL, *Pneumatophorus japonicus*, not the MACKEREL JACK, *Trachurus symmetricus*. For BLACK SEA BASS and some of the large SHARKS a cold slice of MACKEREL is effective, but at times one that has been left in the sun for an hour or so is even better. For smaller fishes, it should be fresh or fresh-frozen and kept cool as long as possible.

Fresh ANCHOVIES, SARDINES, and HERRING are always a good second choice to strips of MACKEREL. SARDINES, TOMMY CROAKER, HERRING and other bait fishes should be scaled when they are to be cut into strips.

There are a number of fresh SHELLFISH sold in markets that can be used for bait. SQUID sold in the markets are not acceptable to the fish when bleached.

FIG. 16. Emmert Brooks halter for marlin: (a) Run lines down. (b) Knot lines. (c) Attach hook to loop.

⤚⤜ FOR MARLIN ⤚⤜

The production of frozen (CALIFORNIA) FLYINGFISH for billfish bait has become big business in supplying the demand for angling in the Sea of Cortez and off southern California.

The old method of burying the hook in this bait, then sewing it up, has lost popularity in favor of the harnessing system. Because the harness hitch is flexible, the billfish can easily turn the bait to go down head first without having to bend the stiff leader.

There are several ways of applying the harness. So far, the most efficient seems to be the "Emmert Brooks halter." With a bit of practice, it can be made rapidly. First, a needle bearing a large fishing line (double) is shoved through the top of the head, in back of the gill covers, and out through the throat, Fig. 16 (a). Cut the bottom lines above the needle, leaving four lines to work with.

After the length has been determined, tie number 1 line at the center of the eye, and repeat with number 2 line on the opposite side. Thread the *top* ends of 1 and 2 through a needle and run it down through the nose vertically. Thread the *bottom* ends of 1 and 2 and shove them up vertically, as shown at (b).

This leaves double lines at the top and bottom. Tie them in front of the snout and again two and a half inches ahead. Loop the end to form a simple bend, insert the hook, and cinch down (c). The hook should be nearer to the mouth.

⤚⤜ TACKLE ⤚⤜

Each of the many angling organizations has its own rules regulating tackle size and weight for its members. The motive to establish the most sporting type of tackle is admirable, but space limitation prohibits us from giving all the various sets of rules. The size, weight, and kind of tackle described herein is calculated for efficiency, particularly for the beginner.

⤚⤜ HOOKS ⤚⤜

A few years ago, when the great schools of game fishes came pressing in along our coast, little thought was given by the average fisherman to the size and weight of his tackle. But as the big fish became scarcer and increasingly more difficult to excite, the angler found that a more subtle technique and less conspicuous gear were necessary. The fish had, it seemed, become more hook-and-leader conscious. Even a small swivel, the angler discovered, was enough to keep some of them at a distance. The large, long-shank siwash type was discarded in favor of the heavy, short-shank hook. Each season a smaller size was tested until it was established that the Nos. 4 to 1 hooks were the most effective for taking many of the very large fishes.

With the reduction in the size of the hooks, the long, finer-gauge leader was found more acceptable. Swivels, large sinkers, and other gadgets were eliminated so that the bait would appear as unencumbered as possible.

The long-shank hook is not only more apparent to the fish than the short-shank but also provides leverage in dislodging it. The main reason for the suggested extra-heavy thickness of the hook is that it is less likely to cut its way out. Figure 17 shows hook sizes and numbers.

The importance of keeping the point of the hook sharp cannot be stressed too heavily. Men who take their fishing seriously examine new hooks carefully and often find that many of them come from the factory with very dull points. If the beginner has not learned to feel the sharpness of the point, a magnifying glass inspection will reveal the condition.

Some of the bottom-feeding fishes, especially those found around deep, rocky reefs have no objection to large hooks. They are accustomed to eating shell-incrusted sea life and are not so apt to notice the hardness of the hook. However, fish that live on softer foods will often try to expel a hook the instant the metal touches the mouth. Many of the smaller species are attracted by the brightness of plated or shiny hooks, but for general purposes dark-colored hooks are better. Hooks with off-set points are not recommended with live bait as the bait is apt to become double hooked.

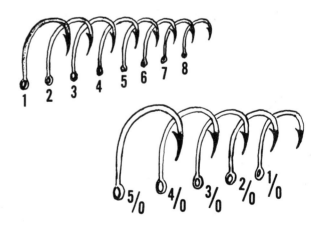

FIG. 17. Hook sizes (actual size) and numbers.

ꙮ BIG GAME HOOKS ꙮ

Following a survey some years ago among big-game anglers of the world, hook manufacturers Mustad, of Oslo, Norway, produced a hook that was considered close to perfect (Fig. 18).

The figure is actual size of a 9/0. The preferred is 7/0. The point is very long, gradually tapering from the curve, with a small barb so the hooks can be set with little effort. The base or curve is very thick and rounded to prevent cutting through the flesh. The shank gradually tapers from the curve to the small, flattened eye. The point is tipped in so that it will be in line with the force applied to set the hook. This one is hand-made of a hard, stainless, alloyed steel. The only drawback is that each hook costs three or four dollars. It should, however, serve as a pattern for manufacturers to follow and give anglers an example in making hook selections for big game.

The longer shank is not objectionable when large baits are used.

A large-size hook is less likely to cut a slip in cheek-hooked fish. But if the fish is given time to swallow the bait, there is no advantage over a strong smaller size, and the smaller hook is less likely to be felt and discharged. With live-bait, the hook is kept to a minimum to avoid weighting the bait down.

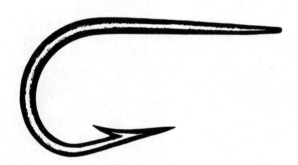

FIG. 18. *"Ideal" big-game hook, made by Mustad.*

In some fish, for example the great SHARKS, the mouth membrane is so tough that the larger hook is more efficient, and the sizes may run on up to 14/0, except when live or small baits are used. On the other hand, when a hook gets below the throat, it is most likely to get imbedded in tough, elastic flesh that will not slit even with a 5/0 hook.

Astute anglers, who have learned to allow the fish ample time to get the bait down, find very small hooks much more efficient.

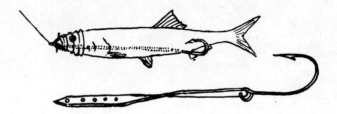

FIG. 19. *Fresh-bait harness for slow trolling.*

A bait harness for SALMON trolling is composed of a long-shank No. 4/0 to 6/0 salmon hook attached to a flat strip of stainless steel three to five inches long. The pointed top end of the strip is inserted up through the anus and on out through the mouth, the hook point barely protruding. A small pin (with a copper wire attached) is inserted down through the jaws of the bait and through one of the small holes in the metal strip. The wire is then wrapped around the jaws, after which the swivel snap-spring is run through a hole near the point of the strip. (Fig. 19.)

Although this rig is designed primarily for SALMON, it can be employed for any type of slow trolling where a fresh whole bait is used. The size of the rig should be selected according to the length of the bait fish.

ꙮ LEADERS ꙮ

While there have been notable improvements in angling equipment in general, the developments in leaders have been revolutionary. Monofilament has replaced gut leader material, and the single wire has been discarded in favor of the nylon or plastic-covered multiple-strand material.

Mono leaders are usually kept below the pound-test of the line. All knots in mono should be cinch-tied with multiple turns.

Figure 20 shows how to secure mono leaders for various purposes. (a) After passing the leader through the hook eye, give the short end a half-dozen or more wraps above the hook, then insert the short end just above the eye and cinch up tightly. (b) To tie onto a line loop, circle the short end around one side of the loop, then around both for a half-dozen turns, then once more around one and cinch down. There are other methods of tying mono, as shown in tackle catalogues. Mono to Dacron is shown in (c), fisherman's knot in (d).

Wire leaders and materials are made by several companies. For Pacific Coast and Sea of Cortez angling, the

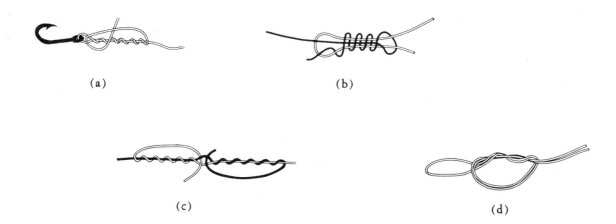

FIG. 20. *Mono leaders: (a) Tied to hook. (b) Tied to line loop. (c) Mono to Dacron. (d) Fisherman's knot.*

Sevenstrand, or Sevalon, seems to have been engineered to keep abreast of the time. This material will not loop and snap off, as a single-strand wire is likely to do. Being made of multiple strands, it is far more flexible, allowing baits to swim about with less restraint, especially when the pound-test is kept down to a minimum. The plastic coating helps in keeping the leader from kinking and corroding, and deadens vibrations that are perceptible to fish. We also found that the blue color is less disturbing to fish.

The ends of made-up Sevenstrand leaders are fused on. For those wishing to make up their own, a kit of easy-to-clamp-on sleeves and a special crimping tool are advisable. Otherwise, the line-snagging ends are not easy to keep out of the way.

When working with light-weight material a doubled loop helps to keep it in shape.

Figure 21 shows how to secure a hook to a wire leader. The short end is first inserted through the hook eye, then looped once (a), then it goes through the eye again and is cinched to size (b), then it's looped twice more and clipped off so it will be barely hidden when the sleeve is shoved down tight to the loop and crimped on (c).

This same procedure (minus the hook) can be followed in forming the loop at the leader top.

While monofilament is more flexible than wire and makes the bait appear less encumbered, there are many occasions when the metal leader is best: when angling for fish with clipper-like teeth or those with a habit of using their rough tail to pop the leader or line; when fishing among rocks.

Metal shorty leaders four to eight inches long are more efficient when sharp teeth is the only problem.

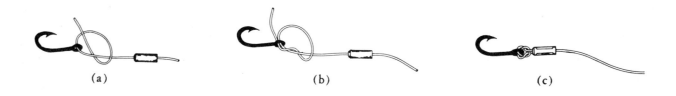

FIG. 21. *Attaching wire leader: (a) Through eye, loop. (b) Through eye. (c) Loop twice, cinch, crimp.*

With live bait they are attached directly to the line with no snaps or swivels. When no sinkers are used swivels do not swivel anyway.

REELS

Today there are special reels for almost every purpose. Some of them constructed for a certain kind of fishing have proven more effective for an entirely different method than originally intended. A good example of this is the reel that was built to fish deep, with a metal line, for SALMON, and which, when loaded with Dacron, turned out to be ideal for trolling MARLIN. This is mentioned to urge the angler to experiment rather than sticking to equipment just because he is accustomed to it.

The reel, a Penn #349, is singled out because it has come close to eliminating the larger reels in trolling for heavy fish. Although it's built with the same gears and is just as sturdy as a 6/0, its spool is 1¼ inches shorter. This means less weight, less thumbing for a level wind, and less tipping from side to side when fighting a fish. Most important, the reel rests snugly and comfortably against the gripping wrist. Along with the strength and reduction of line sizes, it holds enough for almost any purpose.

Large reels are still favored for monstrous SHARK, BROADBILL, and BLACK SEA BASS. Small, conventional squidders and various light-tackle reels are employed for small-game fish when trolling, or for most other angling except casting. In casting, some anglers still prefer the conventional reel, but there is an ever-increasing number who prefer to do all casting with spinning equipment, and no doubt the vast majority will follow when the bugs have been engineered out of present-day spinning reels.

The latest in easy fishing for big game are the Garcia "Ambassadors," a line of light tackle reels that excel in handling and many other ways, especially when you're fishing from a belt.

Factors to consider in a salt-water reel: Retrieve speed; corrosion-proof metals; constancy in brake system; easy take-down features; sturdy gears; close tolerance between spool and housing. Remember that a metal spool is not for casting. Wash or dunk your reel in fresh water after fishing-day. Learn all operations and adjustments at once. Keep the reel oiled, but not the brake washers. When fishing, test the drag often and keep it well below the breaking point of the line. Carry an extra loaded spool. Check all nuts and screws. Keep pressure off the reel by pumping instead of grinding a fish in. Keep the reel from touching sand. It should be taken down, cleaned, and greased, after all shore-fishing.

The sudden introduction and popularity of stronger lines with smaller diameters caught most reel makers napping. A reel with a wide tolerance between the spool flange and the housing allowed the small line to get in and foul up the works, and was discarded as soon as one with less tolerance came out.

LINES

Line trade names, values, and popularity are changing from year to year. At present, Dacron and monofilament are ahead in the race, with braided nylon holding to a close third, in Pacific Coast fishing. There are three totally different reasons for their popularity.

Dacron has little or no stretch, and the hook can be set easily and quickly. A brand made by Gudebrod Bros. Silk Co. is limp, for those who prefer this quality. A more rigid brand is made by the Ashaway Line and Twine Co.

The monofilament material is produced mostly by Dupont and sold under many brand names. A small amount is imported. Its value is opposite that of other lines, when used for spinning. It is springy, a quality enabling it to jump up over the spool flange during the cast. Its elasticity acts as a shock absorber when the hook is set and during the fight, when a small hook would otherwise cut a slit. Mono is also considered less visible or perceptive to many fish species. The disadvantage in using it on a conventional reel is that it is likely to spring up on the spool and cause a birdnest tangle, after working a heavy fish in.

Braided nylon is in-between Dacron and mono. Being slightly elastic, it has that value of the mono, and being limp, it is less likely to tangle.

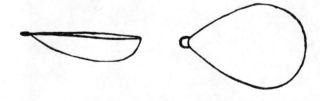

FIG. 22. Rounded spoon sinker slides over rocks.

∾ SINKERS ∾

There are many salt-water fishing conditions that call for various types of sinkers. For bottom fishing the weight is often determined by the force of the current or under-tow. There is the plated, cigar-shaped antimony sinker that is sometimes used as a flash lure ahead of a light-weight feather jig, the crescent-shaped trolling sinker to keep the bait from twisting the line, and the safety surf or anchor sinker with projecting points that dig into the sand. The pyramid and triangle sinkers are also designed to hold against the tide, and the half-flat spoon sinker which is rounded on one side is constructed to slide over submerged rocks and is also recommended for casting. (Fig. 22.)

Then there are the general purpose dollar, cigar-shaped and bank sinkers, and the tenite tear-drop weight for tournament casting. Loop-on, rubber core, clincher or pinch-on lightweight leads should be carried in every tackle box.

Experimentation is necessary in estimating the amount of weight that will be called for in any given spot. The modern angler as a rule uses the lightest weight possible.

A large inexpensive iron breakaway sinker is used in some areas for SALMON trolling.

∾ RODS ∾

Our prediction in the first edition of this volume—that glass rods would likely become the most popular type—has proven true. Laminated wood rods for gigantic monsters, split Tonkin bamboo for fly casting, and the long Calcutta bamboo for jetty fishing are still being made, but are seldom seen by the average salt-water angler along the Pacific Coast. Tubular rods, expertly engineered, with spun glass laminated in crossgrain, have taken over.

When properly constructed, and more importantly, when properly used, glass rods seldom break, and it is the inferior grade only, that takes a "set." No other item in angling tackle has had more scientific study and application. The Sila-Flex line of rods was the first on the Coast to be manufactured scientifically. The Browning-Sila-Flex engineer, Herb Jenks, has continued striving for improvements.

As of 1964, we hear such terms applied as high density, resilience, progressive taper, smooth casting action, durability, and fatigue-proof. In casting rods, the highly flexible tip allows anglers to cast minute baits or lures a great distance. Gradually becoming stronger and more rigid toward the butt, the rod can handle a large fish without bending into a circle.

Trolling rods above the light-tackle size are mounted with AFTCO roller guides, which offer much less friction resistance when a heavy fish is being retrieved.

The tendency toward lighter-weight rods continues. To a degree, the light rod is more efficient in the hands of an experienced angler, and it is always considered more sporting.

With blanks, butts, cork, and hardware available at most tackle stores, the do-it-yourself angler can fit up and wrap his own. The most difficult operation is in learning to apply grips from sheet cork. There is a simpler

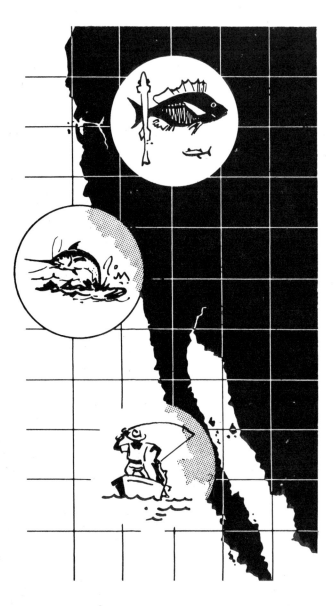

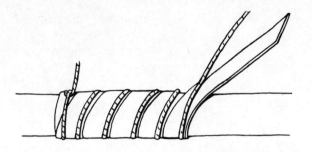

FIG. 23. Rod grip wrapped with glued cork or plastic.

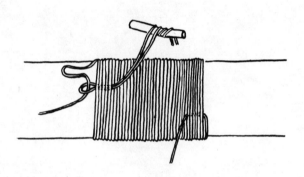

FIG. 24. Thread wrapping pulled under itself.

method of using cork bands, but the more comfortable grip is made of inch-wide strips cut from flat sheets.

The grip size to fit the hand for comfort should first be determined. Cushioning is desirable, but it should not be over or under-size. If over, it can easily be reduced with sandpaper. After cutting the strips and tapering the ends to fit, apply marine glue to the rod and cork. After giving the glue time to set, use a large cord to hold the strip in place as it is wrapped, winding it just tight enough to keep the strip snug. (Fig. 23.) Remove the cord only after the glue has hardened. Then sandpaper the grip to size and bevel the ends.

Wrapping for guides or ferrules and decorating with nylon or Dacron are easily done by using a short length of wire to pull the outer end of the thread under the last few turns, as in Fig. 24.

The color and shape of the thread is maintained by applying a special dope made for that purpose. The rod should not be bent for several hours after wrapping. Unnecessary wrapping will reduce the flexibility of the rod.

With spinning rods, to avoid friction, the bottom guide should be very large and a good distance from the reel. If it's too far, however, the line will bow when casting a very light bait. There's not as much advantage in having a large number of guides as on a trolling rod.

More guides are required on flexible trolling rods than on a rigid one. The guides should be placed close together where the rod bends most to keep the line from being dragged on the rod when large, weighty fish are being worked.

LURES, GIMMICKS, AND GIZMOS

Erratic and flashing lures will attract fish attention, and some species will grab without appraising them, but the greater number of fishes will take time to look them over and shy away. For these more wary or less brave kinds, a lure with little or no action, such as a smooth-running feather or plastic squid, looks more appetizing.

Colors are perceptible to many salt-water species. To some, certain colors are repellant; to others they are attractive. The most desirable are silvery or whitish jigs and feathers. White suggests the belly color of the forage fish. The silver resembles the flakes from a disabled fish.

The feather best suited for large fish and those with cutting teeth is the Compac-type. It slides up on the leader and doesn't get clipped off or chewed up. A triple hook helps keep the mouth open. The chrome head helps in attracting fish.

Spoons, jigs, and other hard lures have come into greater popularity since the advent of spinning tackle, and each year brings a number of new shapes and kinds that prove the best yet. But all too often, some lures attract more fishermen than fish. So far, very few fresh-water plugs have done well in the ocean north of the Mexican border. But south of it, wooden plugs up to 9 inches long get GROUPER, CABRILLA, and other species.

There is a long list of patented gimmicks that have value in tying hooks, wrapping leaders, holding rods, extracting hooks, etc., etc. There are also "fishermen's friend" tools that can be useful in numerous ways. Learning to make good use of these gizmos often requires practice and patience, as just about everything else in our most favored of all sports.

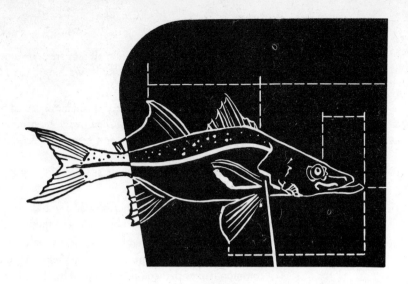

Recognizing and Naming the Fishes

Some confusion still exists in the common names of a few fishes. Two of these, seldom taken within our range but super-abundant in the Sea of Cortez, are to be definitely changed: the (PACIFIC) TENPOUNDER to (PACIFIC) LADYFISH, and the MONTEREY SPANISH MACKEREL to MONTEREY SIERRA.

The California Department of Fish and Game still prefers the names WHITE CROAKER instead of TOMMY CROAKER, and JACK MACKEREL instead of MACKEREL JACK. We could agree on these changes, but not on their calling CHINOOK SALMON "KING SALMON." CHINOOK has been agreed upon and was in common usage in states and provinces north of California long before "KING" was thought up. Nor can we see any reason to follow some of the commercial names the Department has invented for several ROCKFISH, such as "OCEAN PERCH," "SEA BASS," etc.

Fishermen from Italy, Portugal, Spain, China, Russia, and many other countries came and settled in hundreds of separated areas. Each group found fishes resembling those of their homeland and bestowed names in their own language accordingly. As the years passed the misunderstandings grew until finally each of the four provincial and state fish commissions, in the interest of an expanding fishing industry, selected expedient names to fit each of their particular areas. In most instances they followed the most popular usage of the name in their own localities.

J. Edward Gough, D. M. D.

The black sea bass—also miscalled giant bass or California jewfish—is usually easily identified, either with or without such stylish additions.

One of the SALMON, common in all four areas, became "SPRING SALMON" in British Columbia, "CHINOOK" in Washington and Oregon, and "KING SALMON" in California.

Some of the states legalized the names selected by the commissions, but fishermen continued using their own local names. Along the northern California coast alone, the BLACK ROCKFISH, *Sebastodes melanops,* is variously called "BLUE FISH," "WIDOW FISH," "CHERNA," "NERO," "SNAPPER," "BLACK SEA BASS," "BLUE SEA BASS," "BLACK PERCH," and "GRAY ROCK COD."

An angler traveling a short distance would not be able to guess what species were being discussed by anglers in another district.

In 1945 the two noted ichthyologists, Dr. Carl L. Hubbs and W. I. Follett started on the immense task of selecting and creating a list of common names that could be accepted by all concerned. It was thought at first that all interested parties could offer their first choice of names in nomination, then vote on the final selection, but despite an enormous volume of communications it was necessary to hold a series of seminars and meetings to discuss the merits of names.

Although it was the desire of Hubbs and Follett to attack courageously in replacing misnomers and appropriated names, overwhelming common usage made them feel obliged to compromise in some cases. They developed an ingenious device, however, which helped to overcome the objectionable feature in appropriated names. For example: the name "WHITE SEA BASS" became two words, "WHITE SEABASS," thus showing that it was not a true SEA BASS but a member of some other family. "WHITE CROAKER" or "KING CROAKER" were seriously considered for the WHITE SEABASS. Either would have been more fitting, since this species is a member of the CROAKER family, but the usage was so general that it was decided to retain the old name with the new modification.

The names of other fishes such as "JACKSMELT," "LINGCOD," and "TOPSMELT" were so well established that persuading the public to accept new names seemed out of the question. By combining the two names into one, the old sounds are retained but new meaning is given to the printed names.

The angler will find many names that are unfamiliar to him but for the most part they were selected as those most extensively used. Complete new names were found where the old were too misleading. The addition of new attributive or qualifying names was found necessary when another species was already known by the same vernacular outside of our range. For example, "CORBINA" becomes "(CALIFORNIA) CORBINA," with parentheses, there being another CORBINA, but of a different species, outside of our range. This addition establishes the full true name of the fish but its use is not required in the spoken language.

When the parentheses are omitted from the attributive it indicates that there are more than one species within our range, as: "CALIFORNIA SKATE" and "BIG SKATE."

The hyphen is used only when it serves a definite purpose, as in "MAN-EATER" to avoid mispronouncing it as "MANE-ATER." In "SHEEPHEAD" the hyphen serves the extra purpose of calling attention to the missing letter, as the Atlantic species is spelled "SHEEPSHEAD."

The general term "fish" is joined with its attributive because it always constitutes a part of the vernacular, as in "BONEFISH."

Some of the paired names have been shortened when one of the words was found to be exceedingly well established. Thus the word "SHARK" has been dropped from such well known species as SOUPFIN, THRESHER, and HAMMERHEAD.

❧ DESCRIPTION OF THE FISHES ❧

In black and white photography, the light coloring often comes out white and highlights overcome designs. Because of these and other distortions we found that drawings were far more effective in showing the differences between the species. Especially with the addition of the arrows to point out special character variances.

As a fish grows older, the pattern and density of the spots and bars often become faded and are lost in photography. If it were not for the chameleon-like color-changing habit of some of the marine fishes, colored photography would be still better; but since the colorings are not always specific, it would be highly misleading.

The drawings were made to expedite the angler's study and to assist him in identifying a fish in hand. They do not necessarily show all detail such as the exact number of spines and rays in the fins which are described in the text.

When a fish is about to be examined, it should be placed on its right side (FLATFISHES blind side down) with the fins spread and pinned. It can then be compared with the form as shown in the drawings, and the text of the description read and checked with that of the specimen.

❧ EXTERNAL CHARACTERS ❧

At first the sketches showing the different external parts of the anatomy and the terms used in defining them, may seem elaborate and perhaps difficult to remember, but any repeated use will soon show them to be simple. The names of the more obvious parts of the fish's anatomy should properly be included in the angler's vocabulary. In the first sketch, there are twenty terms to remember.

The expression, "length of the base," in measuring the length of the dorsal and anal fins is used to avoid confusing it with the height of the fins. The height of these fins is measured from the base to the tip of the longest ray or spine. The length of the caudal, pectoral, and pelvic fins is measured from the base to the tip of the longest ray. The pelvic and pectoral fins are paired. These and other paired characters are often written in the singular in the descriptions.

In the MACKEREL-LIKE FISHES we find two additional sets of characters. They are the finlets which follow the dorsal and anal fins, and the keel, a hard ridge projecting out from the sides of the caudal peduncle.

In the TROUTS, SMELTS and related fishes, there is an additional character, the adipose fin, a fleshy lump without fin rays situated between the dorsal and caudal fins.

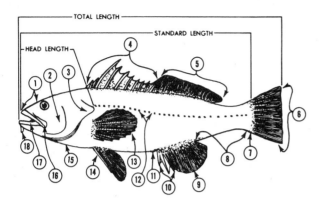

FIG. 25. *Hypothetical spiny-rayed fish: (1) Snout. (2) Preopercle. (3) Opercle. (4) First dorsal fin (spines). (5) Second dorsal fin (soft rays). (6) Caudal fin. (7) Caudal fin base. (8) Caudal peduncle. (9) Anal fin. (10) Anal spines. (11) Anus. (12) Lateral line. (13) Pectoral fin (paired). (14) Pelvic fin (paired). (15) Isthmus. (16) Maxillary or upper jaw. (17) Mandible or lower jaw. (18) Barbel.*

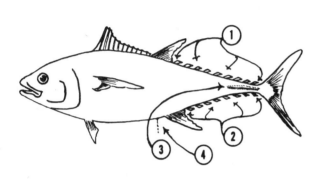

FIG. 26. *Hypothetical tuna: (1) Dorsal finlets. (2) Anal finlets. (3) Keel. (4) Anus.*

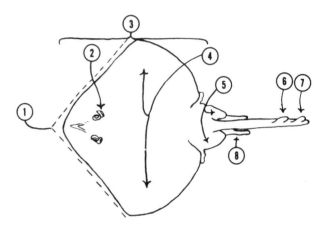

FIG. 28. *Hypothetical skate: (1) Angle of skate. (2) Spiracle. (3) Disk. (4) Pectoral fins (wings). (5) Pelvic fins. (6) 1st dorsal fin. (7) 2nd dorsal fin. (8) Claspers (male).*

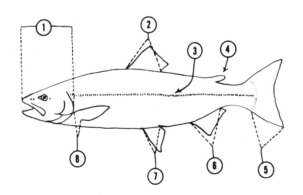

FIG. 27. *Hypothetical salmon: (1) Length of head. (2) Base of dorsal fin. (3) Scale count along lateral line. (4) Adipose fin. (5) Length of caudal fin. (6) Base of anal fin. (7) Base of pelvic fin. (8) Base of pectoral fin.*

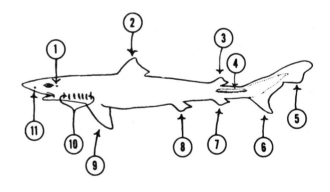

FIG. 29. *Hypothetical shark: (1) Spiracle. (2) 1st dorsal fin. (3) 2nd dorsal fin. (4) Keel. (5) Tail or caudal fin (upper lobe). (6) Tail or caudal fin (lower lobe). (7) Anal fin. (8) Pelvic fins. (9) Pectoral fins. (10) Gill openings. (11) Nostril.*

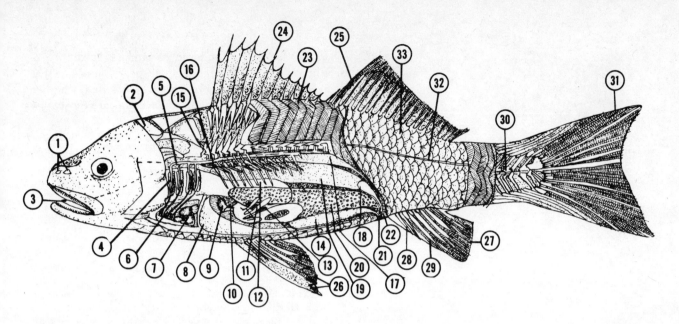

FIG. 30. *Internal structure, hypothetical spiny-rayed fish: (1) Nostrils. (2) Skull. (3) Tongue. (4) Pharynx with gills. (5) Dorsal aorta. (6) Ventral aorta. (7) Heart. (8) Liver. (9) Gall bladder. (10) Coelom. (11) Pyloric caeca. (12) Stomach. (13) Spleen. (14) Intestines. (15) Vertebrae. (16) Ribs. (17) Kidney. (18) Bladder. (19) Air bladder. (20) Gonad. (21) Anus. (22) Urogenital aperture. (23) Trunk muscles. (24) Dorsal fins (spinous). (25) Dorsal fins (soft rays). (26) Pelvic fins. (27) Anal fin. (28) Fin rays (spiny). (29) Fin rays (soft). (30) Caudal vertebrae. (31) Caudal fin. (32) Lateral line. (33) Scales.*

The word disk is better understood when applied to the more round-ish RAYS than to the SKATES which are more or less angular. The word angle as used in describing the SKATES is understood easily when the imaginary line is drawn along the front margin of the cheek and pectoral fin. Claspers, which appear as extensions of the pelvic fins, are sex organs of the male through which the sperm is transferred to the female.

The spiracle is an opening behind the eyes of the SHARKS, RAYS, and SKATES through which water passes to the gills.

✥ KEY TO FISH DESCRIPTIONS ✥

The first name following the number is the true common name of the fish (as selected by Hubbs and Follett). The name (in italics) which follows is the scientific name by which the species is known in practically all languages. The name or names in the following line are sectional, or names by which the species is known in one place or another. (It is hoped they will be speedily discarded.) They are given here for the sake of reference and are listed in the index so that the reader accustomed to their use, may quickly find the species and its true name.

The measurements given of length and weight are the maximum. The average size of the fish is usually much smaller.

Since many of the salt-water fishes change color according to their surroundings, the descriptive color given in this chapter must be considered only as that most prevailing.

The range in which the fish occurs indicates that at least one specimen has been taken that far north or south, but does not necessarily suggest that the species is found in abundance at these extremities. When the range of an individual species indicates that it extends to the tropics, the Sea of Cortez is included, whether mentioned or not. Maximum lengths and weights are those now known. Larger fish will probably be caught.

ᑐᕼᕤ SHARKS AND RAYS ᑐᕼᕤ

CLASS: *Elasmobranchii*—Sharks and Rays. SUBCLASS: *Selachii*—Sharks.

Although 29 species of this subclass have been found in the waters off our coast, only the 20 described herein are of particular interest to the angler.

The skeletal structure of the SHARKS differs from that of the BONY FISHES Osteichthyes, in that it is composed of cartilage rather than bone. Also, instead of being covered with scales, the minute protrusions or knobs of the skin become ossified, forming a layer of thin bony plates of shagreen over the body.

In the males, the pelvic fins appear to be modified to form claspers or sexual organs by which the sperm are transferred to the female. Fertilization is always internal.

Some fishermen mistakenly believe that all SHARKS are a menace and should be destroyed. They do consume a quantity of forage fishes and the young of some good food fishes. A few very large species attack mature SALMON and other game fishes. However, over a period of years the stomach contents of numerous SHARKS have been examined and as a general rule, SQUID and other expendable forms made up the greater part of the bulk.

Because of the commercial value and the growing enthusiasm by anglers for the SHARK as a game and food-fish, we are forced to conclude that none of the common species found along our coast should be wasted. Most of these fishes are wholesome, of excellent flavor and are superior to many of the popular BONY FISHES sold at markets. During World War II, thousands of pounds were colored and sold as SALMON, others as fillets-of-SOLE, HALIBUT, and SWORDFISH. The Anglo-Saxon prejudice against this group of fine fish is ridiculous. Throughout the rest of the world they are prized as a delicacy and cooked in the same manner as any other fish.

With the exception of the THRESHER and BONITO SHARK, all other species within our range up to 100 pounds can be taken on moderately light tackle. Above that weight fairly heavy tackle is advisable. A 6/0-reel; 40-pound-test line; No. 6/0 to 10/0 salmon hook on a ten-foot 50-pound-test wire leader, will suffice.

Baits vary according to locality. A side sliced from a live or fresh mackerel, greenling, midshipman or salmon is usually preferred for large individuals. Owing to the limited vision of the SHARK, the bait should be kept in motion. They will often follow the bait some distance before attacking.

Some of the large species and a few of the smaller SHARKS have similar feeding habits, attacking the bottom forage fishes during the midday hours, rising to feed on the surface in the late afternoon and at night.

They can be located in the open sea by the angular dorsal fin projecting above the surface and by the activities of diving birds and jumping forage-fishes.

While anglers north of Pt. Conception will find a greater number of SHARKS in deep water during fall and winter months, southern California fishermen can locate them at a fairly shallow depth, especially large females in the spring and summer.

Top-feeders should be trolled two feet from the surface; bottom-feeding species, eight to twelve feet above the ocean floor.

SHARKS can sometimes be paralyzed by a heavy blow on the caudal peduncle near tail base.

ORDER: *Cestraciontes.* FAMILY: *Heterodontidae* — Horn Sharks.

1. (California) horn shark   *Heterodontus francisci*

NAMES: Sometimes called BULLHEAD SHARK, PORT JACKSON SHARK. **DESCRIPTION:** Distinguished by the presence of a large spine in the forepart of each of the two dorsal fins; prominent forehead; steep profile; anal fin present. In (PACIFIC) DOGFISH there is no anal fin. **SIZE:** Up to 4 ft. **COLOR:** Brown of varying density with black spots scattered over head, body, and fins. **RANGE:** Occurs from Pt. Conception to Cape San Lucas, Baja California. Abundant south of Pt. Banda. **BAIT & TACKLE:** Feeds principally on mollusks, crustaceans and small fish. Of little interest to anglers. **COMMENT:** Eggs have a horny covering protected by a double spiral flange—seen for sale in curio shops. Of interest to students because of its resemblance and possible close relationship to extinct forms. Most primitive form described in this volume.

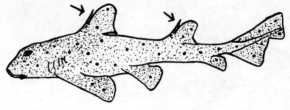

1. (California) horn shark

ORDER: *Notidani.* FAMILY: *Hexanchidae*—Cowsharks. Live and feed near the bottom.

2. Sevengill cowshark   *Notohynchus maculatum*

NAMES: SEVENGILL SHARK, COW SHARK, MUD SHARK. **DESCRIPTION:** Distinguished by the seven gill slits on each side of the body. Body slender, rounded; spiracle nearer eye than gill slits; snout broad, rounded; single dorsal fin; long upper lobe to caudal fin; pelvic fin situated about midway of belly. **SIZE:** Up to 15 ft.; usually 6 ft. **COLOR:** Reddish brown to grayish with many black spots of various sizes scattered over head, body, and fins. **RANGE:** Occurs San Diego to British Columbia in moderately deep water, 10 to 40 fathoms. Seldom south of Pt. Conception. Not abundant. **BAIT & TACKLE:** Taken on large fresh-dead bait or strips of fish; heavy tackle. Hook No. 4/0 to 6/0. Considered one of the most palatable of the SHARKS. **COMMENT:** Caution: Keep fingers away from mouth until fish is dead.

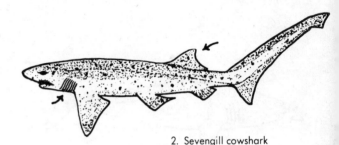

2. Sevengill cowshark

3. Sixgill cowshark   *Hexanchus corinum*

NAMES: SIXGILL SHARK, COW SHARK, MUD SHARK, GRISET. **DESCRIPTION:** Distinguished by the six gill slits on each side of the body; single dorsal fin situated far back on body above anal fin; pelvic fin situated back of middle of belly; short, rounded snout; spiracle large, nearer gill slits than eye; stout, rounded body; long upper lobe to caudal fin. **SIZE:** Up to 15 ft. **COLOR:** Dark gray, sometimes almost black, light streak along sides of body. **RANGE:** Occurs San Diego to Alaska in moderately deep water. More abundant in northern area of range. **BAIT & TACKLE:** Taken on heavy tackle principally during runs of HERRING and other schooling forage fishes, on chrome-plated lures; fresh-frozen strips of herring, sardines, anchovies and squid. Hook No. 4/0 to 6/0. **COMMENT:** An excellent food fish.

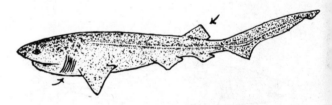

3. Sixgill cowshark

ORDER: *Euselachii.* SUBORDER: *Galei*—True Sharks. Having five gill slits. FAMILY: *Alopiidae*—Threshers. Characterized by long upper lobe of the caudal fin.

4. (Common) thresher   *Alopias vulpinus*

NAMES: THRASHER, LONG-TAIL SHARK. **DESCRIPTION:** Exceedingly long upper lobe to the tail measuring about the same length as the rest of the body; very small anal fin; large pectoral fins; short snout. **SIZE:** Up to 25 ft.; commonly 6 or 7 ft. **COLOR:** Blue-gray to purplish back fading to white belly; fins dark gray to purplish. **RANGE:** Occurs British Columbia to tropics. Abundant south end of range. In shallow water fair-sized individuals found close to shore. **BAIT & TACKLE:** Taken from piers, barges, and in open sea, on small fish, squid, or stripbait. Hook No. 2/0 to 4/0, depending on location. Line must be kept very taut and held as hard as equipment will allow when THRESHER SHARK makes run directly away from the angler. Otherwise will break the line with tail. Good for a fairly exciting fight. **COMMENT:** Stories of this SHARK attacking WHALES with its long tail are false; however, it does thrash schools of forage fishes with the powerful tail. The THRESHER is an excellent food fish.

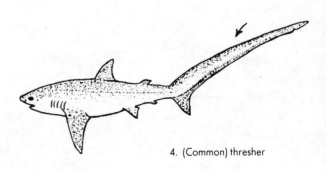

4. (Common) thresher

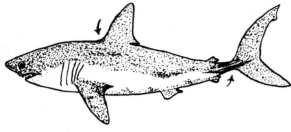

5. Salmon shark

FAMILY: *Lamnidae*—Mackerel Sharks. Streamlined body, slender caudal peduncle, keel on sides of peduncle.

5. Salmon shark   *Lamna ditropis*

NAMES: MACKEREL SHARK, PORBEAGLE, TIGER SHARK. **DESCRIPTION**: Abrupt color demarkation between dorsal and ventral surface; front of the first dorsal fin situated above back portion of pectoral base; prominent keel on sides of caudal peduncle; very large, smooth, fang-like teeth; deep head and body; caudal fin lunate. **SIZE**: Up to 10 ft. **COLOR**: Dark bluish-gray to black back separated from white belly by irregular line along sides. **RANGE**: Occurs from San Diego to Alaska. More abundant in northern part of range. **BAIT & TACKLE**: Taken in same manner as BONITO SHARK. Strip of salmon, herring, kelp greenling, best bait in extreme north. Will take chrome lures at slow troll when following schools of other fishes. Feeds on surface and down to 20 fathoms. **COMMENT**: Equal to BONITO SHARK as a game fish.

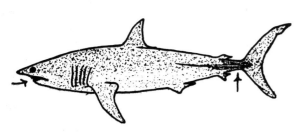

6. Bonito shark

6. Bonito shark   *Isurus glaucus*

NAMES: MACKEREL SHARK, PALOMA, MAKO. **DESCRIPTION**: Long, smooth, fang-like teeth; long, prominent keel on sides of caudal peduncle extending from tail to point above pelvic fins; very small second dorsal and anal fins situated about equal; first dorsal well back of base of pectoral; pointed head; tail lunate. **SIZE**: Up to 15 ft.; 8 ft. within our range. **COLOR**: Dark, metallic-blue back fading to white belly. **RANGE**: Occurs Pt. Conception to Cape San Lucas. Large individuals usually found a mile or more offshore near islands and mouth of bays. **BAIT & TACKLE**: Taken on any live bait or strip of mackerel. The BONITO SHARK is a moody creature, at times allowing himself to be taken without a struggle; then again, fighting as if to rip up the ocean. For this reason medium-heavy tackle is required. Hook No. 6/0 to 10/0, 8 to 10-foot leader. **COMMENT**: Thousands of pounds of BONITO SHARK were sold during the meat scarcity in city markets and served in restaurants as "swordfish" and "sea bass" at fresh-fish prices. Some merchants labeled the big steaks simply as "shark steak" and were amazed at the great number of sales. Considered next to the MARLIN as a game fish. Like its close relative the MAKO SHARK, the BONITO SHARK is noted for its leaps.

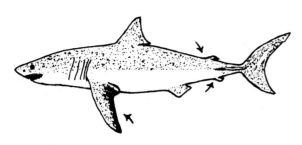

7. White shark

7. White shark   *Carcharodon carcharias*

NAME: MAN-EATER. **DESCRIPTION**: Great depth of body; small second dorsal situated in advance of anal fin; very large, triangular teeth with saw-tooth edges; caudal fin lunate; large pectoral fins situated in advance of base of first dorsal fin. **SIZE**: Up to 37 ft. **COLOR**: Dark, metallic-gray fading to white belly; pectoral fins tipped with blackish. **RANGE**: World's temperate and semi-tropical waters. **COMMENT**: Of special interest to anglers as a gamefish and to divers in that it is dangerous. In the past few years unprovoked attacks along the California coast were reported. Stomach contents of large WHITES captured near Australia produced several large animals.

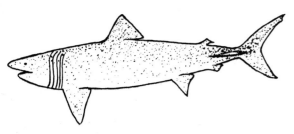

8. Basking shark

FAMILY: *Cetorhinidae*—Basking Sharks.

8. Basking shark   *Cetorhinus maximus*

NAMES: ELEPHANT SHARK, OIL SHARK, BONE SHARK, PELERIN, CAPIDOLI. **DESCRIPTION**: Very long gill slits extending from almost top of head to lower part of throat; deep head and body; small eyes; numerous small, smooth-edged teeth; presence of keels. **SIZE**: Up to 45 ft. **COLOR**: Dark, metallic gray fading to light belly. **RANGE**: Occurs all over the world. Occasionally seen during winter months in schools of 20 to 30 in Monterey and San Simeon Bays. More common during summer months off Washington and British Columbia coast. Because of its enormous size is of negligible interest to anglers. **BAIT & TACKLE**: Small individuals taken by dragging bait along surface. Extra heavy tackle required. **COMMENT**: The flesh is claimed by some people to be of superb quality. The liver is a valuable source of oil. Derives name from its habit of drifting slowly along the surface of the water as if basking in the sun.

FAMILY: *Scyliorhinidae*—Catsharks. Characterized by the upper lobe of the caudal fin being in a straight line with the body.

9. (California) swell shark   *Cephaloscyllium uter*

DESCRIPTION: Broad flat head; first dorsal situated back of middle of body and directly above pelvic fins; second dorsal directly above anal fin; large, rough, placoid scales (plates) on body. Differs from other SHARKS particularly by the odd defense act of inflating its belly with air until its circumference triples. **SIZE:** Up to 3 ft. **COLOR:** Irregular spots and bars across back and sides in varying shades of brown and black with yellowish tinge on belly; covered all over with round, whitish, and dark spots. **RANGE:** Occurs Monterey to Cape San Lucas, Baja California. Abundant south of San Diego in kelp beds. **BAIT & TACKLE:** Occasionally taken in shallow water on live bait. Will take strips of mackerel or fresh-dead anchovies. Hook No. 2/0. **COMMENT:** Caution: The SWELL SHARK is not a food fish. Eating any quantity may cause nausea and diarrhea.

Two other members of this family, the BROWN CATSHARK, *Scyliorhinus brunneus* and FILETAIL CATSHARK, *Parmaturus xaniurus,* are so rare as to be of little interest to anglers.

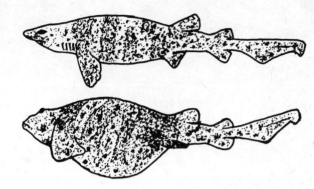

9. (California) swell shark

FAMILY: *Triakididae*—Smoothhounds.

10. Leopard shark   *Triakis semifasciata*

NAME: CAT SHARK (so called because of cat-like pupil of eye). **DESCRIPTION:** Distinguished by the large, dark gray to black bars across back followed by spots on sides and on tail. Fins not pointed as in SICKLEFIN; first dorsal fin well in advance of pelvic fins; base of second dorsal in advance of base of anal fin. **SIZE:** Males up to 3½ ft.; females up to 6 ft. **COLOR:** Iridescent, grayish back fading to lighter belly; bars and spots as above. **RANGE:** Occurs Coos Bay, Oregon, to Turtle Bay, Baja California. Abundant Pt. Dume to Pt. Arena. **BAIT & TACKLE:** Often taken in shallow surf near mass colonies of SAND CRABS, *Emerita analoga.* Also taken on shrimp with shell on, clams, and small strips of mackerel or other fish. Hook No. 1. For offshore, larger individuals, live bait, shrimp, and stripbait kept in motion; hook No. 2/0 to 4/0. **COMMENT:** An exceptionally fine food fish.

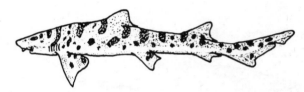

10. Leopard shark

11. Brown smoothhound   *Rhinotriacis henlei*

NAMES: SAND SHARK, DOGFISH, PALOMA. **DESCRIPTION:** Distinguished by the very short, sharp, pointed teeth set in five or more rows; the slender body and caudal peduncle. First dorsal well in advance of pelvic fins, base of second dorsal beginning slightly in advance of anal fin. **SIZE:** Up to 3 ft. **COLOR:** Brownish to brassy back fading to lighter sides and whitish belly. **RANGE:** Occurs Coos Bay, Oregon, to San Quintin Bay, Baja California. **BAIT & TACKLE:** Taken close to shore the year round from piers and boats on small live bait and strips of fish. Hook No. 1/0. **COMMENT:** The most abundant SHARK San Francisco Bay to Humboldt Bay. Is often mistaken for the SOUPFIN but can readily be distinguished by the base of the second dorsal fin being in advance of the anal fin. An excellent food fish.

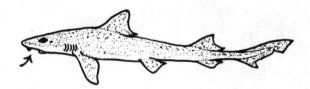

11. Brown smoothhound

12. Gray smoothhound   *Mustelus californicus*

NAMES: MUD SHARK, DOGFISH, SAND SHARK, GRAY SHARK. **DESCRIPTION:** Differs from the BROWN SMOOTHHOUND by the flat, blunt teeth, relatively heavier body and gray coloring. Base of first dorsal fin in advance of pelvic fins; base of second dorsal completely in advance of base of anal fin. **SIZE:** Up to 3½ ft. **COLOR:** Metallic-iridescent dark gray back fading to lighter belly. **RANGE:** Occurs Cape Mendocino to Cape San Lucas, Baja California, and into the Gulf of California. More common south of Dana Point, California. **BAIT & TACKLE:** Taken in bays and sloughs, also in deep water, in same manner as BROWN SMOOTHHOUND. **COMMENT:** Considerable quantities are sold in markets as "grayfish."

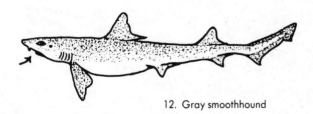

12. Gray smoothhound

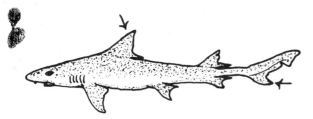

13. Sicklefin smoothhound

13. Sicklefin smoothhound
Mustelus lunulatus

NAMES: GATO, DOG SHARK, SMOOTHHOUND. **DESCRIPTION**: Distinguished by the pointed fins, especially lower lobe of caudal fin; first dorsal fin tall, height equal to length of base; very slender caudal peduncle; base of second dorsal situated slightly in advance of that of anal fin; teeth blunt. **SIZE**: Up to 5½ ft. **COLOR**: Body and fins pale gray, lighter belly. **RANGE**: Occurs Dana Point to tropics in shallow water. **BAIT & TACKLE**: Will take almost any kind of bait. Prefers small live bait or stripbait. Hook No. 2/0 to 4/0. **COMMENT**: Also sold in markets as "grayfish."

FAMILY: *Carcharhinidae*—Requiem Sharks.

14. Bay grayshark
Carcharhinus lamiella

NAMES: BAYSHARK, INJERTO. **DESCRIPTION**: Base of second dorsal fin not in advance of base of anal fin; base of first dorsal nearer base of pectoral than of pelvic fins; absence of spiracles; small eyes. **SIZE**: Up to 15 ft. **COLOR**: Gray back fading to lighter sides and whitish belly. **RANGE**: Occurs Catalina to Mazatlan, Mexico, in shallow waters. Small individuals taken south (seldom north) of border by anglers in pursuit of other large game fishes. **BAIT & TACKLE**: Will take stripbait or whole fresh-dead. **COMMENT**: One gram of liver oil produces 61,000 U.S.P. units vitamin A.

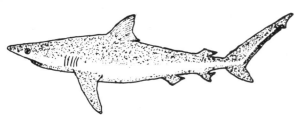

14. Bay grayshark

15. Blue shark
Prionace glauca

NAME: GREAT BLUE SHARK. **DESCRIPTION**: Very long pectoral fin, length equalling twice the height of the first dorsal fin; first dorsal situated about middle of body in advance of pelvic fins; second dorsal directly above anal fin; small, inconspicuous spiracle close behind eye; fifth gill slit above base of pectoral. **SIZE**: Up to 13 ft.; commonly 8 ft. **COLOR**: Grayish to indigo blue on back and fins, whitish belly. **RANGE**: Occurs British Columbia to Cape San Lucas and Gulf of California. Abundant in warm currents south of Pt. Conception. **BAIT & TACKLE**: Taken on medium light tackle near surface on stripbait, sanddabs, squid, sardines, or small live bait. Hook No. 2/0 to 4/0. Will take chrome lure at slow troll. In open ocean, large individuals taken on moderately heavy tackle; side of fresh mackerel best bait. Hook No. 6/0 to 8/0. **COMMENT**: A good food fish, especially when smoked.

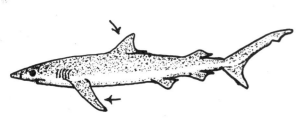

15. Blue shark

16. Tiger shark
Galeocerdo cuvieri

DESCRIPTION: Large head; short snout; pointed upper lobe to caudal fin; heavy body; teeth deeply notched, with saw-tooth edges. **SIZE**: Up to 18 ft. **COLOR**: Grayish brown back fading to lighter belly with numerous irregular darker spots more pronounced on dorsal surface. **RANGE**: Occurs Dana Point to tropics in deep water. **COMMENT**: Because of size and rarity, of little interest to anglers. In many parts of world it is considered a dangerous SHARK.

16. Tiger shark

17. Soupfin
Galeorhinus zyopterus

NAMES: OIL SHARK, TOPE. **DESCRIPTION**: Second dorsal fin situated directly above anal fin, together forming a diamond-shaped symmetrical pattern; a pronounced angular lobule on upper lobe of tail; heavy body; head depressed; long, gradually tapering snout. **SIZE**: Up to 6 ft. **COLOR**: Dark, bluish gray to blackish back fading to lighter sides and whitish belly; pectoral fins blackish; anal, caudal, and dorsal fins tipped with black. **RANGE**: Occurs Vancouver Island to Cape San Lucas in moderately deep to shallow water. Abundant southern end of range. Feeds usually at 8 to 10 feet above bottom in deep water, at varying depths in bays and backwaters. **BAIT & TACKLE**: Taken on fresh stripbait, side of mackerel, whole squid, sardine, herring, and other small fishes. Hook No. 2/0 to 6/0 according to locality. **COMMENT**: Taken for many years by commercial fishermen, first for the fins which were shipped to China, then for the liver. Today considered a fine food fish. Liver valued highly for vitamin A. Protected by law in some bay areas. Gives birth to as many as 30 pups.

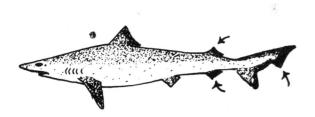

17. Soupfin

18. Hammerhead
Sphyrna zygaena

NAME: AXHEAD SHARK. **DESCRIPTION**: The grotesque formation of the head which flattens out horizontally in the shape of a double-edged ax, with eyes situated on the front corners; first dorsal tall; second dorsal small, not in advance of anal fin. **SIZE**: Up to 18 ft. **COLOR**: Slate-gray back fading to lighter belly. **RANGE**: Point Conception to tropics; abundant in Sea of Cortez and around Mexican islands. Scarce in California waters. **BAIT & TACKLE**: Difficult to persuade with any bait or lure. Feeds on small anchovies, squid, and crustaceans. **COMMENT**: Two other species of this family, rarely occurring within our range, are the *Sphyrna lewini* and *S. tiburo*. The front margin of the head in *S. lewini* is notched. The head of *S. tiburo* resembles a spade in shape.

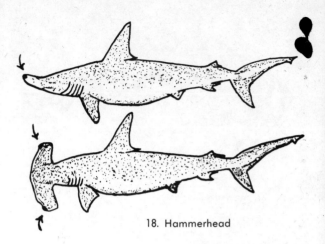

18. Hammerhead

ORDER: *Tectospondyli*. SUBORDER: *Squaloidei*. FAMILY: *Squalidae*—Dogfishes. Having five gill slits on each side of body and no anal fin. Occurs in large schools.

19. (Pacific) dogfish
Squalus suckleyi

NAMES: GRAYFISH, DOG SHARK. **DESCRIPTION**: A hard spine in front of each dorsal fin; long, slender caudal peduncle; slender, rounded body. Differing from the HORN SHARK by the pointed head and absence of anal fin. **SIZE**: Up to 5½ ft. **COLOR**: Gray to brownish back fading to lighter belly; white spots scattered over back of young. **RANGE**: Occurs San Diego to Aleutian Islands. Most abundant SHARK in range. Over-abundant in sounds of Washington and British Columbia. **BAIT & TACKLE**: Taken near surface in shallow to moderately deep water over rocky reefs on small live bait or strips of fish when kept moving. Also takes lures at slow troll. If taken on light tackle, will give good account of its fighting ability. Hook No. 2/0. **COMMENT**: During World War II, few people knew the "grayfish" was SHARK. It became a "special" at the markets and restaurants. A good food fish.

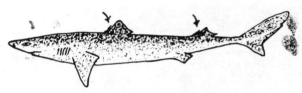

19. (Pacific) dogfish

SUBORDER: *Squatinoidei*. FAMILY: *Squatinidae*—Angel Sharks.

20. (California) angel shark
Squatina californica

NAMES: ANGEL SHARK, MONKFISH. **DESCRIPTION**: The depressed head and body together with the large pectoral and pelvic fins extending horizontally forming a ray-like disk; short, blunt snout; thick, extended tail with two dorsal fins and a pronounced caudal fin; gill openings in deep notch behind head; absence of anal or other fin on flat ventral surface. **SIZE**: Up to 5 ft.; 60 lbs. **COLOR**: Dark brown to blackish, sometimes reddish brown; underside white; fins edged with gray posteriorly. **RANGE**: Occurs Alaska to tropics in shallow water. Common south of Pt. Conception. **COMMENT**: Should not be destroyed. Pectoral fins and tail edible. Do not try to remove hook until lifeless. Has strong jaws. Bears young.

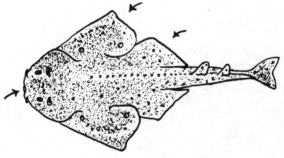

20. (California) angel shark

ORDER: *Batoidei*—Rays. SUBORDER: *Sarcura*. FAMILY: *Rhinobatidae*—Guitarfishes. In the guitarfishes the pectoral fins are attached to the snout forming an angular or circular disk with the head and shoulders as the center. Members of this family give birth to young.

21. Shovelnose guitarfish
Rhinobatos productus

NAME: SHOVELNOSE SHARK. **DESCRIPTION**: Long, pointed snout forming an acute angle; first dorsal fin situated about middle of the very thick tail; presence of a caudal fin; pectoral and pelvic fins extending horizontally, but less than those of other GUITARFISHES; small spines on middle of back, tail, on shoulders, and around eyes; skin covered with fine shagreen. **SIZE**: Up to 5 ft. **COLOR**: Brownish gray back; disk and sides edged with buff; underside pale. **RANGE**: Occurs San Francisco to the tropics in shallow water. Common south of Dana Point, California. Rare north of Pt. Conception. **BAIT & TACKLE**: Taken incidentally on almost any bait and gear when fishing for other forms. **COMMENT**: The fat, heavy tail is edible and should not be wasted.

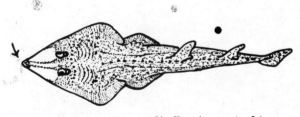

21. Shovelnose guitarfish

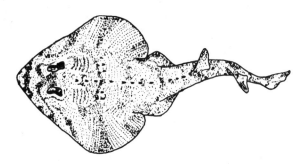

22. Mottled guitarfish

22. Mottled guitarfish *Zapteryx exasperata*

NAME: STRIPED GUITARFISH. **DESCRIPTION:** Distinguished by the presence of dark olive brown to yellowish blotches or bars across snout, back, and tail. First dorsal fin situated in advance of middle of tail; back covered with tubercles and prickles instead of shagreen; slightly rounded snout; low, blunt spines on middle of back and tail, above eyes, and on shoulders. **SIZE:** Up to 3 ft. **COLOR:** Grayish to olive brown with pale undersurface; bars and spots sometimes edged with black. **RANGE:** Occurs La Jolla to tropics. Not abundant north of San Quintin Bay. **BAIT & TACKLE:** Caught incidentally when fishing for other forms. **COMMENT:** Orientals prepare a delectable dish of this fish. It should not be destroyed by anglers as it has a commercial value.

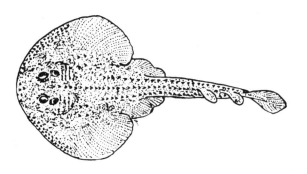

23. (California) thornback

FAMILY: *Platyrhinidae*—Thornbacks.

23. (California) thornback *Platyrhinoides triseriata*

NAME: SHOVELNOSE. **DESCRIPTION:** Distinguished by the three rows of very strong spines extending along back and tail, the rounded snout and circular disk, in contrast to the pointed snouts of GUITARFISHES which it otherwise resembles. Two dorsal fins situated back of the middle of the tail; caudal fin present; skin covered with fine shagreen; prickles on front edge of disk and snout, sometimes around eye; a patch of small spines on each shoulder. **SIZE:** Up to 3 ft. **COLOR:** Light greenish brown to black; belly white or buff. **RANGE:** Occurs Pt. Conception to San Quintin Bay, Baja California (rare north of the Point). Fairly common Dana Point to Ensenada. **BAIT & TACKLE:** Taken on sandy bottoms on stripbait. Hook No. 1. **COMMENT:** Edible.

FAMILY: *Rajidae*—Skates. (7 or 8 members of this family occur within our range.)

In the SKATES the snout and the connecting pectoral and pelvic fins are extended horizontally to form what is termed the disk. The frontal, outer margin is more or less triangular, while the margin from the tip of the pectoral posteriorly forms somewhat of a semi-circle or angle. The mouth, nostrils, gill slits, and anus are situated on the flattish ventral surface. There may be many small spines along top and sides of tail but never a long, sharp spine as in the STINGRAYS. Two small dorsal fins are situated near the end of the tail. The caudal fin, if present, is so small as to be considered absent in this text. A large spiracle is situated close behind each eye.

The pair of appendages (apparent in some of the sketches) extending back from underneath the pelvic fins are claspers (sex organs of the male).

SKATES feed on the bottom and are taken on small live bait, shrimp, squid, and stripbait. Hook No. 1 to 2/0. SKATES have the habit, when hooked, of cupping the edges of the disk, forming a vacuum on the bottom. They are therefore sometimes difficult to pry loose.

The pectoral fins, marketed as "wings," are cooked in various ways and are considered a delicacy by Orientals and many Europeans.

SKATES are oviparous. They deposit their eggs in leather-like cases from three inches to a foot long. Each case contains from 1 to 7 eggs.

Since the coloring is so variable and for lack of other obvious identifying characters, an added line (drawn for comparative purposes) from tip of pectoral fin to tip of snout will help to show the variations of the outer margin angle between the species. The large spots (sometimes absent) at or near base of pectoral fins are called "eye spots" (not to be associated with the spiracles or eyes).

SKATES using the pectoral fins as wings fairly fly through the water.

24. California skate · *Raja inornata*

DESCRIPTION: Frontal outer margin slightly concave near snout and between cheek and pectoral tip (drawn line touching tip of snout, cheek, and pectoral tip); posterior margin curving; snout sharp and pointed forming acute angle; pectoral tips slightly curved; single row of spines from about center of back to first dorsal fin, a short row above each eye; in males a row near tip of pectorals; small, weak spines or prickles on outer edge of pectorals, center of back, and sides of tail. **SIZE**: Up to 2½ ft. **COLOR**: Dark-greenish to brown; eye spots small, pale, surrounded by small, dark spots. **RANGE**: Occurs Ensenada to British Columbia in bays and backwaters as well as in moderately deep water. Rare north of Eureka. **COMMENT**: One of the most important of the SKATES in the fresh fish markets of California.

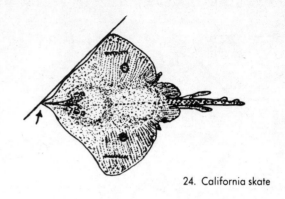

24. California skate

25. Big skate · *Raja binoculata*

DESCRIPTION: Frontal outer margin slightly concave (drawn line not touching margin between pectoral tip and tip of snout); outline posteriorly, angular, not rounded; pectoral tips pointed; snout pointed; head depressed; spines along top of tail; one spine midway and back of eyes. **SIZE**: Up to 7 ft. **COLOR**: Dull brown to very dark gray; eye spots (at center of base of pectorals) large, very dark, surrounded by lighter ring which is encircled by small, white spots; many white spots size of eye scattered over body; ventral surface white. **RANGE**: Occurs San Diego to Alaska. More abundant north of Pt. Conception. **BAIT & TACKLE**: Will take live bait up to one foot, also shrimp, clams or strips of fish. Hook No. 4/0 to 6/0.

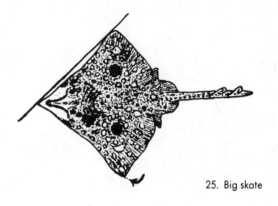

25. Big skate

26. Longnose skate · *Raja rhina*

DESCRIPTION: Frontal margin deeply concave (drawn line touching snout and near tip of pectoral); posterior outline curved; very long, sharp, pointed snout forming an acute angle; pectoral tips somewhat rounded; spines on top of tail, one in middle of back; in males a patch near each pectoral tip. **SIZE**: Up to 4½ ft. **COLOR**: Dark brown with darker mottlings, light spots scattered over body; eye spots small, a dark ring encircled by small, light spots; ventral surface bluish. **RANGE**: Occurs Cedros Island to Alaska. **COMMENT**: One of the most abundant SKATES in northern California and Oregon and frequently seen in fish markets.

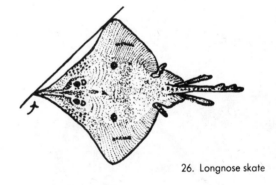

26. Longnose skate

27. Starry skate · *Raja stellulata*

NAMES: PRICKLY SKATE, CHEAP SKATE. **DESCRIPTION**: Frontal margin protruding at cheek (drawn line touching cheek and near tip of pectoral fin); posterior outline circular; snout slightly pointed; large spines from between spiracles in continuous row along center of back and top of tail to first dorsal fin; smaller spines over body and sides of tail; area between eyes soft and fleshy. **SIZE**: Up to 2½ ft. **COLOR**: Grayish brown with many darker spots over body; eye spots large, dark centers ringed with yellow and encircled with small, dark spots; eye spot sometimes followed by dark, round spot. **RANGE**: Occurs San Diego to Alaska in deep water. Common north of Pt. Arena. **COMMENT**: Considered the most palatable of the SKATES.

Two other species, the MONTEREY SKATE, *Raja montereyensis*, and the ROUGH-TAIL SKATE, *R. trachura*, are so seldom taken as to be of negligible interest to anglers. There are two other very rare species, the *Raja kincaidi* and *R. abyssicola*.

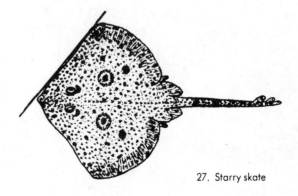

27. Starry skate

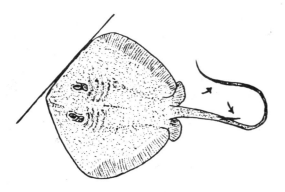

28. Diamond stingray

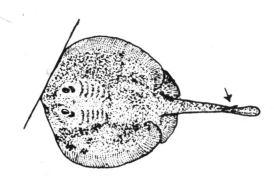

29. Round stingray

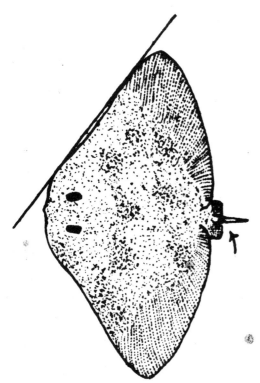

30. (California) butterfly ray

SUBORDER: *Masticura*—Whiptailed Rays. FAMILY: *Dasya-tididae*—Stingrays.

The main reason for describing members of this family is to warn the angler of their danger and to help him to quickly distinguish them from the edible SKATES which they resemble. In the species described here, a powerful poison is secreted along sides of the sting or spine situated on top of the tail. Serious injury may result from their sting. (For first-aid apply iodine or alcohol at once, then soak injured part in very hot epsom salts solution.)

At present it seems that all STINGRAYS should be reduced. All should be killed before removing hook.

28. Diamond stingray   *Dasyatis dipterurus*

NAMES: PACIFIC STINGRAY, RAT-TAILED STINGRAY, STINGAREE. DESCRIPTION: Distinguished from the SKATES which it resembles by the long, whip-like tail, 1½ times the length of the body, with the long, sharp sting, or spine on top, and by the absence of dorsal or caudal fins. The chief resembling feature to SKATES being the somewhat diamond-shape. SIZE: Up to 6 ft. COLOR: Bluish brown, without the contrasting color marks of the ROUND and BUTTERFLY STINGRAYS. RANGE: Occurs British Columbia to tropics. Not common north of Dana Point. COMMENT: Of interest to anglers principally in that it is very dangerous.

29. Round stingray   *Urolophus halleri*

NAME: STINGAREE. DESCRIPTION: The almost circular disk; tail being shorter than disk; presence of a caudal fin; absence of dorsal fins; long, sharp spine on top of tail; skin smooth, with few spines. SIZE: Up to 20 in. COLOR: Dark brown or slaty-brown above with spots or blotches; undersurface yellow. RANGE: Occurs Pt. Conception to tropics. COMMENT: This species lives on the bottom in bays, sloughs, and sandy beaches and because of its abundance, presents a hidden threat to surf anglers and swimmers. Is often caught by anglers fishing for other forms.

30. (California) butterfly ray   *Gymnura marmorata*

NAMES: BUTTERFLY STINGRAY, ANGEL SHARK, BAT RAY, EAGLE STING RAY. DESCRIPTION: Distinguished from other RAYS and SKATES on the Pacific Coast by the very small, short tail; the body, including pectoral fins, being about twice as wide as it is long; the spine or sting on top of tail very small in comparison. SIZE: Width to 5 ft. COLOR: Back dark brown or grayish olive, sometimes of varying shades with patterns of dark and light spots; disk bordered with buff; underside white. RANGE: Occurs Pt. Conception to the tropics. Common south of San Diego.

FAMILY: *Myliobatididae*—Eagle Rays.

31. Bat ray   *Myliobatis californicus*

NAMES: BAT STINGRAY, EAGLE RAY. DESCRIPTION: Head projecting out above and past angle of pectoral fins; large eyes on sides of head; single dorsal fin situated on top of tail just ahead of long, sharp spine. SIZE: Up to 150 lbs. COLOR: Entirely black or greenish black; undersurface white, edged with gray. RANGE: Occurs Cape Mendocino to the tropics in shallow water, bays, and sloughs. COMMENT: Seldom taken by anglers.

These giant BAT RAYS should be reduced whenever possible because of their menace to crabs, lobsters, and all kinds of edible shellfish. By the powerful sweep of their wings (pectoral fins), while swimming near the bottom, they create a suction in the sand thereby exposing the mollusks which they then devour.

SUBORDER: *Narcaciontes*. FAMILY: *Torpedinidae*—Electric Rays.

32. Electric ray
Torpedo californica

DESCRIPTION: Distinguished from the ROUND STINGRAY by having two dorsal fins on the tail and by absence of spine. Differing from SKATES (for which it is often mistaken) by having a pronounced caudal fin and by the almost circular disk, also by the short, stout tail and blunt snout. Skin entirely smooth; absence of scales, spines, or prickles. SIZE: Up to 3 ft., 50 lbs. COLOR: Bluish gray to brownish gray with black spots. RANGE: Occurs British Columbia to southern California in moderately deep water. Abundant in widely separated areas. COMMENT: This RAY is capable of delivering a strong electric shock, especially if touched at two points at one time. It is said that the discharge from a large individual is sufficient to knock a man down.

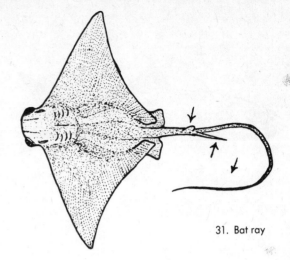

31. Bat ray

SUBCLASS: *Holocephali*. Members of this intermediate subclass have fish-like shapes but are more closely related to the sharks and rays. Like them they have a cartilaginous skeleton, rather than the hard skeleton structure of the bony fishes. ORDER: *Chimaeroidei*. There is but one known family in this order. FAMILY: *Chimaeridae*—Chimaeras.

33. Ratfish
Hydrolagus colliei

NAMES: RABBITFISH, GOATFISH, KING-OF-THE-HERRINGS, WATER HARE, CHIMAERA, ELEPHANT FISH. DESCRIPTION: Distinguished by the large ugly head; long body tapering gradually to a pointed tail; mouth small; teeth prominent; upper lip notched; rounded snout; single gill opening covered with fleshy flap; skin smooth, scaleless; large, triangular pectoral fins; two dorsal fins, the first with one large spine, the second deeply notched; caudal fin lance-shaped. Males have a club-shaped appendage between eyes and a long clasper behind each pelvic fin. SIZE: Up to 3 ft.-2 in. COLOR: Various shades of metallic brown and gray. RANGE: Occurs Alaska to San Quintin Bay, usually in deep water (40 fathoms); shallow water during summer and fall months. Abundant north of Pt. Arena. BAIT & TACKLE: Taken incidentally when fishing for other forms, on almost any bait. Hook No. 1 or 1/0.

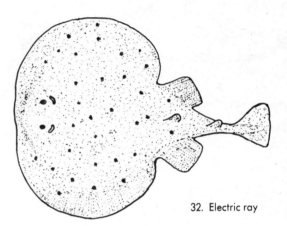

32. Electric ray

❧ SOFT-RAYED FISHES ❧

CLASS: *Osteichthyes*—Bony Fishes. SUBCLASS: *Teleostomi*—Ray-finned Fishes. A fish is a cold-blooded animal with a spinal column, adapted to life in the water, breathing by means of gills which are attached to bony gill arches, with limbs that are developed as fins. Differing from sharks and rays by having a bony skeleton instead of cartilage. Usually with scales or slick skin instead of the rough shagreen of the sharks and always having a heavy opercle over gills and a single-slit gill opening. ORDER: *Isospondyli*—Soft-rayed Fishes. SUBORDER: *Elopoidea*—Herring-like Fishes. FAMILY: *Elopidae*—Ladyfishes. Having a single dorsal fin on middle of back; no adipose or other dorsal finlet.

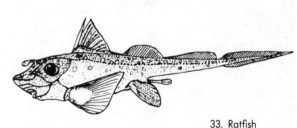

33. Ratfish

34. (Pacific) ladyfish
Elops affinis

NAMES: JOHN MARIGALE, TENPOUNDER, BONEFISH, BIG HERRING, MULLET. (Mistaken for MULLET by inexperienced fishermen. MULLET is a SPINEY-RAYED FISH.) DESCRIPTION: Slender body; projecting lower jaw; bone-plated throat; deeply forked caudal fin; single, spineless dorsal fin. SIZE: Up to 3 ft. COLOR: Steel blue back, white belly. RANGE: Large LADYFISH reportedly caught in San Diego Bay and in inlet below Ensenada some years ago, may have been the larger MILKFISH, *Chanos chanos*, which ranges up Baja's Pacific Coast in warm years. It is rarely hooked. LADYFISH are superabundant throughout Sea of Cortez. BAIT & TACKLE: Taken on small feathers, bucktails, and other lures. Also takes small LIVE BAIT and CRUSTACEANS. Best in muddy water near shore and in inlets. Hook No. 4 to 2.

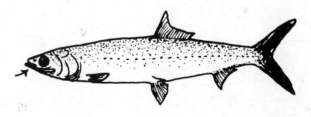

34. (Pacific) ladyfish

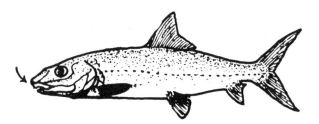

35. Bonefish

SUBORDER: *Albuloidei.* FAMILY: *Albulidae* — Bonefishes. Having a single dorsal fin, no adipose fin.

35. Bonefish
Albula vulpes

NAMES: LADYFISH, SILVER-SHUTTLE, MULLET, BANANA FISH. **DESCRIPTION:** Shaped something like the LADYFISH except for thicker body, projecting upper jaw, larger head, and larger scales. **SIZE:** Up to 2½ lbs. **COLOR:** Steel blue back fading to white belly. Young, transparent and ribbon-shaped. **RANGE:** Occurs Monterey Bay to tropics. Follows the tide into sloughs and backwaters. Often found in company with MULLET feeding on crawfish, soft-shell crabs, and other crustaceans. **BAIT & TACKLE:** Can be taken on small lures, live bait, shrimp, sand crabs, crawfish, and stripbait. Hook No. 4 to 2.

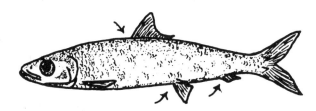

36. (California) round herring

SUBORDER: *Clupeoidei.* FAMILY: *Dussumieriidae*—Round Herrings. Having no adipose fin. The lateral line is suggested by a very few pores on the forepart of the body and therefore will be considered as absent in this text.

36. (California) round herring
Etrumeus acuminatus

NAME: JAPANESE HERRING. **DESCRIPTION:** The short base of the anal fin and base of the pelvic fin being situated back of point below base of the dorsal fin distinguishes the ROUND HERRING from the SARDINE and (PACIFIC) HERRING. Head long; body round; absence of lateral line; absence of striae on gill cover. **SIZE:** Up to 10 in. **COLOR:** Bright silver with brown spot on all back scales. **RANGE:** Occurs Dana Point to Cape San Lucas. **COMMENT:** An important bait and forage fish.

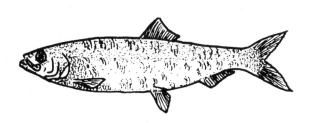

37. (Pacific) herring

FAMILY: *Clupeidae*—Herrings. Having a single dorsal fin, no adipose fin.

37. (Pacific) herring
Clupea pallasi

NAME: HERRING. The QUEENFISH is miscalled "HERRING" in southern California. **DESCRIPTION:** Dorsal fin on middle of back; absence of scales on head; absence of ridges on opercle; absence of lateral line; projecting lower jaw; absence of blackish spots on sides of body as in SARDINE and SHAD; maxillary reaching back to point below center of eye; fleshy appendage at base of each pelvic fin. Body deeper than SARDINE, measuring four times standard length. **SIZE:** Up to 1½ ft. **COLOR:** Bluish green to purple back, silver belly. **RANGE:** Occurs Ensenada to Aleutian Islands in bays and brackish waters to open ocean. Not abundant south of Pt. Conception. **BAIT & TACKLE:** Taken from piers on snag lines at daybreak or at night on fly or very small lure when strong light is used. **COMMENT:** As a bait fish, the HERRING rates as one of the best. It also constitutes one of the fundamental sources of food for the game fishes especially in northern waters. Of considerable commercial importance and will continue so if not overfished. It is too valuable to be reduced for oil or meal. This fish deposits eggs on various kinds of sea vegetation.

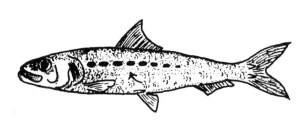

38. (Pacific) sardine

38. (Pacific) sardine
Sardinops caerulea

NAMES: CALIFORNIA SARDINE, PILCHARD. The young called "FIRECRACKERS" by anglers. **DESCRIPTION:** Closely resembling (PACIFIC) HERRING to casual observer. Differing in having raised ridges (striae) running down across gill covers and black spots on sides of body. Body elongate; head compressed; absence of teeth; lower jaw slightly projecting or equal; small, single dorsal fin situated slightly forward of middle of back; caudal fin deeply forked; two specialized, large scales on each side of tail; body depth 5 times standard length. **SIZE:** Up to 14 in. **COLOR:** Greenish to dark blue back, fading to silver belly; one or more rows of round to oblong black spots along sides of body. **RANGE:** Once a superabundant population spawned successfully in Southern California. Less abundant on up to Alaska. Despite scientific warnings, cannery and private purse seiners overfished and destroyed this population, a tragic example of commercial greed. Two small groups of Mexican SARDINES are surviving but are expected to be depleted soon; one near Sebastian Vizcaino Bay, another in the Midriff of the Cortez.

39. (American) shad
Alosa sapidissima

DESCRIPTION: Deep body with a sharp, saw-tooth edge on breast and belly; coarse striae on gill cover; large scales; single dorsal fin middle of back; pair of specialized large scales on each side of tail; no scales on head; no visible lateral line; body depth 3½ times standard length. SIZE: Up to 13½ lbs. COLOR: Deep bluish back, fading to silver belly, with row of dark to blackish spots on sides of body, decreasing in size posteriorly. RANGE: Occurs Vancouver Island to Ensenada. Abundant in separated areas north of Pt. Conception. Introduced from the Atlantic in 1871 into the Columbia and Sacramento Rivers. Is an ocean fish that ascends rivers in early spring to spawn. BAIT & TACKLE: Taken near surface at mouth of large streams and inlets on small strips of fish, sea worms, and small lures, sometimes flies. Hook No. 4. COMMENT: The roe is highly prized. The flesh excellent when baked.

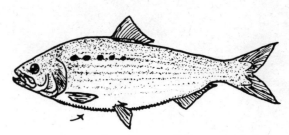

39. (American) shad

FAMILY: *Engraulididae*—Anchovies. Having no adipose or lateral line. Members of this family are of vital importance as sources of food supply for most predatory fishes, which display their preference for them by deserting other schools of forage fish to follow chum-trail of anchovies. These fishes are delicate and incapable of great speed or agility. They must therefore remain in great schools to avoid annihilation.

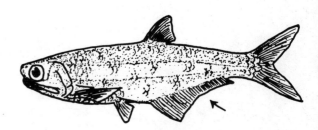

40. Deepbody anchovy

40. Deepbody anchovy
Anchoa compressa

NAMES: SPRAT, SARDINUS. DESCRIPTION: Deep, thin body; single dorsal fin; large mouth; eyes near end of snout; length of base of anal fin being half again as long as head. SIZE: Up to 6 in. COLOR: Pale, translucent green; a bright, horizontal, silvery stripe beginning above eye and running full length of body. RANGE: Occurs Pt. Conception to Morro Bay and in Gulf of California. Not abundant north of Dana Point.

41. Slough anchovy
Anchoa delicatissima

NAME: SOUTHERN ANCHOVY. DESCRIPTION: Length of head not greater than depth of body; length of base of anal fin not less than length of head; no scales on head; single dorsal fin; large mouth; eyes near end of snout. SIZE: Up to 5 in. COLOR: Greenish and translucent; silvery band along sides. RANGE: Los Angeles harbor to Todos Santos Bay, Baja California.

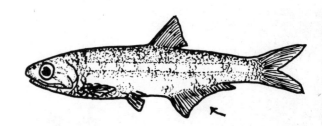

41. Slough anchovy

42. Northern anchovy
Engraulis mordax

NAME: CALIFORNIA ANCHOVY. The young are called "PINHEADS" by anglers. DESCRIPTION: Very large mouth; head longer than depth of body; eyes near end of snout; base of anal fin shorter than head; short, single dorsal fin. SIZE: Up to 8½ in. COLOR: Opalescent or metallic-blue back with bluish reflections; silver on sides and belly. RANGE: Occurs Vancouver Island to Cape San Lucas. COMMENT: Most important if all forage fishes and can be expected to follow the SARDINE to extinction. There is no scientific proof that this ANCHOVY can survive the present predation by its enemies, when man is included.

SUBORDER: *Salmonoidei*. FAMILY: *Osmeridae*—Smelts.

A family of small fishes with slender bodies; moderately small scales; a well-developed lateral line; a single soft-rayed dorsal fin and a dorsal adipose fin. The males are smaller than the females and have comparatively larger fins.

Spawning occurs in gravel and sandy surfs or in fresh water. Most of the species are excellent food fishes. Also especially important as bait and forage fish.

Some species of the SILVERSIDE family, Atherinidae, are called "SMELTS." They are SPINY-RAYED FISHES and differ from the TRUE SMELTS by having two dorsal fins, the first composed of spines, the second of soft rays; no adipose fin and no lateral line.

NOTE: The line of numerals following the names of the fishes describes the dorsal and anal fins. Thus: d. 10 to 14; a. 15 to 19 indicates that there are 10 to 14 soft rays in the (d) dorsal, and 15 to 19 soft rays in the (a) anal fin.

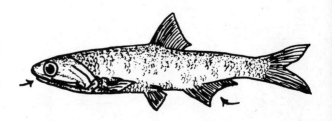

42. Northern anchovy

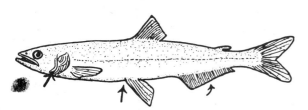

43. Candlefish

43. Candlefish · *Thaleichthys pacificus*

NAMES: EULACHON, ULCHEN. DESCRIPTION: d. 11 to 13; a. 20 to 23. Differing from other members of the SMELT family in that the origin of the pelvic fin is situated in advance of the middle of the body and ahead of the base of the dorsal fin; also by the well-defined ridges (striae) on the opercle. SIZE: Up to 12 in. COLOR: Bluish-brown back to silvery-white belly. RANGE: Occurs California to British Columbia in mouth of streams and backwaters, spring and early summer. More common north of Columbia River. BAIT & TACKLE: Caught on snag lines or with dip nets at high tide. Sometimes taken on flies. COMMENT: Is excellent as bait fish. Dies after spawning. Considered by many as having a better flavor than TROUT. The name "CANDLEFISH" because of the richness in oil. Was used by native Indians as a lamp by simply setting a dried one afire.

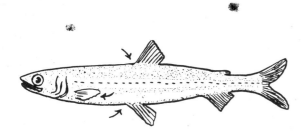

44. Night smelt

44. Night smelt · *Spirinchus starksi*

NAMES: WHITEBAIT, SAND SMELT, NIGHTFISH. DESCRIPTION: d. 6 to 10; a. 15 to 17. Distinguished by the pelvic fin being attached at about middle of the body, origin beginning slightly ahead of origin of dorsal fin; no scales on head; small teeth in roof of mouth; pointed snout; maxillary reaching past eye. SIZE: Up to 10 in. COLOR: Silvery stripe on sides, otherwise very pale green. RANGE: Occurs Pismo Beach to Straits of Juan de Fuca, year round. Abundant north of Pt. Arena to Columbia River. BAIT & TACKLE: Taken during spawning runs at night with snag lines and dip nets at high tide. COMMENT: Makes excellent bait.

Two other members of this family, the LONG-FINNED SMELT, *Spirinchus dilatus,* occurring from Eureka to Alaska, are taken during fall months. Is distinguished by the extra large fins.

The other species, *Allosmerus attenuatus,* found in about the same location, closely resembles *S. starksi.* Differs in having larger teeth and slightly longer pectoral fin. Is also known as WHITEBAIT. Taken in same manner.

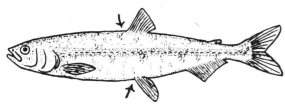

45. Surf smelt

45. Surf smelt · *Hypomesus pretiosus*

NAMES: SILVER SMELT, DAY-FISH, SURF FISH, PERLIN. DESCRIPTION: d. 9 or 10; a. 14 to 16. Differing from *S. starksi* in that the pelvic fin is smaller and is set back of the origin of the dorsal fin; very small teeth on tongue and vomer; maxillary reaching only to middle of eye. SIZE: Up to 10 in. COLOR: Pale green with silver belly; a pronounced metallic stripe along sides becoming dark when removed from water. Male becomes brown on back at spawning time. RANGE: Occurs Pt. Conception to Alaska, year round. Very abundant north of Pt. Arena. BAIT & TACKLE: Taken in surf and in mouth of streams by amateur fishermen with squaw nets, dip nets, rakes, or by hand at high tide. COMMENT: An important forage fish.

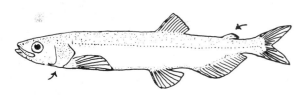

46. (Pacific) capelin

46. (Pacific) capelin · *Mallotus catervarius*

DESCRIPTION: d. 12 or 13; a. 17 to 20. Distinguished from other SMELTS by the very small scales; large adipose fin and rough opercle. Body elongate; long head; pointed snout; enlarged scales on lateral line of males during spawning period. SIZE: Up to 6 in. COLOR: Olive green back fading to silver sides and belly; black dots on opercle. RANGE: Occurs Oregon to Alaska. Abundant north of Juan de Fuca Straits. BAIT & TACKLE: Taken on sandy beaches by hand when they come in to deposit eggs in the sand during September and October. COMMENT: The eggs are adhesive and become attached to the gravel or large grains of sand, to be covered by the wave action at extreme high tides. Important forage fish for SILVER SALMON.

FAMILY: *Salmonidae*—Trouts.

There are five species of SALMON that are native to the Pacific. They are very closely related and belong in the same genus, *Oncorhynchus,* which in turn is closely related to the ATLANTIC SALMON and the sea-going TROUTS in the genus, *Salmo,* and the CHARS in the genus, *Salvelinus.*

The external characters of these fishes are so similar, counts and measurements so often overlapping that positive identification of some of the species is very difficult. Even scale and gill raker counts can not be depended upon unless all characters are considered.

A simple method of distinguishing the difference between the CHINOOK SALMON, SILVER SALMON, and RAINBOW (STEELHEAD) TROUT is by an examination of the mouth cavity. In the CHINOOK, the mouth cavity, tongue, and gums are all dark; in the SILVER, the crown of the gum is white, the mouth cavity and tongue are dark; in the STEELHEAD TROUT, the whole mouth cavity, tongue, and gums are light.

In all species the body is stout; lateral line pronounced; adipose fin well developed; scales small; a large fleshy appendage at base of each pelvic fin. The colors before entering fresh water range from bright blue to green on the back with silver on belly. These colors as well as the shape of the jaws, head, and body begin changing soon after entering fresh water.

All of the SALMONS are anadromous by nature, living in salt water but entering streams to spawn. All die shortly after spawning. Some become land-locked, spending the life cycle in fresh water.

For the sake of brevity the great range of baits, tackle, localities, and methods of taking the various species has been limited in this chapter to those most commonly used.

The SEA TROUTS like the SALMONS are anadromous but do not die after spawning. Some species return to fresh water to spawn as many as seven times. The young descend to the sea in the third or fourth year. Some remain to spend their lives in fresh water.

It will be noticed that there are 12 or less rays in the anal fin in the TROUTS, while in the SALMONS the anal ray count is usually 13 or more. On rare occasions a SILVER SALMON may be found with 12 rays.

Although the SEA TROUTS are voracious feeders in salt water very little angling technique has been developed for taking them in the open ocean.

The ATLANTIC SALMON, *Salmo salar,* was introduced into northern Pacific waters but has not as yet shown indications of becoming established.

47. Brown trout   *Salmo trutta*

NAMES: LOCH LEVEN, CHAR. DESCRIPTION: d. 10 to 13; a. 9 or 10; adipose small, slender. Distinguished by the distinct black spots encircled by a ring of pink or red, extending along sides below lateral line. Deep caudal peduncle; maxillary extending to point equal to back margin of eye; no teeth on back of tongue. SIZE: Up to 3 ft. and 30 lbs. COLOR: Brown to tan, silvery sides and belly, numerous black spots on back, top of head, cheeks, and on perpendicular and longitudinal fins. RANGE: Occurs Eureka, California, to Vancouver Island. Not abundant. BAIT & TACKLE: Taken occasionally in brackish water near mouth of streams in same manner as CUTTHROAT. COMMENT: The BROWN TROUT was successfully introduced into rivers of Victoria Island in 1932 from Wisconsin and Montana.

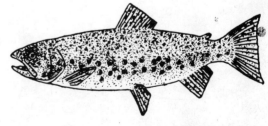

47. Brown trout

48. Cutthroat trout

48. Cutthroat trout — *Salmo clarki*

NAMES: BLUEBACK, COASTAL CUTTHROAT TROUT, SEATROUT, BLACKSPOTTED TROUT, CUTS, HARVEST TROUT. **DESCRIPTION**: d. 8 to 11; a. 9 to 11. Distinguished by the bright red dash on inner edge of mandible and on the underside of the lower jaw. Maxillary extending to point well back of eye; body rounded; head relatively long; caudal peduncle long, deep; adipose fin small, slender. **SIZE**: Up to 2½ ft. **COLOR**: Greenish to greenish blue on back; silvery sides and belly; many moderately large spots over head, body, dorsal, caudal, anal, and adipose fins. **RANGE**: Occurs Cape Mendocino to Alaska. More abundant north of Astoria, Oregon. Some individuals found in streams and lakes do not migrate to salt water. Found in salt and brackish waters seasonally—one run in early spring to meet the young SALMON, the other in fall and winter to spawn. **BAIT & TACKLE**: Taken in brackish water on small stripbait, crawfish tails, ghost shrimp, and other crustaceans; also on a wide range of lures at slow troll. Hook No. 2.

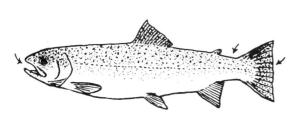

49. Rainbow (steelhead) trout

49. Rainbow (steelhead) trout — *Salmo gairdneri*

NAMES: STEELHEAD RAINBOW TROUT, SUMMER SALMON, HARDHEAD, SALMON TROUT, STEELHEAD TROUT. **DESCRIPTION**: d. 11 or 12; a. 9 to 12. Distinguished from the SALMONS by the long, deep caudal peduncle and the twelve or less rays in the anal fin. Adipose fin small, slender; head comparatively short; caudal fin almost straight; maxillary extending back to point below center of eye. Differing from CHINOOK and SILVER SALMONS by having white mouth cavity. **SIZE**: Up to 2 ft. 9 in. and to 36 lbs. **COLOR**: In salt water, steel blue back, silvery sides and belly; small, black spots on head, back, dorsal, adipose and caudal fins. At spawning time red stripes appear on sides (more pronounced in males). **RANGE**: Occurs Ensenada to Alaska. Abundant north of Pt. Arena. They arrive off the mouth of streams in the southern section about a month before the winter rains start, September or October, and remain until the small streams swell or break the sea barriers, December or January. They begin entering the larger streams earlier. It is during these runs that the anglers take them. **BAIT & TACKLE**: They can be caught occasionally by casting in sandy surfs near the mouth of streams on stripbait and shrimp. In brackish water they will take lightweight moving lures and flies. Also taken on crawfish tails, sea worms, ghost shrimp, and salmon egg clusters. Hook in accordance to size of fish in run. No. 4 to 1. **COMMENT**: Spawns after third year.

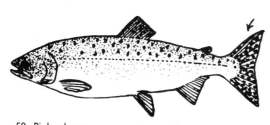

50. Pink salmon

50. Pink salmon — *Oncorhynchus gorbuscha*

NAMES: HUMPBACK, HADDO. **DESCRIPTION**: d. 10 to 15; a. 13 to 17. Rakers on first gill arch 26 to 34; scales on lateral line small, 170 to 229. Distinguished by the very large black oval or irregular spots on back and whole of caudal fin. Caudal peduncle slender (slightly longer than in CHINOOK and SILVER but not as deep or long as in TROUTS); caudal fin slightly furcate; teeth small, loosely set. **SIZE**: Up to 2½ ft. **COLOR**: Steel blue to bright gray with the large, black spots on back and on caudal fin; silvery belly; sides of males reddish; females greenish on sides, sometimes with dusky stripes. Flesh, pink. **RANGE**: Occurs La Jolla to Alaska. Abundant north of Straits of Juan de Fuca. **BAIT & TACKLE**: Feeds chiefly on crustaceans and small live fishes in salt water. Will occasionally take lures, crawfish tails or stripbait at slow troll. Hook No. 4 to 2. **COMMENT**: The PINK matures in two years.

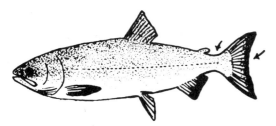

51. Chum salmon

51. Chum salmon — *Oncorhynchus keta*

NAMES: HAYHO, CALICO SALMON, DOG SALMON. **DESCRIPTION**: d. 10 to 13; a. 13 to 17. Rakers on first gill arch widely separate, short, fatty, smooth, numbering 19 to 26; scales on lateral line 126 to 151. Distinguished by the black tips on the pectoral, anal, and caudal fins; whitish on dorsal and pelvic fins. Long, slender caudal peduncle (not as long as in TROUTS); teeth large, conical, rigid; adipose fin small, slender; caudal fin furcate. **SIZE**: Up to 3 ft. 2 in. **COLOR**: Metallic blue with very small, sparse speckling; absence of spots on back; silvery sides and belly. Flesh, pale pink. **RANGE**: Occurs Cape Mendocino to Alaska. Abundant north of Astoria. **BAIT & TACKLE**: Hook No. 4. **COMMENT**: Matures about fourth year.

52. Chinook salmon
Oncorhynchus tschawytscha

NAMES: KING SALMON, SPRING SALMON, TYEE, QUINNAT. Young males called JACKS. DESCRIPTION: Fins: d. 10 to 14; a. 15 to 19. Rakers on the first gill arch 20 to 28; scales on lateral line 131 to 151. Distinguished in salt water by the dark mouth cavity, tongue and gums. Small, short, caudal peduncle (as compared to the long, deep caudal peduncle of the RAINBOW [STEELHEAD] TROUT); short caudal fin with the upper and lower rays stout and rigid; head conical; teeth loosely set, pointed, moderately large; adipose fin comparatively short and fleshy. SIZE: Up to 4 ft. 10 in. and to 100 lbs. COLOR: Greenish to dark blue or blackish, fading to silvery belly; many black spots (less than size of eye) on back, dorsal fin and both lobes of caudal fin. Flesh, pink to red, sometimes white. RANGE: Occurs San Diego to Alaska. Rare south of Pt. Conception. Fairly abundant north of Monterey. BAIT & TACKLE: For locality, bait, and method of taking, see chapters on "Marine Angling Boats" and "Privately-owned Craft." Hooks from 1 to 6/0. COMMENT: Spawns third to eighth year. Usually fourth or fifth.

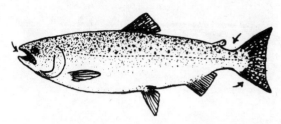

52. Chinook salmon

53. Silver salmon
Oncorhynchus kisutch

NAMES: COHO, COMO SALMON, SILVERSIDE, SKOWITZ. DESCRIPTION: d. 9 to 13; a. 12 to 17. Rakers on first gill arch widely spaced, rough, 19 to 25; scales on lateral line 121 to 126. Distinguished by the light gum crown and dark tongue and mouth cavity. Small, short caudal peduncle as compared to RAINBOW (STEELHEAD) TROUT; head conical; teeth small, sharp, rigid; adipose fin small, slender. SIZE: Up to 3 ft. and 30 lbs. COLOR: Metallic blue to greenish (blue predominant) on back; silver on sides, caudal peduncle and on belly; many small, black spots (smaller than in CHINOOK SALMON) on back, dorsal fin, and upper lobe of caudal fin (differing from CHINOOK in which spots are larger and on both lobes of caudal fin). Flesh, pink. RANGE: Occurs Cabo Colnett to Alaska—rare south of Pt. Conception, gradually becoming more abundant north of Coos Bay. BAIT & TACKLE: For baits and methods of taking, see chapters on fishing from "Marine Angling Boats" and "Privately Owned Craft." Hooks from 2 to 4/0. COMMENT: Returns to fresh water to spawn in second or third year, rarely fourth.

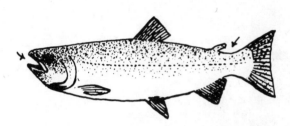

53. Silver salmon

54. Sockeye salmon
Oncorhynchus nerka

NAMES: RED SALMON, BLUEBACK SALMON, REDFISH, RED ALASKA SALMON, SILVER TROUT, KOKANEL. DESCRIPTION: d. 11 to 16; a. 13 to 17. Rakers on first gill arch large, slender, rough, and closely set, numbering 30 to 39; scales on lateral line 125 to 139. Distinguished by the small, black specks on back; absence of larger spots. Small, short caudal peduncle; teeth small, sharp, loosely set; head conical; adipose fin fleshy, slender; caudal fin moderately furcate. SIZE: Up to 33 in. and 15½ lbs. COLOR: Blue to greenish with fine specks on back; head brighter green; silver belly; back of males flushed reddish; females with yellowish blotches, sometimes dark red. Flesh very deep red. Because of red meat and flavor, is prized for canning. RANGE: Occurs Eureka to Aleutian Islands. Abundant Washington and British Columbia. BAIT & TACKLE: Occasionally taken in salt water around islands, in swift currents, and at stream entrances, on stripbait, spinner, worms, crawfish tails, ghost shrimp, and lures, trolled near bottom at 3 miles per hour. Hooks range from 4 to 1/0. Little technique yet developed for taking this one. COMMENT: Spawns third to eighth year, usually fourth or fifth.

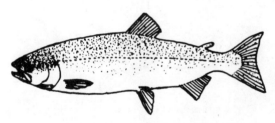

54. Sockeye salmon

55. Dolly Varden
Salvelinus malma

NAMES: WESTERN CHAR, REDSPOTTED CHAR, DOLLY VARDEN TROUT, BULL TROUT. DESCRIPTION: d. 10 or 11; a. 9 or 10; adipose fin slender, small. Distinguished by the small, well-separated, pale yellow spots on back, becoming red on sides and belly. Maxillary extending well past eye; body comparatively slender and rounded; eyes large. SIZE: Up to 20 lbs. COLOR: Greenish brown to light brown on back fading to silvery sides and belly; spots as above. RANGE: Occurs Eureka to Alaska in salt and brackish water near streams. More abundant in northern part of range. BAIT & TACKLE: Taken on flies and other small lures. Also on stripbait, herring, stickleback, anchovy and shrimp. Hook No. 3 to 1. COMMENT: An excellent game fish.

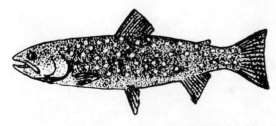

55. Dolly Varden

TROUTS & SALMONS   109

56. (Pacific) saury

ORDER: *Synentognathi.* FAMILY: *Scomberesocidae*—Sauries.

56. (Pacific) saury   *Cololabis saira*

NAMES: SAURY, SOURBELLY, SOURFISH, SKIPPER, GARFISH. DESCRIPTION: d. 9 to 12; a. 12 to 14. Long, slender body; jaws sharp and beak-like; lower jaw flexible; single dorsal fin situated far back and past origin of anal fin, both followed by six finlets; lateral line low on belly. SIZE: Up to 14 in. COLOR: Dark green back, fading to silver belly. RANGE: Occurs Alaska to Pt. Banda, Baja California, in channel waters and open sea, traveling in great schools. Abundant whole range. COMMENT: Important forage fish. Should prove good bait fish if exploited. Feeds near surface. No exact technique yet developed for its capture by anglers. A favorite food fish in Japan. Often seen in open ocean jumping two or three feet above surface when pursued by large fishes.

57. (California) needlefish

FAMILY: *Belonidae*—Needlefishes.

57. (California) needlefish   *Strongylura exilis*

NAMES: GARFISH, BILLFISH. DESCRIPTION: d. 14 to 16; a. 16 to 18. Jaws forming a long, pointed needle-like beak; body very slender, rounded; dorsal and anal fins situated far back on body; teeth sharp, fine. SIZE: Up to 3½ ft. COLOR: Green on back, silver on belly; a bluish stripe along sides. Greenish bones, white meat. RANGE: Occurs Pt. Conception to Cape San Lucas and in Gulf of California. Abundant south of San Diego. BAIT & TACKLE: Very difficult to hook with lures. Feather best at slow troll. More readily taken on small stripbait or squid. Hook No. 4. COMMENT: An excellent food fish.

A small but important forage fish, the TUBESNOUT, *Aulorhynchus flavidus,* has a shorter beak than the NEEDLEFISH. It occurs in great abundance from Alaska to Baja California.

58. (California) flyingfish

FAMILY: *Exocoetidae*—Flyingfishes.

58. (California) flyingfish   *Cypselurus californicus*

DESCRIPTION: d. 12; a. 10. Readily distinguished by the long, spreading pectoral fins which serve as gliding wings, sustaining it above water for some time. There are three species on the Pacific Coast, two of them, the *Fodiator acutus* and the *Exonautes rondeletii* are seldom seen north of Ensenada. The (CALIFORNIA) FLYINGFISH differs from the others in having larger eyes, a projecting lower jaw and in being much larger. Is said to be the largest of all the FLYINGFISHES. SIZE: Up to 18 in. COLOR: Blue on back and sides, silver on belly. RANGE: Occurs Pt. Conception to Cape San Lucas. COMMENT: Especially good as bait for large game fishes. Used extensively in kite fishing. Quantities shipped to Hawaii for MARLIN bait. A good food fish.

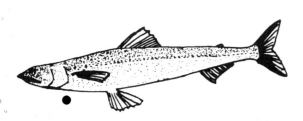

59. (California) lizardfish

ORDER: *Iniomi.* FAMILY: *Synodidae*—Lizardfishes.

59. (California) lizardfish   *Synodus lucioceps*

DESCRIPTION: d. 11 or 12; a. 12. The long, slender body and shape of head somewhat resemble those of a lizard, hence the name. Front base of dorsal fin situated slightly back of pelvic fin base; pectoral reaching base of pelvic fin; dorsal finlet above anal fin; area between eyes slightly concave; mouth large. SIZE: Up to 23 in. COLOR: Greenish brown with brassy luster on back halting abruptly at lateral line; sides and belly light gray; blackish stripes along lateral line; some blackish reticulations or criss-cross lines running at angles from lateral line across back; lower jaw and pelvic fins yellow. RANGE: Occurs San Francisco to San Quintin Bay in moderately shallow water. COMMENT: Not common. Taken incidentally by anglers fishing for other forms. Edible.

ORDER: *Apodes*—Eel-like fishes. SUBORDER: *Colocephali*.
FAMILY: *Muraenidae*—Morays.

60. (California) moray — *Gymnothorax mordax*

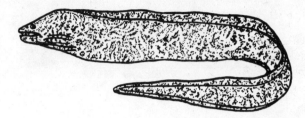

60. (California) moray

NAMES: MORAY, CONGER EEL, MARINA, MURAENA, MORAY EEL. **DESCRIPTION**: Eel-shaped body extremely long and slender; absence of scales; absence of pelvic and pectoral fins; dorsal and anal fins hardly more than fleshy ridges; sharp, pointed teeth set in well-developed jaws. **SIZE**: Up to 5 ft. **COLOR**: Dark brown with many small, lighter spots; vague light streaks on belly. **RANGE**: Occurs Pt. Conception to Pt. Eugenia, Baja California, along rocky coast line and in kelp beds. **BAIT & TACKLE**: Taken on mussels, shrimp, stripbait and clams on No. 2/0 hooks or from under rocks with large eel hook on long stick. **COMMENT**: Very ferocious in or out of water. Excellent food fish.

ORDER: *Cyprinodontes*. FAMILY: *Cyprinodontidae*—Killifishes.

61. (California) killifish — *Fundulus parvipinnis*

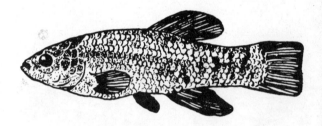

61. (California) killifish

DESCRIPTION: d. 13 or 14; a. 10 or 11. First rays of single dorsal fin situated about middle of back, directly above anus; caudal peduncle deep, long; head pointed; mouth small. Fins large in males, small in females. **SIZE**: Up to 4 in. **COLOR**: Dark to light green back fading to yellowish belly. **RANGE**: Occurs Pt. Conception to San Quintin Bay in bays and backwaters. **COMMENT**: Important forage and bait fish.

ORDER: *Anacanthini*. FAMILY: *Merlucciidae*—Hakes.

62. (Pacific) hake — *Merluccius productus*

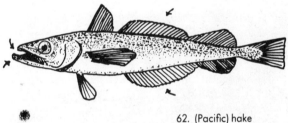

62. (Pacific) hake

NAMES: HAKE, WHITEFISH, HADDOCK, BUTTERFISH, OCEAN WHITEFISH, MELLUSA, POPEYE, SILVER HAKE. **DESCRIPTION**: 1st d. 10 or 11; 2nd d. 41; a. 40 to 43. Differing from other cod-like fishes in having a large mouth; projecting lower jaw; two separated, soft-rayed dorsal fins, the first short, the second long and deeply notched forming a symmetrical pattern with the long anal fin; the caudal peduncle very small in comparison. Small scales; head with W-shaped ridges; large eyes; lateral line slanting from top of opercle to middle of body, then straight; maxillary extending to point past pupil of eye. **SIZE**: Up to 3 ft. **COLOR**: Iron-gray to black back with darker specks; silver sides and belly; jet black inside mouth. **RANGE**: Occurs Alaska to Cape San Lucas year round. Abundant from Monterey to British Columbia, in moderately shallow to deep water. **BAIT & TACKLE**: Taken on strips of fish, squid, shrimp or other crustaceans. Hook No. 2/0 to 4/0. **COMMENT**: A fine food fish if kept cool and damp; otherwise flesh will soften.

FAMILY: *Gadidae*—Codfishes. Having barbel on tip of lower jaw, sometimes minute or absent. True cods inhabit cold water.

63. (Walleye) pollack — *Theragra chalcogramma*

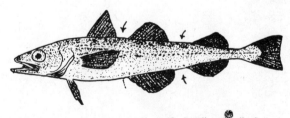

63. (Walleye) pollack

NAMES: WHITING, ALASKAN POLLACK. **DESCRIPTION**: 1st d. 10 to 13; 2nd d. 12 to 18; 3rd d. 14 to 20; 1st a. 15 to 22; 2nd a. 15 to 21. Dorsal fins well separated; third dorsal and second anal forming symmetrical pattern; lateral line curving up toward first dorsal, then down and straight from middle of body; body elongate; head pointed; lower jaw slightly projecting; large eyes; minute barbel on tip of lower jaw, though sometimes absent; anus below gap between 1st and 2nd dorsal fins. **SIZE**: Up to 3 ft. **COLOR**: Olive green to brown on back; silver sides; white belly; dusky or black on fins. Young with two or three yellow bands along sides. **RANGE**: Occurs Eureka to Alaska. Abundant in rather shallow water north of Columbia River. **BAIT & TACKLE**: Crustaceans and strips of herring or greenling. Will also take flesh of mollusks. Hook No. 1/0 to 2/0.

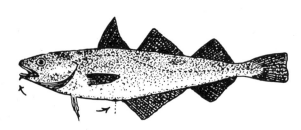

64. (Pacific) tomcod

64. (Pacific) tomcod *Microgadus proximus*

NAMES: TOMCOD, PICIATA. South of Pt. Conception the TOMMY CROAKER is miscalled "TOMCOD." **DESCRIPTION**: 1st d. 11 to 14; 2nd d. 17 to 20; 3rd d. 18 to 20; 1st a. 20 to 25; 2nd a. 18 to 21. Typical COD goatee or barbel at tip of lower jaw, barbel length about equal to diameter of pupil of eye; three separate dorsal fins; two separate anal fins; lateral line beginning to curve upward midway of body; anus directly below first dorsal fin. **SIZE**: Up to 12 in. **COLOR**: Gray back with brownish tinge fading to white belly; dusky on tips of fins, except first anal and pelvic. **RANGE**: Occurs Pt. Conception to Alaska. Very abundant north of Pt. Arena. **BAIT & TACKLE**: Taken year round in bays and backwaters on almost any bait if kept in motion. Strips of fish, shrimp, clams or sea worms. Hook No. 2. **COMMENT**: Is a bottom feeder. Must be kept cool and damp.

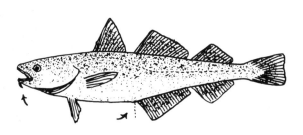

65. Pacific cod

65. Pacific cod *Gadus macrocephalus*

NAMES: ALASKA COD, COD, GRAY COD, TRUE COD. **DESCRIPTION**: 1st d. 11 to 14; 2nd d. 14 to 21; 3rd d. 14 to 20; 1st a. 16 to 24; 2nd a. 14 to 19. Differs from other Pacific members of this family in having a very long barbel on tip of lower jaw, length equal to diameter of eye; and the first dorsal being situated well in advance of anus. Body elongate, stout, moderately compressed; last two dorsal fins forming symmetrical pattern with anal fins; head large; snout blunt; eyes small in comparison. **SIZE**: Up to 3 ½ ft. **COLOR**: Brown to gray on back, fading to light belly; numerous small spots on back and sides; fins dusky; vertical fins tipped with whitish. **RANGE**: Occurs Eureka to Alaska. Taken by anglers in rather shallow water, where forage fishes are abundant. Migrates from deep water (130 fathoms) to very shallow places around docks and piers during summer months. **BAIT & TACKLE**: Shrimp, herring or other small fresh-dead bait, strips of fish, and crustaceans. Hook No. 2/0 to 4/0. **COMMENT**: Is a bottom feeder. Must be kept cool and damp to retain firmness and flavor.

↬ *FLATFISHES* ↫

ORDER: *Heterosomata*—Flatfishes.

When hatched and for a short time thereafter, the FLATFISHES swim upright and resemble other normal fishes in appearance. A metamorphosis takes place in which one eye migrates over toward the other, finally both are on one side. This side becomes somewhat rounded and darker in color and is called the "eye side." The underside, remaining light in color and almost flat, is referred to as the "blind side." In this order the adult fishes rest flat on the bottom and swim in a horizontal position with the "blind side" down. The single dorsal fin extends from the snout or top of head to the short caudal peduncle; the anal fin from a point just under or shortly back of the base of the pectoral fin to match the posterior end of the dorsal fin. The very small pelvic fins attached on or near the edge of the abdominal ridge are situated under or in advance of the base of the pectoral fin. All fins are composed of soft rays. A single spine in advance of the anal fin occurs in some species.

FLATFISHES generally feed on or near the bottom, sometimes following the food some distance above the ocean floor and occasionally rising to the surface in pursuit of schools of small fishes. These FLATFISHES are in far greater abundance than the angler suspects. Vast numbers are missed because of a general lack of knowledge of acceptable bait and technique of hooking them.

While this order comprises five families, only two are of particular interest to anglers of the Pacific Coast: the families, Bothidae, and Pleuronectidae.

In the meetings held by Hubbs and Follett on nomenclature, the common names of the FLATFISHES were the most troublesome of all the salt-water forms. It was found that there was no more logic in calling them "FLOUNDERS" than "SOLES." Their decision to follow common usage in this case appeared to be the only course that would be followed by anglers as well as scientists.

The use of the French name "SOLE" (so named because of its flatness) was established by the early Europeans who settled along our coast. To them these fishes resembled the SOLES they had known, both in looks and flavor.

Just why the family Pleuronectidae should ever have been called FLOUNDERS is not quite clear, since there was originally only one member known as FLOUNDER, or FLUNDRA, and it differed greatly from the others in a number of respects. This FLOUNDER was very small and it ascended fresh-water streams of northern Europe. Sometime prior to 1900 all FLATFISHES were thought to be in the family, Pleuronectidae.

It should be noted that the SANDDABS and FLOUNDERS are more often sinistral (left-eyed) while the SOLES and TURBOTS are almost always dextral (right-eyed).

The color description given refers to the eye side except when stated otherwise.

FAMILY: *Bothidae*—Left-eyed Flounders. Most members of this family are sinistral (eyes and coloring on left side of body); others may be either sinistral or dextral (eyes and coloring on left or right side of body).

66. Bigmouth sole · *Hippoglossina stomata*

NAMES: BIGMOUTH HALIBUT; BIGMOUTH FLOUNDER. DESCRIPTION: Sinistral or dextral (eyes as often on right as on left side of head). Large mouth; maxillary reaching past lower eye; large eyes separated by bony ridge curved upward; very large, abrupt arch at front of lateral line; teeth very fine. SIZE: up to 20 in. COLOR: Brown tinged with blue, lighter blue and brown spots. RANGE: Pt. Conception, California to Bahia Conception, Baja California. BAIT & TACKLE: Taken in moderately shallow water on shrimp, strips of fresh sardine or mackerel and live bait. Hook No. 1/0 or 2/0 short-shank.

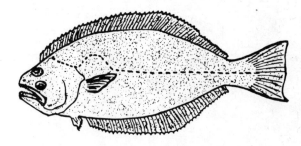

66. Bigmouth sole

67. California halibut · *Paralichthys californicus*

NAMES: BASTARD HALIBUT, CHICKEN HALIBUT, SOUTHERN HALIBUT, ALABATO. DESCRIPTION: Sinistral or dextral. Small eyes, separated by broad, flat area; small pectoral fin, half as long as head; lateral line forming high arch over pectoral fin; large, vicious-looking mouth with needle-pointed teeth and strong, square jaw (a good place to keep fingers away from); maxillary extending past eye. SIZE: Up to 3½ ft. and 75 lbs. COLOR: Blind side white, colored side muddy brown, sometimes mottled or splotched with lighter shades, at times found with definite small white spots. RANGE: Monterey Bay to Magdalena Bay. Taken year round south of border. Summer months best. Appearing north of border in shallow waters in February; caught as late as December from marine angling boats, barges, and piers. Occasionally found in backwaters. Not common north of Pt. Conception. Abundant south of San Diego. BAIT & TACKLE: A large range of baits is acceptable to this HALIBUT. It favors live anchovies in shallow water and queenfish out away from shore. If these are not available, small fresh-dead or stripbait will attract it if kept moving near the bottom. Hook No. 2 to 1/0 short-shank.

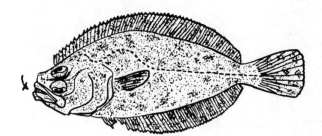

67. California halibut

68. Fantail sole · *Xystreurys liolepis*

NAMES: LONG FINNED FLOUNDER, FANTAIL HALIBUT, FANTAIL FLOUNDER. DESCRIPTION: Sinistral or dextral. The long, pointed pectoral fin about the same length as the head; long, rounded caudal fin, a high arch in the lateral line just above pectoral fin and a short, blunt snout distinguish the FANTAIL from other FLATFISHES. Large eyes, separated by a narrow, scaly ridge; maxillary reaching point below middle of eye. SIZE: Up to 15 in. COLOR: Brown, blotched or mottled with reddish brown or black; bars or stripes across pectoral fin; dark blotches on dorsal, anal and caudal fins. RANGE: Occurs Pt. Conception to Mazatlan in bays and backwaters during summer months. BAIT & TACKLE: Taken on small live bait, stripbait or meat of shellfish when kept in motion. Hook No. 1 or 2.

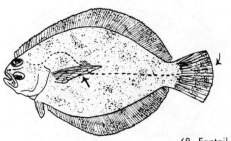

68. Fantail sole

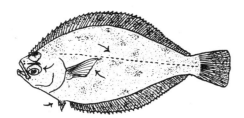

69. Pacific sanddab

69. Pacific sanddab *Citharichthys sordidus*

NAMES: SANDDAB, MOTTLED SANDDAB, MEGRIM, SOFT FLOUNDER. **DESCRIPTION:** Sinistral. Scales large in comparison to size and easily removed; lower eye longer than snout; nearly straight lateral line; offset pelvic fins, the one on eye side attached on ridge of abdomen, the one on blind side attached to side of ridge; pectoral fin shorter than head; space between eyes concave, rising to a ridge above lower eye. **SIZE:** Up to 2 lbs. and 12 in. **COLOR:** Brownish to light olive, mottled with deeper color; anal, dorsal and caudal fins blackish. **RANGE:** Occurs British Columbia to Cape San Lucas over sandy bottoms offshore. Seems to be very abundant throughout whole range. **BAIT & TACKLE:** Taken on strips of herring, anchovy, strips from belly of tommy croaker, or bits of shrimp at depth of 10 to 80 fathoms. Hook No. 2.

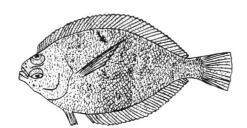

70. Longfin sanddab

70. Longfin sanddab *Citharichthys xanthostigma*

NAMES: SANDDAB, SOFT FLOUNDER, CATALINA SANDDAB. **DESCRIPTION:** Sinistral. Distinguished from other SANDDABS by the long pectoral fin which is longer than the head. Eyes longer than snout, separated by narrow, concave area; nearly straight lateral line; eye side pelvic fin on ridge of belly. **SIZE:** Up to 12 in. **COLOR:** Light olive brown to grayish, irregular dark dots and numerous yellow spots over body. **RANGE:** Occurs Cape San Lucas to Pt. Conception in moderately deep to deep water. Very abundant south of Pt. Dume. **BAIT & TACKLE:** Taken on strips of sardine, anchovy, mackerel, belly of tommy croaker, squid, and bits of shrimp. Hook No. 2.

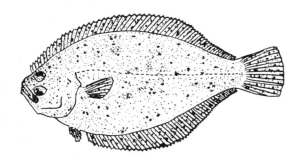

71. Speckled sanddab

71. Speckled sanddab *Citharichthys stigmaeus*

NAME: SAND DAB. **DESCRIPTION:** Sinistral. Distinguished from other SANDDABS in that the lower eye is not longer than the snout, and by the speckled coloration. Pectoral fin shorter than head; absence of ridge between eyes, area flat; pelvic fin on ridge of belly; nearly straight lateral line; maxillary extending to middle of lower eye. **SIZE:** Up to 8 in. **COLOR:** Olive brown; body and fins sparsely covered with fine black specks. **RANGE:** Occurs Alaska to San Quintin Bay in moderately shallow to deep water. Common throughout range. **BAIT & TACKLE:** Taken in same manner as PACIFIC SANDDAB. Hook No. 6. **COMMENT:** The three Pacific species in the genus, *Citharichthys,* differ considerably from the ATLANTIC SAND DAB, *Hippoglossoides platessoides,* in the family Hippoglossidae.

FAMILY: *Pleuronectidae*—Right-eyed Flounders. With one exception, the STARRY FLOUNDER, *Platichthys stellatus,* all members of this family normally are dextral (eyes and colored surface on right side of body).

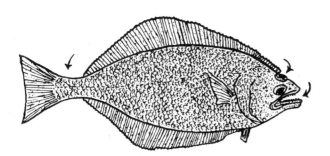

72. Arrowtooth halibut

72. Arrowtooth halibut *Atheresthes stomias*

NAMES: ARROWTOOTH SOLE, FRENCH SOLE, LONG-JAWED FLOUNDER, ENGLISH FLOUNDER, BASTARD HALIBUT, TURBOT. **DESCRIPTION:** Dextral. Distinguished by the long maxillary which extends well past lower eye; large, deciduous scales; teeth with small, arrow-like tips; long, slender caudal peduncle; head and body elongate; upper eye entering into margin of profile; caudal fin lunate; lateral line gradually curving upward over pectoral fin. **SIZE:** Up to 30 in. **COLOR:** Small dark spots on blind side; eye side greenish brown; edges of scales tipped with darker brown. **RANGE:** Occurs Monterey to Aleutians. Abundant north of Coos Bay, Oregon. Taken in deep water during winter months and in shallow water during summer and fall months. **BAIT & TACKLE:** Shrimp, strips of fish, and lures. Hooks No. 1/0 or 2/0. **COMMENT:** Often found in company with PACIFIC HALIBUT.

73. Pacific halibut
Hippoglossus stenolepis

NAMES: NORTHERN HALIBUT, ALABATO, RIGHT HALIBUT, HALIBUT. DESCRIPTION: Dextral, rarely sinistral. Outline of the dorsal fin differs somewhat from that of other FLATFISHES. Starting just above the upper eye, it remains short until it passes above base of pectoral fin, runs up to a point and recedes, almost forming a triangle, then continues evenly short again to caudal peduncle. Anal fin follows same pattern giving diamond shape to fish. Lateral line forming high arch over pectoral fin; scales narrow and smooth; snout pointed; caudal fin slightly furcate; maxillary extending to point about middle of lower eye; no spine before anal fin. SIZE: Females up to 500 lbs. and over 8½ ft.; males up to 50 lbs. and 4½ ft. COLOR: Brown, often with pale blotches on eye side; white on blind side. RANGE: Occurs Pt. Arena, California, to Aleutian Islands in moderately deep to deep water, becoming increasingly abundant toward northern end of range. Larger individuals along edges of offshore banks at 10 to 100 fathoms. BAIT & TACKLE: Heavy tackle is required at this depth; 4/0 to 6/0 hook; large stripbait or whole fresh-frozen sardine, herring, or squid. Fish weighing up to 40 pounds (sometimes larger) occur in very shallow water during spring and summer months, where they are taken on light tackle in same manner as CALIFORNIA HALIBUT; hook No. 1 to 2/0; small stripbait, whole anchovy, shrimp, or other fresh or live-bait fishes. From surf, docks, piers, and boats, will sometimes take bright lures. COMMENT: Spawning takes place below 200-fathom level. One large female may produce two and a half million eggs.

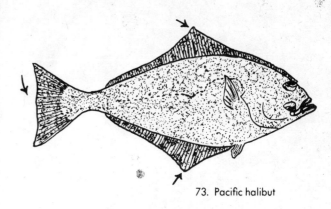

73. Pacific halibut

74. Slender sole
Lyopsetta exilis

NAMES: ROUGH SOLE, SLENDER FLOUNDER. DESCRIPTION: Dextral. Very slender body; head narrow, pointed; large, rough scales on both sides of body; slight arch at front of lateral line; pectoral fin much shorter than head; the short maxillary extending to middle of eye, and the rough scales on the blind side, distinguish this species from *Atheresthes stomias,* which it otherwise resembles. SIZE: Up to 1 ft. COLOR: Light brown; dark spots on edge of scales; pelvic fins yellowish; others dusky; blind side often orange or yellowish. RANGE: Occurs Ensenada to Alaska in moderately deep water near rocky areas. Shallow water north of California. Abundant north of Columbia River. BAIT & TACKLE: Taken on ghost shrimp, strips of fish or squid. Hook No. 2 or 1.

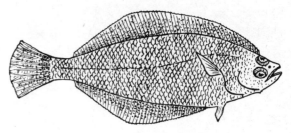

74. Slender sole

75. Petrale sole
Eopsetta jordani

NAMES: CALIFORNIA SOLE, ENGLISH SOLE, JORDAN'S FLOUNDER, BRILL. DESCRIPTION: Dextral. Small scales; large head and mouth; slight arch at front of lateral line; maxillary extending to point midway lower eye; scales on blind side very smooth. SIZE: Up to 20 in. COLOR: Olive brown; dusky blotches on dorsal and anal fins. RANGE: Occurs Ensenada to Alaska. Abundant north of Monterey. BAIT & TACKLE: Comes in shallow water during summer months where it can be caught with a wide variety of baits, such as ghost shrimp, stripbait, fresh or frozen anchovies, crustaceans and clams. Hook No. 1. COMMENT: An excellent food fish. Is particularly prized by Chinese for "hom yee" (salt fish). Mexicans call it "PETRALES,''meaning rocky. The name *"jordani"* is in honor of Dr. David Starr Jordan.

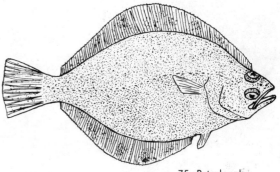

75. Petrale sole

76. Sand sole
Psettichthys melanostictus

NAMES: FRINGE SOLE, SANDDAB, SPOTTED FLOUNDER. DESCRIPTION: Dextral. Differing from other FLATFISHES in that the first few rays of the dorsal fin stand out unattached to each other except near the base and are more than twice the length of the eye. Caudal peduncle short and deep; pectoral fin much shorter than head; small branch to lateral line; eyes small; maxillary reaching back below middle of lower eye. SIZE: Up to 20 in. COLOR: Grayish brown to light green, covered with blackish specks or small spots on eye side. RANGE: Occurs Pt. Conception to Sitka, Alaska, on sandy bottoms in deep water, except during summer months when it comes into moderately shallow water. Abundant in northern part of range. BAIT & TACKLE: Taken on small live bait, stripbait, rock worms, crustaceans, and mollusks. Hook No. 1. COMMENT: A highly prized food fish.

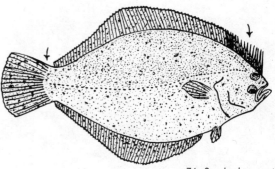

76. Sand sole

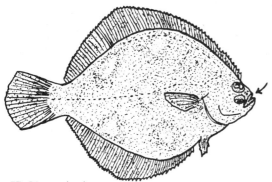

77. Diamond turbot

77. Diamond turbot *Hypsopsetta guttulata*

NAMES: DIAMOND FLOUNDER, HALIBUT, SOLE. DESCRIPTION: Dextral. Scales extending out onto fin rays on eye side. The depth of the body measuring half that of full length, including caudal fin. Very small mouth; pectoral fin shorter than head; no high ridge between eyes; lateral line with a long branch running along base of dorsal fin; maxillary extending to forepart of eye. SIZE: Up to 18 in. and to 4 lbs. COLOR: Dark brown with lighter, bluish blotches. RANGE: Occurs Cape Mendocino to Cape San Lucas and into Gulf of California in shallow water. Most abundant TURBOT found in southern backwaters. BAIT & TACKLE: Taken on small live bait, mussels, clams, stripbait, and small crustaceans. Same technique and gear as for small CALIFORNIA HALIBUT. Hook No. 2.

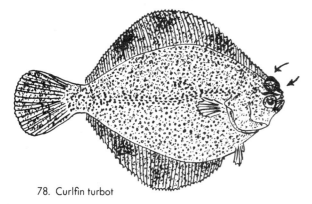

78. Curlfin turbot

78. Curlfin turbot *Pleuronichthys decurrens*

NAMES: CALIFORNIA TURBOT, CURLFIN SOLE, SANDDAB. DESCRIPTION: Dextral. The deep head, oval body and high spreading dorsal and anal fins, forming overall disk-shape; nine to twelve of dorsal rays beginning on blind side at point equal to corner of mouth; large, protruding eyes close to end of snout, with a bony ridge between them—a definite blunt spine at either end; lateral line with an upper branch along base of dorsal fin extending half the length of body; very small mouth; well separated scales imbedded in tough skin. SIZE: Up to 12 in. COLOR: Yellowish brown with grayish-brown blotches on body, very dark on fins. Differing from *P. coenosus* and *P. verticalis* in having no large black spot on lateral line. RANGE: Occurs Pt. Conception to British Columbia in moderately deep to shallow water. Most abundant TURBOT found in northern California. BAIT & TACKLE: Taken on stripbait, meat of shellfish, and crustaceans if kept in motion. Hook No. 2.

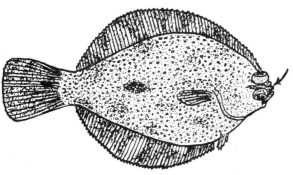

79. Hornyhead turbot

79. Hornyhead turbot *Pleuronichthys verticalis*

NAMES: SHARPRIDGE FLOUNDER, SANDDAB. DESCRIPTION: Dextral. Deeply imbedded scales, tough skin; eyes separated by high, spiny, very sharp ridge, with two sharp spines at front and one at back end, spine above lower eye extending over mouth; dorsal fin not extending past eye; first five rays of dorsal fin on blind side; branch of lateral line running from head along base of dorsal fin; no teeth on eye side; caudal peduncle deep; mouth small, maxillary extending only to front of lower eye. SIZE: Up to 10 in. COLOR: Chocolate brown with blotches of lighter brown and gray; dark blotch on lateral line; fins gray with irregular dark or black mottlings. RANGE: Occurs Pt. Reyes to Cape San Lucas and in Gulf of California in moderately shallow water. Abundant south of San Diego. BAIT & TACKLE: Taken on stripbait, shrimp, and strips of squid. Hook No. 2.

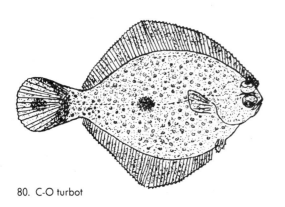

80. C-O turbot

80. C-O turbot *Pleuronichthys coenosus*

NAMES: MOTTLED TURBOT, POPEYE SOLE, C-O SOLE. DESCRIPTION: Dextral. High dorsal and anal fins; first five or six rays of dorsal on blind side, not extending past eye; body ovate; eyes large and protruding, separated by a high, sharp, bony ridge; one bony, blunt spine near rear edge of eyes pointing downward; lateral line with branch along base of dorsal fin; mouth small; snout short; lips thick; scales deeply imbedded, barely touching each other. SIZE: Up to 14 in. COLOR: Dark brown to black; a black spot about size of eye on middle of lateral line; dark spot and bar sometimes present on caudal fin. RANGE: Occurs Alaska to San Quintin Bay, mainly in deep water but small individuals occasionally are taken in bays and backwaters during summer months. Fairly abundant Washington and British Columbia. BAIT & TACKLE: Bits of shrimp, squid, stripbait, sea worms, or fresh-dead bait, kept moving. Hook No. 1 or 1/0.

81. Spotted turbot
Pleuronichthys ritteri

DESCRIPTION: Dextral. Large, protruding eyes separated by low, bony ridge with two or more blunt, bony protuberances at front end and one at hind end pointed downward; dorsal with five or more rays on blind side; lateral line running to upper eye before turning to branch up. **SIZE:** Up to 9 in. **COLOR:** Grayish brown; light spots about head and body; two or three large dark spots on back, one near base of dorsal, another on or near lateral line, the third sometimes above base of anal fin; fins mottled. **RANGE:** Occurs principally in and near San Diego Bay. **BAIT & TACKLE:** Taken on strips of fish and very small live bait when tail-hooked. Hook No. 2 to 4.

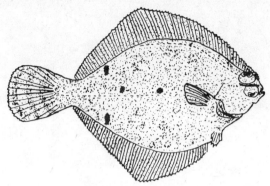

81. Spotted turbot

82. Butter sole
Isopsetta isolepis

NAMES: SCALY-FIN SOLE, SCALY-FIN FLOUNDER, ROCK SOLE, BELLINGHAM SOLE. **DESCRIPTION:** Dextral. Body covered with very rough scales, extending up on fins on eye side; small eyes, separated by narrow, flat, scaly area; slight arch at front of lateral line, a branch of which runs along front part of dorsal base; teeth on blind side; mouth small. **SIZE:** Up to 18 in. **COLOR:** Gray, mottled with yellowish or green; fins sometimes tipped with yellow. **RANGE:** Occurs Pt. Conception to Alaska in moderately deep water near mouth of streams over silt and sandy bottoms. Abundant in Washington and British Columbia. **BAIT & TACKLE:** Taken in same manner as C-O TURBOT. Hook No. 1 or 1/0.

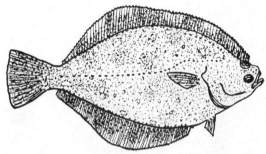

82. Butter sole

83. English sole
Parophrys vetulus

NAMES: SHARPNOSE SOLE, LEMON SOLE, COMMON SOLE, CALIFORNIA SOLE, POINTED NOSE SOLE. **DESCRIPTION:** Dextral. Very pointed head; slender body; teeth on blind side of lower jaw; eyes large, separated by narrow, high ridge; a long branch of lateral line along dorsal fin base. **SIZE:** Up to 21 in. **COLOR:** Yellowish brown; dorsal and anal fins tipped with dark; yellowish to white on blind side. **RANGE:** Occurs Ensenada to Alaska over sandy or muddy bottoms. Comes into moderately shallow water during summer months north of Pt. Arena. Abundant in northern region. **BAIT & TACKLE:** Taken in rather deep water on ghost shrimp, fresh stripbait, clam siphons, rock worms, and small crabs. Hook No. 1 or 2. **COMMENT:** Rated as most delicately flavored of all FLATFISHES.

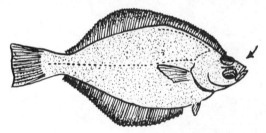

83. English sole

84. Rock sole
Lepidopsetta bilineata

NAMES: GRAVEL SOLE, DOUBLE-LINE SOLE, ROUGH-BACK SOLE. **DESCRIPTION:** Dextral. Abrupt arch at front of lateral line, a short branch of which runs along base of dorsal fin; dorsal fin beginning in front of upper eye; eyes separated by flat, scaly area; body half as wide as long if fins not included; scales rough on eye side. **SIZE:** Up to 18 in. **COLOR:** Dark brown with lighter brown spots and mottlings; irregular dark streaks on dorsal, anal, and caudal fins; blind side sometimes reddish or yellowish. **RANGE:** Occurs Pt. Conception to Arctic in shallow water near eel-grass beds and in gravelly surfs. Abundant north of Coos Bay. **BAIT & TACKLE:** Taken same manner as other small FLATFISHES on ghost shrimp, crabs, rock worms, clam siphons. Hook No. 4 to 1. Small individuals taken in backwaters on small lures.

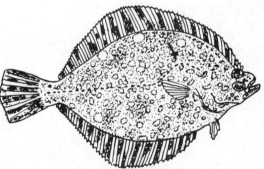

84. Rock sole

85. Dover sole
Microstomus pacificus

NAMES: SLIPPERY SOLE, RUBBER SOLE, CHINESE SOLE, SLIME SOLE, SMEAR DAB, LEMON SOLE. **DESCRIPTION:** Dextral. Distinguished by the very slippery mucous secretion over body, and by the black or very dark brown fins. Females sometimes only tipped with these colors. Teeth only on blind side, closely set; body slender; lower eye slightly in advance of upper; gill opening extending barely above pectoral base; lateral line curving slightly over pectoral; mouth small; caudal peduncle short; maxillary barely reaching front of eye. **SIZE:** Up to 24 in. **COLOR:** Greatly variable, from blackish to many shades of brown and greenish yellow, often mottled with yellow or green; dark on blind side varying in density. Males usually darker than females. Occasional individual found with dull red blotches. **RANGE:** Occurs Pt. Conception to Arctic. Abundant north of Pt. Arena. **BAIT & TACKLE:** Taken at 75 fathoms and in moderately shallow water near mouth of streams during summer months on ghost shrimp or stripbait kept in motion near bottom. Hook No. 1.

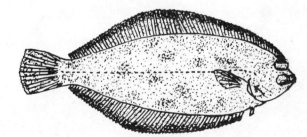

85. Dover sole

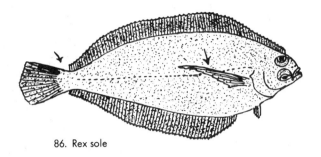

86. Rex sole

86. Rex sole
Glyptocephalus zachirus

NAMES: WITCH SOLE, LONG-FINNED SOLE. DESCRIPTION: Dextral. The very long; slender pectoral fin on the eye side being longer than the head, the short caudal peduncle and the bulging, rounded snout distinguish the REX from other FLAT-FISHES. Body slender and smooth; lateral line almost straight; mouth very small; maxillary extending back under front of lower eye. SIZE: Up to 1½ ft. COLOR: Light brown; dark brown to dusky on fins. RANGE: Occurs Pt. Dume to Aleutians. Seldom taken south of Monterey. Moderately deep to deep water. Abundant north of Pt. Arena. BAIT & TACKLE: Shrimp, ghost shrimp, squid, or stripbait. Hook No. 1 or 1/0.

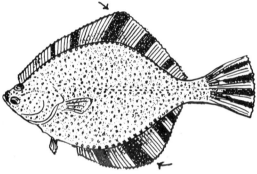

87. Starry flounder

87. Starry flounder
Platichthys stellatus

NAMES: GREAT FLOUNDER, ROUGH-JACKET, GRINDSTONE FLOUNDER, EMERY FLOUNDER, FLOUNDER. DESCRIPTION: Dextral or sinistral. Readily distinguished by the alternating orange and black stripes on fins. Eyes small; slight arch to lateral line with no accessory branch; rough, spinous plates scattered over body, formed of small scales. SIZE: Up to 3 ft. COLOR: Dark brown with orange and black stripes on dorsal, anal and caudal fins. RANGE: Occurs Ensenada to Arctic. BAIT & TACKLE: Taken by anglers in backwaters and around mouth of streams preferably on fresh stripbait, especially eelpout and sculpin, ghost shrimp, clam siphons, mollusks and small fishes, but will take almost any kind of bait if kept moving. Hook No. 2 to 1/0. Same gear and technique as for CALIFORNIA HALIBUT. COMMENT: Caught year round. Most abundant of all the FLATFISHES occuring in northern bays. The young ascend fresh-water streams for some distance. About 60 per cent of this species are sinistral (left-eyed). Other members of this family are dextral.

ᏯᏯ *SPINY-RAYED FISHES* ᏯᏯ

SUPERORDER: *Acanthopterygii*—Spiny-rayed Fishes. Having spiny rays in the fins or having descended from spiny-rayed fishes. ORDER: *Percomorphi*. SUBORDER: *Perchesoces*.

Most of the fishes in this order have dorsal and anal fins that contain both spiny and soft fin rays. Pelvic fins (may be absent) with 1 hard spine and less than 6 soft fin rays. Anal fin having from 1 to 3 hard spines followed by a varying number of soft fin rays. Anterior portion of dorsal fin having a number of hard spines followed by soft fin rays posteriorly. Caudal fin having less than 18 soft rays.

NOTE: The hard spines in the dorsal and anal fins are indicated by Roman numerals; the soft rays, in Arabic numerals. For example: 1st d. V; 2nd d. I & 9; a. I & 22, indicate that the first section of the dorsal fin has five hard spines; the second section of the dorsal fin, one hard spine and nine soft rays; the anal fin, one hard spine and twenty-two soft rays.

FAMILY: *Atherinidae*—Silversides.

Having two dorsal fins; the first with weak spines, the second with soft fin rays, differing from the TRUE SMELTS which have a single, soft-rayed dorsal and a small dorsal adipose fin. Differing also from the family, Osmeridae, by the absence of a lateral line.

88. (California) grunion
Leuresthes tenuis

NAMES: SMELT, LITTLE SMELT, LEAST SMELT. DESCRIPTION: 1st d. V; 2nd d. 1 & 9; a. I & 22. Distinguished by the very slender body; the small first dorsal fin containing only five flexible spines and situated slightly back of point above the anus. Absence of teeth; upper jaw greatly extendible when lower jaw pulled down. SIZE: Up to 7 in. COLOR: Back ashy green down to the thin blue and silver lateral stripe, belly silver. RANGE: Occurs on sandy beaches, Monterey to San Juanico Bay. Abundant south of Ventura. COMMENT: Captured by hand when they come in on extremely high, summer evening tides to deposit their eggs. Occurring March to September on full and dark moons. By a remarkable arrangement of nature, some of the eggs ripen in the female exactly at these high tides which repeat every two weeks of the season.

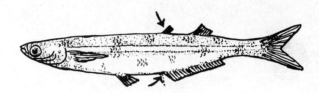

88. (California) grunion

89. Jacksmelt
Atherinopsis californiensis

NAMES: SILVERSIDE, HORSE SMELT, BLUE SMELT, CALIFORNIA SMELT. DESCRIPTION: 1st d. IX; 2nd d. I & 12; a. I & 23. Distinguished by the small scales; large body; presence of teeth that are not forked; jaws equal; first dorsal situated well in advance of anus. Has comparatively smaller pectoral than the TOPSMELT. SIZE: Up to 18 in. COLOR: Greenish above with bluish tinge; silver belly; blue lateral stripe with lighter blue upper border. RANGE: Occurs Puget Sound to Magdalena Bay. Abundant Eureka to Ensenada. Taken year round, about piers and kelp beds. BAIT & TACKLE: Small pieces of mackerel, anchovy or other fish, clams, mussels, and pile worms. Hook No. 3. COMMENT: The possibility of two races of this species being separated by Pt. Conception may explain the size difference. Those taken south of the Point seldom exceed 13 inches in length.

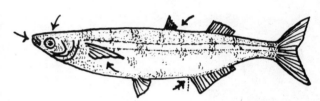

89. Jacksmelt

90. Topsmelt
Atherinops affinis

NAMES: BAY SMELT, RAINBOW SMELT, PANZAROTTI, SILVERSIDE, CAPRON, JACK. DESCRIPTION: 1st d. VI; 2nd d. I & 11; a. I & 22. Distinguished by the comparatively longer pectoral fin which is longer than the head; upper jaw slightly projecting; large eyes; first dorsal situated slightly in advance of anus; minute, forked teeth; snout comparatively blunt. SIZE: Up to 12 in.; average 7 in. COLOR: Greenish-gray back above a thin, bright blue lateral stripe; silver below. RANGE: Occurs from the mouth of the Columbia River to Magdalena Bay close to shore in large schools. Abundant south of Pt. Arena. BAIT & TACKLE: Taken with snag line after chumming with pieces of fish or on No. 5 hook baited with bits of fish or mussel.

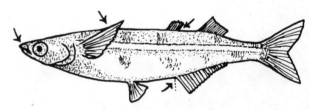

90. Topsmelt

FAMILY: *Mugilidae*—Mullets.

91. (Striped) mullet
Mugil cephalus

NAME: MULLET. DESCRIPTION: 1st d. IV; 2nd d. I & 8; a. II or III & 8. Two well-separated dorsal fins, the first containing four spines and situated in advance of the middle of the body; broad, convex area between eyes; very large scales; small mouth; small teeth; highly set pectoral fin; absence of lateral line; short snout. SIZE: Up to 2½ ft. COLOR: Gradually blending from grayish-green back to silver belly; darkly tipped scales forming parallel lines along body. RANGE: Occurs San Francisco Bay to tropics in mouth of streams, bays, and sloughs. Abundant San Diego south. BAIT & TACKLE: Can be caught where tide flows over sandy shoals with cotton, flour, and banana made into small doughballs (try adding garlic). No. 10 hook. Some claim to have taken them on flies in irrigation canals in floating foam.

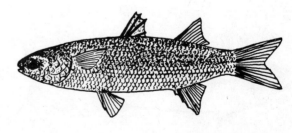

91. (Striped) mullet

92. (California) barracuda *Sphyraena argentea*

NAMES: BARRACUDA, SCOOTER, LOG BARRACUDA, SCOOT, SNAKE, BARRY. DESCRIPTION: 1st d. V; 2nd d. I & 9; a. I & 8. The length of the BARRACUDA and its sharp, pointed head distinguish it from other Pacific fishes. Strong, fang-like teeth; sharp, projecting lower jaw; row of raised, well-set scales along lateral line. SIZE: Up to 4½ ft. and 12 lbs. COLOR: Dark gray back, silver below lateral line; yellow caudal fin. RANGE: Alaska to Magdalena Bay. Abundant along west coast of Baja California and up to Pt. Conception from April to December, appearing for a month or so above Pt. Conception. BAIT & TACKLE: Taken on sardine, anchovies, or stripbait. At times prefers mixed, colored feathers to all other lures or baits. No. 2 to 1/0 short-shank hook. COMMENT: A very popular fish with open-ocean anglers. Good for a quick, hard fight when taken with light tackle.

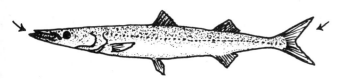

92. (California) barracuda

SUBORDER: *Scombroidea*—Mackerel-like Fishes. A group of related fishes having symmetrical streamlined bodies tapering to a very small caudal peduncle with a widely forked caudal fin. FAMILY: *Cybiidae*—Spanish mackerels.

93. Sierra grande *Scomberomorus sierra*

NAME: SPANISH MACKEREL. DESCRIPTION: 1st d. XVII; 2nd d. 15; a. 11 & 15. Four to six rows of yellow, orange, or bluish spots along each side of body; jaws equal; large teeth; lateral line wavy; eight or nine finlets following second dorsal and anal fins; slender body; first dorsal fin low. Has less than 13 gill rakers below gill arch while *S. concolor* has more than 14. SIZE: Up to 5½ ft. and 14 lbs. COLOR: Dark, metallic blue back fading to silver belly; first dorsal black; anal fin whitish; underside of pectoral black; front, yellowish with blackish border; caudal fin black. RANGE: Abundant along coast of Baja California and in Sea of Cortez. Reported north of Ensenada but its occurrence north of San Quintin Bay is doubtful. Was most likely MONTEREY SIERRA, *S. concolor*. Both species were nearly depleted by over-netting in 1967 but a 5 year moratorium gave them a partial comeback by 1975.

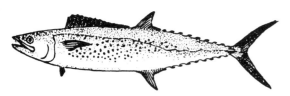

93. Sierra grande

94. Monterey sierra *Scomberomorus concolor*

NAMES: The MACKEREL JACK, *Trachurus symmetricus*, is often mistakenly called "SPANISH MACKEREL". DESCRIPTION: 1st d. XVII; 2nd d. 16; a. II & 16. Eight or nine finlets following rayed dorsal and anal fins. SIZE: Up to 30 in. COLOR: Some of them have steel blue on back with no streaks or spots, but majority are dark with two rows of brown spots on sides. Otherwise resembles SIERRA. RANGE: Was very abundant in Monterey Bay in the Eighties but disappeared completely. For many years few have been caught north of Ensenada. Abundant north end of Cortez. BAIT & TACKLE: Taken on various small lures, small white feather (¼-oz) best, when trolled at 8 to 10 knots on surface. Live bait, stripbait and shrimp. Hook No. 1/0. A highly rated game fish. COMMENT: This fish is considered among the world's most palatable food fishes.

94. (Monterey) sierra

95. (California) bonito *Sarda lineolata*

NAMES: OCEAN BONITO, STRIPED TUNA, SKIPJACK. DESCRIPTION: 1st d. XVIII; 2nd d. I & 12; a. II & 11 or 12. Ten or eleven narrow, black or blackish stripes extending obliquely along the back; very short interspace between the first and second dorsal fins; eight or nine finlets following second dorsal and six or seven following anal fin; soft keel on each side of caudal peduncle. SIZE: Up to 40 in. and 25 lbs. COLOR: Dark greenish-blue to violet back with the darker stripes fading to silver belly, with an overall metallic luster. RANGE: Occurs from Vancouver Island to tropics, year round. Not common north of Pt. Conception. BAIT & TACKLE: Taken on live bait; anchovies, sardine, squid, or strip of mackerel kept moving; occasionally on hard lures (chrome) or feathers. Hook No. 1 or 1/0 to 2. Small BONITO come close to shore in schools. COMMENT: Generally preferred as baked, broiled, or smoked fish.

95. (California) bonito

96. (Pacific) mackerel *Pneumatophorus japonicus*

NAMES: GREENBACK, GREEN-JACK, ZEBRA, STRIPED MACKEREL, AMERICAN MACK-EREL. **DESCRIPTION**: 1st d. VIII to X; 2nd d. I & 12; a. II & 11. Distinguished by the long inter-space between the dorsal fins, the first containing eight to ten long spines; twenty-five to thirty blackish to dark green irregular bars and spots zig-zagging across back, followed by irregular spots on sides; lateral line wavy; absence of keels on caudal peduncle; five to six finlets following second dorsal and anal fins; very small, loose scales covering body. **SIZE**: Up to 25 in. and 6¼ lbs. **COLOR**: Metallic green to bluish back (the bars darker), gradually fading to silver belly. **RANGE**: Occurs Alaska to tropics. Most abundant from Santa Barbara to Ensenada. July to November plentiful in shallow water, scarce February through May. **BAIT & TACKLE**: Eats almost anything, prefers strips of fresh sardine, mackerel or its "straw-berry" (pyloric caeca), live anchovy or other small fishes; also taken on small lures. Should be bled as soon as taken and kept damp and cool. Hook No. 1. **COMMENT**: Previously not respected, now becoming a prized game fish. Cooked in same man-ner as BONITO. Very prolific—a single female may produce as many as half a million eggs which are pelagic and hatch within three days.

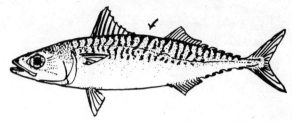

96. (Pacific) mackerel

97. (Oceanic) skipjack *Katsuwonus pelamis*

NAMES: SKIPJACK, OCEAN BONITO, TUNA, STRIPED TUNA, SKIPPY. **DESCRIPTION**: 1st d. XV or XVI; 2nd d. I and 13 to 15; a. II & 12 to 14. Four or five longitudinal, dark stripes along lower part of body, none on back; absence of scales except in the area of the corselet (around and above pectoral fin); anus longitudinal slit, not rounded as in TUNAS; small caudal peduncle with low keel on either side; small triangular pectoral fin, shorter than length of head; seven to eight finlets following dorsal fin; six to eight, usually seven, following anal fin; angle of the preopercle rounded; absence of an air bladder. **SIZE**: Up to 3 ft. and 43 lbs; rarely over 2 ft. **COLOR**: Dark to light metallic blue back fading to silver belly, the stripes varying from dark blue to brownish. **RANGE**: Occurs Vancouver Island to the Galapagos. Abundant south of Ensenada. Rare north of Pt. Conception. Comes to our coast when water becomes warm, August to November. Swims at about 25 miles per hour. **BAIT & TACKLE**: Takes lure better than live bait when chumming is done prop-erly. Feather, bone, or chrome lures. Troll at 8 miles per hour. Anchovies, sardine, smelt, squid and stripbait. Hook No. 1 or 1/0, when live bait is used. **COMMENT**: Sometimes found in company with YELLOWFIN TUNA. Another species, BARRI-LETE SKIPJACK, *Euthynnus lineatus,* is miscalled "BONITO" because of dark stripes along back. Has dark flesh. **RANGE**: Santa Barbara (in warm years) to tropics; superabundant in the Sea of Cortez.

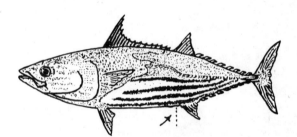

97. (Oceanic) skipjack

In the TUNAS within our range the body is rounded, the forepart deep, tapering sharply from the second dorsal and anal fins to a very small caudal peduncle, with keel on sides. Seven to nine finlets follow the second dorsal and anal fins, rarely more than eight. The head is conical; caudal fin lunate; lateral line almost straight, curving upward from above the base of the pectoral fin.

The color given for each species must be considered as the most prevailing since a like color may appear on any one of the species. The characters in an occa-sional individual may sometimes resemble those in another species more closely than its own.

The major identifying characters occurring in the various species are in the length of the pectoral fin; the shape of the anus; and the outline of the posterior margin of the opercle. In separating the BLUEFIN from the YELLOWFIN all three char-acters should be carefully studied and compared.

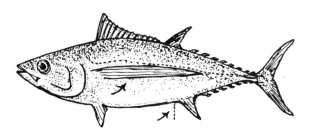

98. Albacore

98. Albacore   *Thunnus alalunga*

NAMES: LONG-FINNED TUNA, ABREGO. **DESCRIPTION:** 1st d. XIII or XIV; 2nd d. II & 13 or 14; a. II & 12 or 13. Distinguished from other TUNAS by the exceptionally long pectoral fins which reach back to or past the anal fin. Shape of anus, round; angle of preopercle, square; seven or eight finlets following anal and second dorsal fins. **SIZE:** Up to 4 ft. and 104 lbs. **COLOR:** Dark steel-blue back fading to silver belly (not specific); flesh white. **RANGE:** Occurs Alaska to Cedros Island. South of Pt. Conception comes within 3 or 4 miles offshore; at Eureka, 15 to 20; Coos Bay, 20 to 25. Fluctuating north of Columbia River. Abundant along whole range. Best months July to October. Seldom near shore, but usually in the marginal line between the green shore waters and the deep blue, open-ocean water in temperatures 58° to 60° F. **BAIT & TACKLE:** Taken on anchovies, sardine, herring, saurie, and other small live bait. Hook No. 1/0 or 2/0 on 4 foot, 32-pound-test dark wire leader. For trolling, light feather first choice. Will take bone or chrome jig at 8 to 10 miles per hour.

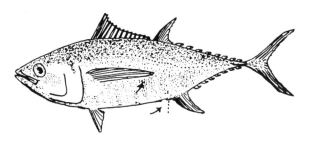

99. Yellowfin tuna

99. Yellowfin tuna   *Neothunnus macropterus*

NAME: YELLOW-FINNED ALBACORE. **DESCRIPTION:** 1st d. XII to XIV; 2nd d. II & 12 to 14; a. II & 12 or 13. The pectoral fin reaching back to base of second dorsal fin but not to anal fin; oval or tear-drop shape of the anus; angle of the preopercle, square; eight or nine finlets following second dorsal fin, seven or eight following anal fin. **SIZE:** Up to 450 lbs. **COLOR:** Metallic dark blue back fading to light-grayish belly; fins yellow; an indistinct gold stripe running to caudal (not specific). Fades soon after taking from water. **RANGE:** Occurs Santa Barbara Channel to tropics, June to August along coast of Baja California, August to November around islands north of border. Not common north of border. Fluctuating according to temperature of water (favors warm water). **BAIT & TACKLE:** Same gear, bait, and method as for large BLUEFIN. Hook No. 1 or 1/0 for immature fish; No. 6/0 to 8/0 for large individuals.

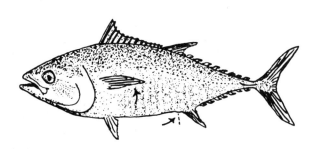

100. (California) bluefin tuna

100. (California) bluefin tuna   *Thunnus saliens*

NAMES: LEAPING TUNA, GREAT TUNNIE, TUNNY. **DESCRIPTION:** 1st d. XIII or XIV; 2nd d. II & 13; a. II & 12 or 13. The short pectoral fin which reaches only to the eleventh or twelfth dorsal spine; the angle of the preopercle, rounded; shape of anus, round; eight or nine finlets following second dorsal, seven or eight following anal fin. **SIZE:** Up to 250 lbs. Pacific Coast; 1600 lbs. Atlantic species. **COLOR:** Deep iridescent-blue back with small, silvery spots on metallic-silver belly; finlets yellowish; other fins dusky tinged with yellowish green (not specific). The flesh grayish, at times pinkish. **RANGE:** Occurs Oregon to Guadalupe Island some miles at sea and near islands. Seldom taken north of Pt. Conception. Abundant south of Santa Barbara Island. Is never taken when school of KILLER WHALES is near. **BAIT & TACKLE:** Kite fishing (originated by George Farnsworth in 1909, with flyingfish as bait) is still used in pursuit of the large TUNAS. Can be taken on sardine, small mackerel, or anchovy. Small individuals taken on feather, bone, and chrome jigs. Hook No. 4 to 1; 5-foot, 27-pound-test leader; no sinker or swivel. May to December; July and August best. Occasionally located at depth of about 100 feet where they seem to ignore size of hook and gear. **COMMENT:** Another species, the BIG-EYED TUNA, *Parathunnus mebachi,* found near Guadalupe Island, is distinguished by the very large eye, the albacore-like pectoral fin, and in having an oval anus.

FAMILY: *Istiophoridae*–Billfishes.

101. Striped marlin   *Makaira audax*

NAMES: PACIFIC MARLIN, SWORDFISH, SPEARFISH, SPIKEFISH, SAILFISH. **DESCRIPTION:** Upper jaw extended to form a round spear in contrast to the longer, flat, sword-like extension of the upper jaw of the SWORDFISH. Long dorsal fin extending almost full length of back; short second dorsal; presence of pelvic fins; two small keels on each side of caudal peduncle; long, narrow imbedded scales. **SIZE:** Up to 13½ ft. and 692 lbs. **COLOR:** Purplish-blue back fading to silver belly; light blue bars extending down from back and on to belly; dorsal fin violet with brighter blue spots; pectoral fin dark gray edged with black. **RANGE:** Occurs Santa Cruz Island to Manzanillo, Mexico. Taken off California Coast May to November—September best. **BAIT & TACKLE:** Taken on moderately light to heavy tackle. Attracted by teaser lure when baited with mullet, flyingfish, mackerel or sardine. Hook No. 6/0 to 9/0. **COMMENT:** A furious fighter, capable of leaps above the surface and thousand-foot runs.

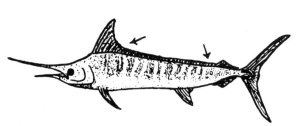

101. Striped marlin

FAMILY: *Xiphiidae*—Swordfishes.

102. Swordfish — *Xiphias gladius*

NAME: BROADBILL SWORDFISH. **DESCRIPTION:** Upper jaw greatly extended to form a sharp-edged flat sword, differing in this respect from the MARLINS and PACIFIC SAILFISH, *Istiophorus greyi,* which is encountered south of our range. Tall, curved dorsal fin extending less than one third length of back; single wide keel on sides of caudal peduncle; absence of pelvic fins; absence of scales. **SIZE:** Up to 1000 lbs.; under 600 lbs. So. Calif. **COLOR:** Purplish back fading to silver-gray belly; crossbars absent. **RANGE:** Occurs Santa Cruz Island to tropics. Taken from June to November out around offshore islands. **BAIT & TACKLE:** Flyingfish, mackerel, small barracuda slowly trolled on surface. Live bait effective south of Mexican border. Hook No. 9/0 to 12/0; 9/0 reel of 500-yard capacity; 70-pound-test line. **COMMENT:** Not plentiful within our range.

102. Swordfish

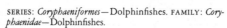

SERIES: *Coryphaeniformes*—Dolphinfishes. FAMILY: *Coryphaenidae*—Dolphinfishes.

103. (Common) dolphinfish — *Coryphaena hippurus*

DESCRIPTION: Single dorsal fin extending from top of the short head almost to caudal fin; mouth flush with the high, straight forehead, the male forehead more bulging than that of the female; anal fin extending half the length of body. **SIZE:** Up to 6 ft. and 82 lbs. **COLOR:** Brilliant blue or green above, with bright blue dots; this fish is capable of 11 body color changes. **RANGE:** Occurs in open sea, Canadian border to tropics. **BAIT & TACKLE:** Taken readily on live bait, flyingfish, and white feathers, knucklehead, and other rapid-trolled lures. Hook No. 1/0 to 4/0. **COMMENT:** This is not the porpoise-like mammal DOLPHIN, *Delphirus delphi.*

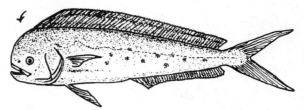

103. (Common) dolphinfish

SERIES: *Stromateiformes.* FAMILY: *Stromateidae*—Butterfishes.

104. (California) butterfish — *Palometa simillima*

MARKET NAME: POMPANO. Not a true POMPANO of the family Carangidae. **DESCRIPTION:** d. III & 45 to 47; a. III & 40 to 44. Deep compressed oval body; long dorsal and anal fins forming symmetrical pattern; long, pointed pectoral fin; absence of a pelvic fin; forepart of head rounded in profile; caudal peduncle short and slender; lateral line straight; deeply notched caudal fin. **SIZE:** Up to 11 in. **COLOR:** Iridescent-greenish to blue back fading to silver belly. **RANGE:** Occurs British Columbia to Magdalena Bay in bays and backwaters. More common Pt. Arena to San Diego. **BAIT & TACKLE:** Taken on small stripbait, bits of mussel, clam, and sea worms. In spring and early summer found in deeper water offshore, at which time bits of squid is best bait. Hook No. 6.

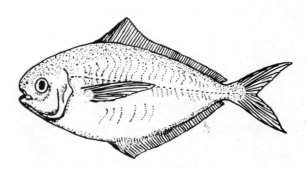

104. (California) butterfish

SERIES: *Carangiformes.* FAMILY: *Carangidae*—Jacks.

105. (California) yellowtail — *Seriola dorsalis*

NAMES: YELLOWTAIL, AMBERJACK. **DESCRIPTION:** 1st d. V or VI; 2nd d. I & 35 to 39; a. III & 21. Distinguished by the conspicuous bright, brassy to metallic, yellow lateral stripe extending from snout to caudal fin. Deeply forked caudal fin; slender caudal peduncle; first dorsal low, less than half the height of the second; second dorsal extending almost to caudal fin base; low keel on sides of caudal peduncle; short pectoral fin; pointed snout. **SIZE:** Up to 5 ft.; 80 lbs. **COLOR:** The bright, metallic blue to greenish back abruptly halted by the lateral stripe; belly silvery; caudal fin yellow. **RANGE:** Occurs in schools from Pt. Conception to Guadalupe Island. Best grounds around islands of Baja California and Gulf of California where they are taken year round. Appearing off southern California coast in large numbers about May, Catalina Island around June. **BAIT & TACKLE:** Sardine, anchovie, butterfish, smelt, other small fish, and squid. Often following school of fish very close to shore. When hungry will take lures, feather, jig or stripbait at fast troll. Hook No. 4 to 1 short-shank; 5-foot 32-pound-test wire leader. **COMMENT:** Gamy, hard strike, good for one terrific run, and a half dozen shorter ones.

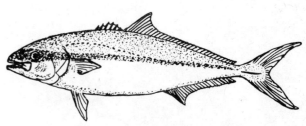

105. (California) yellowtail

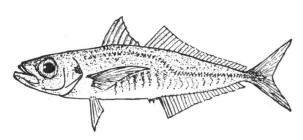

106. Mackerel jack

106. Mackerel jack — *Trachurus symmetricus*

NAMES: Market name JACK MACKEREL. HORSE MACKEREL, SPANISH MACKEREL. Is not closely related to the true MACKEREL family, Scombridae, or to the SPANISH MACKEREL family, Cybiidae. **DESCRIPTION:** 1st d. VIII; 2nd d. I & 31; a. III & 27. Short interspace between the two dorsal fins, first dorsal about the same height as the second; second dorsal and anal fins extending almost to caudal fin base; caudal fin deeply notched; spiny shields extending along lateral line forming ridge posteriorly; long pectoral fin; projecting lower jaw; snout blunt. **SIZE:** Up to 30 in. **COLOR:** Green to bluish with iridescent luster mottled with lighter on back becoming silvery on belly. **RANGE:** Occurs Pt. Arena to tropics, more abundant south of Pt. Conception. **BAIT & TACKLE:** Taken on small strips of anchovy, sardine, or bits of shrimp, 6 to 12 feet below surface. Hook No. 4. An excellent food fish. **COMMENT:** Another larger member of this family, the SCAD, *Decapterus hypodus,* occurring south of San Diego is abundant south of Guadalupe Island. Differs from MACKEREL JACK by having a single finlet following the dorsal and anal fins.

ᑲᕝᕕ BASSES ᑲᕝᕕ

SERIES: *Perciformes*—Perch-like Fishes. **FAMILY:** *Serranidae*—Basses. Having projecting lower jaw, ten or eleven spines in the dorsal fin; three spines in the anal fin; pectoral fins low on the body. In the author's conception the shapeliness of the head, body, and fins of these BASSES comprises the perfect, typical, fish form—a model by which all other forms in the class *Osteichthyes* could be compared.

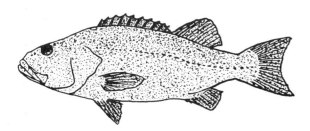

107. Striped bass

107. Striped bass — *Roccus saxatilis*

NAMES: ROCK BASS, ROCK FISH, STRIPER. **DESCRIPTION:** 1st d. IX; 2nd d. I & 12; a. II & 11. Distinguished by the seven or eight blackish, horizontal stripes on back and sides; small eyes; small pectoral fin; the two dorsal fins contiguous; caudal fin notched. **SIZE:** Up to 80 lbs. Average 10 lbs. or less. **COLOR:** Brassy-tinged greenish to blue back; silvery between the blackish stripes on sides; silver belly; fins pale. **RANGE:** Occurs Umpqua River, Oregon, to Dana Point, year round. More abundant Coos Bay to Monterey Bay. Migrating from open ocean to fresh water, seasonally. **BAIT & TACKLE:** Anchovies, stripbait, fresh sardine, herring, or shrimp. Hook No. 1 to 2/0. Will take lures in brackish waters. **COMMENT:** Introduced from Atlantic and planted in San Francisco Bay in 1879.

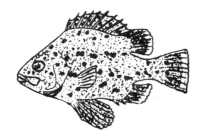

108. (California) black sea bass

108. (California) black sea bass — *Stereolepis gigas*

NAMES: CALIFORNIA JEWFISH, GIANT BASS, B.S. BASS. The BLACK ROCKFISH, *Sebastodes melanops,* is erroneously called BLACK SEA BASS. **DESCRIPTION:** d. XI & 9 to 11; a. III & 7 to 9. Dorsal fin continuous, deeply notched between spinous and soft-rayed sections; spines of the first dorsal less than half the length of the soft rays; pectoral fin comparatively small; body heavy, robust; head depressed; mouth large; area between eyes wide; caudal fin slightly furcate. **SIZE:** Up to 7½ ft.; 600 lbs. **COLOR:** Dark brown to black on back, lighter belly. **RANGE:** Occurs Farallon Islands to islands and banks off of Baja's west coast and Sea of Cortez. Caught on bottom near kelp beds sometimes fairly close to shore. **BAIT & TACKLE:** Taken on live barracuda, mackerel, sardine, mullet, or fillet sliced from either. Very heavy tackle required; 72-pound-test line; chain leader; hook No. 14/0. **COMMENT:** Liver said to be toxic during certain seasons.

The drawing of the young of the BLACK SEA BASS will illustrate the great difference in the body shapes between the young and the mature fish. The descriptions given in this volume, with few exceptions, are those of the mature fish. By comparison the total length of the adult is about 3 times the depth of the body. While the depth of the body of the young, at this stage of development, is almost equal to the length. The comparative fin sizes will also show the extreme differences.

109. Broomtail grouper
Mycteroperca xenarchus

NAMES: GARUPPA, GRAY BROOMTAIL, PINTO BROOMTAIL, SPOTTED BROOMTAIL.
DESCRIPTION: d. XI & 16 to 18; a. III & 11. Distinguished by the sawtoothed caudal fin. Dorsal fin continuous, not deeply notched between the spinous and soft-rayed sections; spines of first dorsal comparatively tall; soft rays of dorsal and anal fins longer and more numerous than in the BLACK SEA BASS which it otherwise resembles. SIZE: Up to 75 lbs. COLOR: Brownish to dark-bluish back fading to lighter belly; head, fins, and body covered with small, reddish-brown spots. These spots and colors are not to be depended upon for identifying this fish since unlike the leopard, it does change its spots, sometimes ridding itself of them entirely. A few years back there was thought to be three species of this BROOMTAIL, but later it was discovered to be a protean artist passing through three different phases: GRAY BROOMTAIL (without contrasting color or markings), PINTO BROOMTAIL (greenish body with dark oblong rings with light centers), and SPOTTED BROOMTAIL (with distinct round reddish spots). RANGE: South of San Quintin Bay, this fish is found in great abundance over rocky reefs. BAIT & TACKLE: Can be taken on stripbait, live-bait or lure trolled at 6 to 8 knots. Hook No. 4/0. COMMENT: Captured as far north as Catalina Island by fin divers.

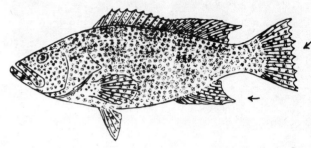

109. Broomtail grouper

110. Baya grouper
Mycteroperca jordani

NAME: GARUPPE DE BAYA. DESCRIPTION: d. XI & 17 to 19; a. III & 11. Back edge of caudal fin straight; dorsal fin continuous, spinous section low, incised; base of anal fin long; profile straight; scales comparatively small. SIZE: Up to 6 ft; 280 lbs. COLOR: Blackish to olive-gray back to light brown; light olive to yellowish belly; four series of dark, oblong, olive blotches along body (two other phases as in BROOMTAIL); sides of head with more or less indistinct, wavy, black streaks. As in the BROOMTAIL these markings are not specific. RANGE: Found as far north as Pt. Dume but is more abundant south of San Quintin Bay and in the Cortez. Seldom taken by anglers north of San Diego.

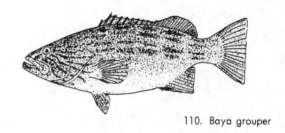

110. Baya grouper

111. Kelp bass
Paralabrax clathratus

NAMES: ROCK BASS, SAND BASS, CALICO BASS, BULL BASS, CABRILLA. DESCRIPTION: d. X & 13 or 14; a. III & 7 or 8. Single dorsal fin deeply notched between the sections; the third and fourth spines of about equal length and taller than the soft-rayed section; caudal fin straight; pectoral fin large. SIZE: Up to 20 in. COLOR: Dark gray or brownish on back; upper sides mottled with brownish blotches; underside tinged with yellow; fins yellowish. Markings less distinct in older fish. RANGE: Occurs San Francisco to Abreojos Pt. in and around kelp beds year round. May to October best. More abundant south of Pt. Conception. BAIT & TACKLE: Anchovies, queenfish, tommy croaker, shrimp, and squid; at times queenfish best bait. Will take lure if kept from tangling in kelp. Hook No. 1. Bottom and surface feeder. COMMENT: Not a migrating fish and should not be taken less than 12 inches. This limit is not to be applied to several small rockfish mistakenly called "bass" by party-boat crews.

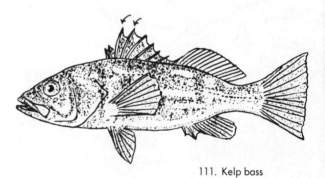

111. Kelp bass

112. Sand bass
Paralabrax nebulifer

NAMES: KELP BASS, JOHNNY VERDE, ROCK BASS. DESCRIPTION: d. X & 13 to 15; a. III & 7 or 8. Third spine of dorsal fin much longer than the fourth and twice the length of the second, differing in this respect from the KELP BASS; also the dorsal fin is not as deeply notched between the sections. Caudal fin straight; pectoral fin large. SIZE: Up to 22 in. COLOR: Dull gray with greenish tinge on back with irregular dark mottling and oblique bars; small, golden-brown spots on cheeks and snout; gray or whitish belly. Coloring fades in older fish. RANGE: Occurs Monterey to Magdalena Bay year round, on sandy bottoms near kelp beds and among rocks. Abundant south of Pt. Conception. BAIT & TACKLE: Taken on stripbait, live anchovies, queenfish, small sardine, tommy croaker, shrimp, and mussels. Usually feeds near bottom. Hook No. 1.

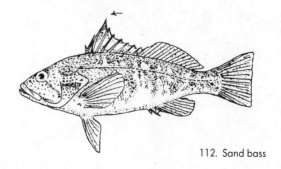

112. Sand bass

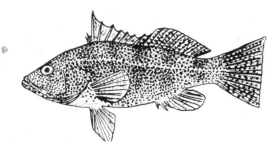

113. Spotted bass

113. Spotted bass — *Paralabrax maculatofasciatus*

NAMES: SPOTTED SAND BASS, SPOTTED CABRILLA, PINTA CABRILLA, ROCK BASS. **DESCRIPTION**: d. X & 13; a. III & 7. Differing from the KELP and SAND BASSES in being completely covered with reddish-brown spots. Third spine of dorsal fin longer than fourth; dorsal fin not deeply notched between sections; caudal fin straight; pectoral fin large. **SIZE**: Up to 18 in. **COLOR**: Gray, greenish-brown back gradually becoming white on belly; six or seven dusky bars down across sides; lips yellowish; spots as above. **RANGE**: Occurs Pt. Conception to Mazatlan in bays, sloughs, and stream entrances. More abundant south of San Diego. **BAIT & TACKLE**: Taken on strip-bait, clams, mussels, rock worms, shrimp, and small live bait. Hook No. 1 or 2.

FAMILY: *Xenichthyidae*—Salemas. The only member of this family found in California.

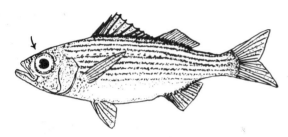

114. (California) salema

114. (California) salema — *Xenistius californiensis*

NAMES: BIG-EYE BASS, STRIPED BASS. **DESCRIPTION**: 1st d. XI; 2nd d. I & 12; a. III & 10. Distinguished by the lateral stripes and the very large eyes, being about one-third the length of the head. Shapely bass-like body; long, pointed pectoral fin; first and second dorsals barely separated; head and snout short. **SIZE**: Up to 12 in. **COLOR**: Three reddish stripes running parallel with and above lateral line, three or four below; bluish back; silver belly. **RANGE**: Occurs Monterey to Cape San Lucas. More common south of Dana Point. Abundant in Gulf of California. **BAIT & TACKLE**: Taken around kelp, piers, and jetties on stripbait, anchovies and other small live bait, shrimp, razorback and other clams. Hook No. 2.

FAMILY: *Haemulidae*—Grunts.

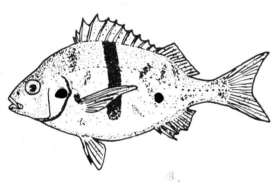

115. (California) sargo

115. (California) sargo — *Anisotremus davidsoni*

NAMES: BLUE BASS, PERCH, CHINA CROAKER. **DESCRIPTION**: d. XI or XII & 15; a. III & 10 or 11. Distinguished by the black band across back and sides. Body deep; small, thick-lipped mouth; fine, single-pointed teeth in jaws. **SIZE**: Up to 20 in. **COLOR**: Silver with grayish tinge on back; belly silver; dark blotches sometimes on head and dorsal surface; edge of opercle black; dark spot at base of pectoral fin. **RANGE**: Occurs Pt. Conception to Pt. Eugenia. **BAIT & TACKLE**: Taken during hot summer months on mussels and strips of fish. Hook No. 4.

⚬⚭ CROAKERS ⚬⚭

FAMILY: *Sciaenidae*—Croakers. Having a lateral line which extends back onto the caudal fin; straight caudal fin; two dorsal fins, the first usually triangular in shape. Members of this family produce a peculiar croaking sound, hence the name croaker. Inhabit waters over sand or mud, seldom over rocky bottoms.

116. Black croaker — *Cheilotrema saturnum*

NAMES: BLACK PERCH, BLACK BASS, BLUE BASS, CHINESE CROAKER, CHINAFIN CROAKER, SURF FISH. **DESCRIPTION**: 1st d. IX or X; 2nd d. I & 26 or 27; a. II & 7 or 8. Distinguished from other members of this family by the jet-black spot on the upper angle of the opercle and the dark coloration. Short pectoral fin, much shorter than length of head; projecting upper jaw; two dorsal fins barely connected; the two anal spines, stout; body deep. **SIZE**: Up to 16 in. **COLOR**: Dusky to blackish with reddish to coppery reflections; belly silver with dark specks; a vague, pale band across body; fins dusky, tips of pelvics and anal black; black spot on opercle. **RANGE**: Occurs Santa Barbara to Cape San Lucas, and into Gulf of California. Not abundant north of San Diego. Caught along sandy beaches, around piers, also near kelp in coves and bays. **BAIT & TACKLE**: Soft-shell sand crabs, sea worms, shrimp, and mussels. Hook No. 2. **COMMENT**: This species, like other members of this family, retreats to deep water in winter.

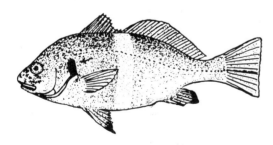

116. Black croaker

117. Spotfin croaker
Roncador stearnsi

NAMES: SPOT, GOLDEN CROAKER, SURF FISH. **DESCRIPTION**: 1st d. X; 2nd d. I & 24; a. II & 8. Distinguished by the long, pointed pectoral fin which is longer than the head and the large, black spot at base of fin. Short, rounded snout; projecting upper jaw; absence of barbel on lower jaw. **SIZE**: Up to 24 in. **COLOR**: Metallic gray or brassy back, fading to silvery belly. Appears golden in water. **RANGE**: Occurs Pt. Conception to San Juanico Bay. July to late fall best. Taken in depressions along sandy surfs and in "croaker holes" in bays and sloughs; late afternoon and evening high tides more favorable. **BAIT & TACKLE**: Pile worms, sand worms, softshell sand crabs, mussels, clams, and shrimp with shell on. Nylon leader; hook No. 2 or 1. **COMMENT**: Ranks second only to (CALIFORNIA) CORBINA in esteem of surf anglers. Spawns July to August.

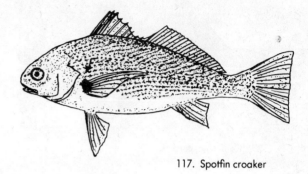
117. Spotfin croaker

118. Tommy croaker
Genyonemus lineatus

NAMES: KINGFISH, TOMMY, TOM COD, WHITE CROAKER, HERRING, PASADENA TROUT, CHENFISH, CARBINETTE. Commonly miscalled "TOMCOD" by southern California fishermen. Is not closely related to the true COD family, Gadidae. **DESCRIPTION**: 1st d. XII or XIII; 2nd d. I & 21 to 24; a. II & 11 or 12. A conspicuous black spot under upper base of pectoral fin is the noticeable difference between the TOMMY CROAKER and the small YELLOWFIN CROAKER which it resembles. Two spines in front of anal fin; several minute barbels sometimes present on lower jaw, never a large, single one. **SIZE**: Up to 13 in. **COLOR**: Metallic-brassy back fading to silvery belly, more or less dusky or bluish; indistinct, wavy lines following rows of scales upward and backward; all fins except pelvics pale yellowish with grayish or dusky base; first dorsal slightly darker. **RANGE**: Occurs Vancouver Island to Cedros Island. Most abundant of all fishes around piers year round south of Pt. Conception. **BAIT & TACKLE**: Taken easily on strips of fresh or salt fish, clams, shrimp, or live bait. Occasionally taken in very deep water. Hook No. 1. **COMMENT**: The TOMMY CROAKER is the most abused of all fishes of southern California by barge and pier fishermen who usually catch them, bounce them on the deck and kick them back in, not aware that they are considered a most desirable food fish by many people. Thousands of pounds are caught by commercial fishermen and sold in the public markets. Another mistaken idea is that the "TOMMY" in some way drive HALIBUT away. The truth is the opposite. HALIBUT and other fishes feed on the small "TOMMY" and follow schools of them in near piers. The TOMMY CROAKER is an excellent bait for the KELP BASS. An important forage fish.

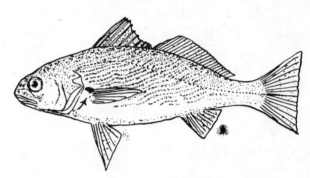
118. Tommy croaker

119. Yellowfin croaker
Umbrina roncador

NAMES: GOLDEN CROAKER, SURF FISH. **DESCRIPTION**: 1st d. X; 2nd d. I & 25 to 28; a. II & 7. Distinguished by the conspicuous, single, fleshy barbel at tip of lower jaw. Upper jaw projecting; two dorsal fins barely connected by low membrane; snout rounded; anal spines strong, second large and half the length of the first soft ray; absence of black spot on opercle or pectoral fin. **SIZE**: Up to 16 in. **COLOR**: Metallic green to grayish back with brassy or golden reflections fading to silver belly; undulating bluish to greenish lines extending obliquely back over sides and back; cheeks whitish; fins brassy yellow or orange, dorsal fins slightly dusky. **RANGE**: Occurs Pt. Conception to Cape San Lucas and into Gulf of California year round, in depressions in sandy surfs to a mile or so offshore. Common south of Pt. Dume. Abundant in Baja California. Also around old piers and other structures. High tides in surf, low tides offshore. Late summer and fall months best. Early evening and night more favorable. **BAIT & TACKLE**: Mussels, shrimp, soft-shell sand crabs, rock worms, pile worms, and clams. Will take small anchovies (pinheads), stripbait, or shrimp offshore. Hook No. 1 or 2.

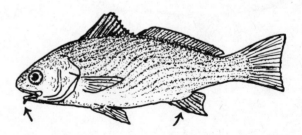
119. Yellowfin croaker

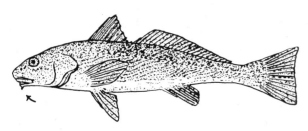

120. (California) corbina

120. (California) corbina *Menticirrhus undulatus*

NAMES: CALIFORNIA WHITING, CORVINA, SURF FISH. **DESCRIPTION:** 1st d. X; 2nd d. I & 24 to 26; a. I seldom II, & 8. Long, slender body; small eyes; short, fleshy barbel on tip of lower jaw; large, low-set pectoral fin; one or two slender, weak spines in the anal fin; upper jaw projecting; snout rounded; absence of air bladder. **SIZE:** Up to 20 in. **COLOR:** Dark, metallic blue back, fading to lighter sides and whitish belly; fins dusky. **RANGE:** Occurs Pt. Conception to Cape San Lucas and in Gulf of California year round, summer and fall best, in depressions of shallow, sandy surfs and bays. Seldom found among rocks. Feeds on bottom 2 to 20 feet deep. **BAIT & TACKLE:** Pile worms, soft-shell sand crabs, rock worms, mussels, soft clams, and shrimp. Hook No. 2 or 1; 4 foot 20-pound-test nylon leader. **COMMENT:** Most highly esteemed fish by surf anglers south of Pt. Conception. This species rests on bottom, at times using pelvic fins to shuffle along.

121. Queenfish *Seriphus politus*

NAMES: HERRING, HERRING CROAKER. Not closely related to the HERRING family, Clupeidae. **DESCRIPTION:** 1st d. VII to IX; 2nd d. I & 18 to 21; a. II & 20 to 23. First and second dorsal fins widely separated, the first containing less than ten spines (differing from other CROAKERS in this respect). Body compressed; projecting lower jaw; large mouth; large eyes; base of anal fin long, nearly equalling length of second dorsal base. **SIZE:** Up to 1 ft. **COLOR:** Metallic blue to bronze back, sometimes with brassy reflections; silver belly; upper base of pectoral fins dusky. **RANGE:** Occurs Eureka to Cedros Island. Abundant south of Pt. Conception. In shallow water around piers and over sandy bottoms. Often found in company with TOMMY CROAKER but is more difficult to catch. **BAIT & TACKLE:** Small individuals are caught by chumming with small pieces of fish and then jigged on snag lines. Large individuals are taken on a No. 2 hook baited with a narrow strip of mackerel or other fish about two inches long by dropping it to the bottom, then slowly pulling it up to the surface. They will also take grunion and other small live bait, shrimp, clams or squid. **COMMENT:** A highly respected food fish, fine-grained and delicately flavored. Must be kept damp and cool. North of Pt. Conception the size of the head of the QUEENFISH appears smaller than that of those south of the Point. This does not signify that they are of a different species, but may be regarded as a different race of the same species. Because of decrease in numbers, this species should not be commercialized.

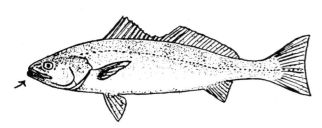

121. Queenfish

122. White seabass *Cynoscion nobilis*

NAMES: WHITE SEA BASS, WHITE CROAKER, KING CROAKER, WEAKFISH. Is of the family, Sciaenidae, and not closely related to the true BASSES, Serranidae. The young are often miscalled "SEA TROUT." **DESCRIPTION:** 1st d. X or XI; 2nd d. I & 21 to 23; a. II & 8 or 9. Large, elongated body; small canine teeth in upper jaw; large mouth; lower jaw projecting; eyes small; pectoral fin small; base of anal fin comparatively short. **SIZE:** Up to 4 ft.; 80 lbs. Seldom over 60 lbs. **COLOR:** Steel blue to gray back fading to silvery sides and belly; dark spot on inner base of pectoral fin. Young have three to six dark, indistinct bars across back. **RANGE:** Occurs Alaska to north end of Sea of Cortez. Most abundant along southern California and northern Baja California coast. **BAIT & TACKLE:** Taken near kelp beds and over shallow submerged banks, and on edges of banks on live bait, sardine, anchovies, small mackerel, and stripbait. Will take lures at slow troll. Feeds near surface at night and near bottom during day. Hook No. 1 to 2/0. A schooling fish. **COMMENT:** Although this fish has been terribly depleted, it appears to be increasing in last few years. Fifty years ago the WHITE SEABASS was abundant in San Francisco area, but is seldom seen there today. This fish is separated from the SHORTFIN CORVINA which has 2 or 3 very large canine teeth in upper jaw, while the SEABASS has patches of very small teeth in roof of mouth.

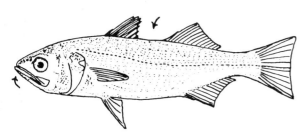

122. White seabass

FAMILY: *Branchiostegidae*—Blanquillos.

123. Ocean-whitefish
Caulolatilus princeps

NAMES: BLANQUILLO, WHITEFISH, BLANKA. The only member of this family on our Pacific Coast. Is not closely related to the fresh-water ROCKY MOUNTAIN WHITE FISH, *Prosopium williamsoni*. DESCRIPTION: d. IX & 24; a. II & 23. Distinguished by the very long base of the single dorsal fin, last spines and first rays of equal length without notch between them; long base of anal fin originating about middle of body; caudal fin slightly lunate; caudal peduncle rounded, slender. During spawning time males have bulging, fatty forehead. SIZE: Up to 44 in. COLOR: Rich brown to yellowish back fading to lighter belly; dorsal and anal fins with bluish stripe, pectoral bluish with yellow stripe. RANGE: Occurs Monterey to tropics year round over rocky bottoms and around kelp beds, shallow water in summer, deep in winter. Abundant south of Pt. Banda. Feeds four to six feet from bottom. BAIT & TACKLE: Shrimp, crabs, lobster, squid, mussels, abalone, stripbait, and small live bait. Hook No. 4/0 long-shank in deep water; No. 1/0 or 2/0 short-shank in shallow water.

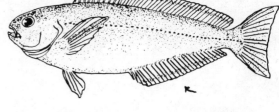

123. Ocean-whitefish

FAMILY: *Girellidae*—Nibblers.

124. Opaleye
Girella nigricans

NAMES: BLUE-EYE, GREEN FISH, BLUE PERCH, BLACK PERCH, GREEN PERCH, OPALEYE PERCH, JACK BENNY. Although often miscalled "PERCH," the OPALEYE is not closely related to that family. DESCRIPTION: d. XIII or XIV & 12 to 14; a. III & 12. Distinguished from other fishes along our coast by the bright, opalescent-blue eyes. Deep caudal peduncle; caudal fin straight; three spines and twelve very long rays in the anal fin; base of soft-rayed section of dorsal short and with twelve to fourteen long rays; profile of head and snout rounded. SIZE: Up to 7 lbs. COLOR: Dark to olive-green back becoming grayish brown to greenish on belly. The young have one to three whitish or yellowish spots below middle of dorsal fin. RANGE: Occurs Eureka to Cape San Lucas in white water around rocks. Abundant south of Santa Barbara Island. BAIT & TACKLE: Mussels best bait. Will take a moss-like sea growth (sold at some bait shops) for the minute sea animals on it. Sometimes will accept shrimp, soft clams, or bits of mackerel. Hook No. 5 or 6.

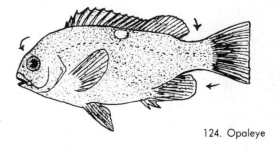

124. Opaleye

FAMILY: *Kyphosidae*—Rudder Fishes.

125. Zebraperch
Hermosilla azurea

NAMES: CONVICT FISH, PERCH. DESCRIPTION: d. XI & 11; a. III & 10 or 11. While the shape of the body and many of the external characters resemble the SALT-WATER PERCHES, it is not closely related to the family, Embiotocidae. Distinguished chiefly by the twelve vertical, blackish bars across back and sides. Body oblong-ovate; scales large; dorsal fin continuous; anal spines strong; head and mouth small; slight depression above eyes. SIZE: Up to 1 ft. COLOR: Light tan or gray to bluish with vertical black bars; a black spot on edge of opercle; fins dark. RANGE: Occurs Dana Point to Cape San Lucas among rocks and rank growth sea vegetation in very shallow water. Common south of San Diego. Sometimes seen in company with the SEAPERCHES. BAIT & TACKLE: Will take mussel or shrimp on hook No. 4 to 6.

125. Zebraperch

FAMILY: *Scorpididae*—Halfmoons.

126. (California) halfmoon
Medialuna californiensis

NAMES: BLACK PERCH, BLUE PERCH, CATALINA BLUE PERCH. Not closely related to PERCH family, Embiotocidae. Sold as PERCH in markets. DESCRIPTION: d. X & 21 to 25; a. III & 16 to 19. Distinguished by the small black eyes; single dorsal fin, with spinous section very low; second soft-rayed section and anal fin scale-covered; pectoral fin small; profile curved; caudal fin moderately furcate. SIZE: Up to 1 ft. COLOR: Slate-black back to very dark green, fading to lighter sides (sometimes mottled); belly whitish. RANGE: Occurs Monterey to Turtle Bay year round in shallow white water along rocky shores where it is often found in company with OPALEYE and dark-colored PERCHES. At times found in abundance out around kelp beds feeding near surface. BAIT & TACKLE: Mussels, shrimp, rock worms, and bits of fish. Hook No. 4.

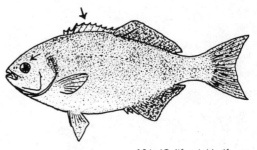

126. (California) halfmoon

ORDER: *Cataphracti*—Mail-cheeked Fishes. FAMILY: *Scorpaenidae*—Scorpionfishes (Rockfishes).

There are 52 species in this family within our range. Some inhabit such deep water (down to or below 600 fathoms) as to be of little interest to anglers. The 39 species described here could almost be divided into two groups: One inhabiting the shallow, rocky places; the other remaining in moderately deep (20 to 50 fathoms) to deep (50 to 200 fathoms) water.

The young of some of the deep-water species frequent shallow places. In the colder waters at the northern end of our range and the region south of Punta Banda, a number of mature deep-water species venture from the depths to moderately shallow water. One species, the BLACK ROCKFISH, *Sebastodes melanops,* becomes a top-feeder on occasions. The others, with few exceptions, feed a short distance above the ocean floor.

The prevailing method for catching the deep-water species in southern California is by the use of heavy hand-lines, which are standard equipment on some sportfishing boats. The angler is usually required to bring his own rig, consisting of a 50-pound-test wire leader long enough to accommodate a half dozen hooks (sizes 6/0 to 8/0) on 8-inch nylon leaders. An increasing number of anglers, especially those in the northern end of our range, consider it more sporting to use their own heavy tackle; a heavy, short rod, a No. 6 to 8 reel of 500-yard (60-pound-test line) capacity, and a sinker heavy enough to hold against the currents. A split piece of garden hose clamped around the rod protects it from friction on the rail. Tackle for the shallow-water species is described individually. All can be taken on fresh stripbait. Squid or shrimp is favored in some areas. The shallow-water species will take mollusks and crustaceans. The BLACK ROCKFISH and a few others will take a lure at slow troll.

In this family the shapely body resembles that of a BASS. In some species the head and shoulders are large. A bony structure extends from under the eye back across the cheek just under the skin. There are prominent spines on the gill covers and usually on the snout and head; III stout spines in the anal fin, and I spine and 5 rays in the pelvic fins. The body is covered with scales. The flesh is white.

The eyes of the deep-water species are normal under the tremendous pressure of their habitat but when suddenly brought to the surface the reduced pressure causes their eyes to bulge out of all proportion. This must be considered in comparing the fish in hand with the description given herein. There are also variations in color within a species, and therefore the color given in the description is not to be taken as specific. A number of species of this family have such similar characters that distinguishing them is very difficult. Furthermore the characters may vary considerably. A species may be described as having the pectoral fins reaching back as far as the anus but above a certain age this may not hold true. All characters should therefore be considered when there is some doubt as to the identity.

The shallow-water species are much more abundant than anglers suspect. The red-colored species (the SCORPIONFISH excepted) are seldom found in shallow places.

For many years the Fish Commissioners of the West Coast states have earnestly tried to establish "ROCKFISH" as an addition to the species' name. Their hope was to eliminate the term "ROCK COD." These fishes are definitely not CODS, do not resemble them, and are not closely related to the COD family, Gadidae. It was our contention that the name "COD" tacked on to this group of fishes would weaken the whole program. Just before going to press we made a tour of the coast and found the anglers even more anxious than the commissions to get rid of misapplied or appropriated names. With the exception of a few conservative fishermen everyone seems to agree to the final choice of "ROCKFISH" instead of "ROCKCOD."

The common names finally adopted for the individual species were based first on popular usage, second on descriptive value, and third on habitat. Some of the names that were directly appropriated from long-established names of other fishes, such as "RED SNAPPER," "BLACK SEA BASS," "GROUPER," and "BLUEFISH," were discarded or partially so. Some compromises were necessary because of popular usage. The newly created names are plain and comprehensive. As examples: "PINK ROCKFISH" and "BLACKMOUTH ROCKFISH" were selected as most descriptive, and "KELP ROCKFISH" because of its habitat.

127. (California) scorpionfish — *Scorpaena guttata*

NAMES: Market name, SCULPIN. It is a SCORPIONFISH and not a true SCULPIN of the family, Cottidae. **DESCRIPTION**: d. XII & 9 or 10; a. III & 5 or 6. Differs from members of the family, Cottidae, by the scale-covered body, presence of three, strong spines on front of anal fin; spinous section of dorsal fin deeply incised, and the large pelvic fins. True SCULPINS, in contrast, having scales, if present at all, below lateral line; no spines in the anal fin; spinous section of dorsal fin not deeply incised, and small pelvic fins. The number of small cirri (fleshy flaps) about the body, head, snout, and above the eyes distinguishes the SCORPIONFISH from other members of this family. Eyes set high on head; blunt snout; numerous sharp spines about the head and cheeks. **SIZE**: Up to 1½ ft. **COLOR**: Variable, more often reddish brown on back with many small, round, brown to green spots sometimes extending onto belly; belly pink; pelvic fins reddish with dark spots, all others with dark bars or spots. **RANGE**: Occurs Monterey Bay to Cape San Lucas and in Gulf of California in moderately deep to very shallow water, around piers, barges, breakwaters, and docks, but is more plentiful over rocky reefs. Abundant south of Pt. Conception. **BAIT & TACKLE**: Caught on small live bait, stripbait, shrimp, mussels, and clams. Hook No. 1 or 1/0. **COMMENT**: A prized food fish. Great care should be taken when handling the SCORPIONFISH as a wound inflicted by the fin spines may cause intense pain. An application of ammonia will often give relief.

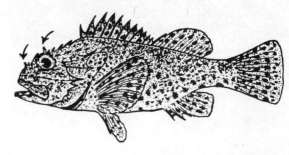

127. (California) scorpionfish

128. Bocaccio — *Sebastodes paucispinis*

NAMES: SALMON GROUPER, ROCK COD, GROUPER. **DESCRIPTION**: d. XIII & 13 to 15; a. III & 9 or 10. Slender body; long narrow head; lower jaw greatly projecting, extending out past profile of head; large knob under tip of jaw; space between eyes broad and convex; no spines on top of head. Deep notch between first and second sections of dorsal fin, being almost separated. **SIZE**: Up to 36 in. and to 20 lbs. **COLOR**: Dark brown back, fading to reddish, pale pink or white belly; everywhere flushed with red; many black spots sometimes present; lower jaw tipped with black. These colors become less pronounced in large individuals. **RANGE**: Occurs British Columbia to San Diego in deep water. One of the most abundant of the ROCKFISHES south of Pt. Conception. **BAIT & TACKLE**: Strips of fresh fish, small fresh-dead such as herring, sardine, and young mackerel. Will also take strips of squid or salt bait. Hook No. 6/0 to 8/0. The young appear in moderately shallow water in June. **COMMENT**: "BOCACCIO" means big mouth.

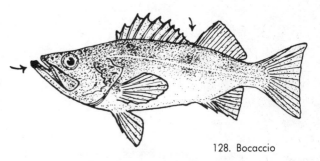

128. Bocaccio

129. Chilipepper — *Sebastodes goodei*

NAME: RED ROCK COD. **DESCRIPTION**: d. XIII & 13 to 15; a. III & 8 or 9. The brick-red to pinkish-red coloring on the back fading to a pink belly, with a distinct, clear pink stripe along the lateral line, helps to distinguish the CHILIPEPPER. Slender body; projecting lower jaw; space between eyes wide and convex; absence of spines on top of head; maxillary extending to pupil of eye. **SIZE**: Up to 22 in. **RANGE**: Fort Bragg to Turtle Bay. Found in moderately shallow water south of Pt. Banda.

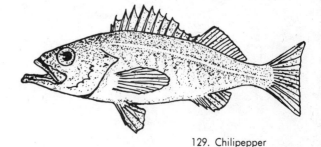

129. Chilipepper

130. Blue rockfish — *Sebastodes mystinus*

NAMES: PRIESTFISH, BLACK SNAPPER, BLACK BASS, BLACK ROCK COD, BLUEFISH, NERI. **DESCRIPTION**: d. XIII & 15 to 17; a. III & 9 or 10. Distinguished by the spinous section of the dorsal fin being much shorter than the soft rays; absence of spines on top of the head and the dark coloration. Space between eyes broad and convex; eyes small; maxillary extending past pupil of eye. **SIZE**: Up to 20 in. **COLOR**: Very dark bluish to slate-gray back fading to lighter belly; fins uniformly dark to blackish. Abdominal cavity black to dusky white in large specimens. In *S. melanops* it is white. **RANGE**: Occurs Pt. Santo Tomas, Baja California, to the Aleutian Islands. Abundant Pt. Arena to Columbia River in shallow to moderately deep water. **COMMENT**: Another species, *S. melanops,* closely resembles the BLUE ROCKFISH.

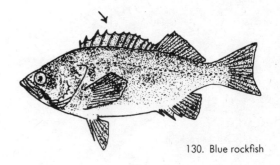

130. Blue rockfish

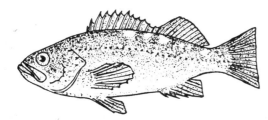

131. Bass rockfish

131. Bass rockfish   *Sebastodes serranoides*

NAMES: OLIVE ROCKFISH, SUGAR BASS, SUGARFISH. **DESCRIPTION:** d. XIII & 15 or 16; a. III & 8 or 9. Differing from *S. flavidus* principally by having a greenish caudal fin, a more slender body and smaller eyes. Long, slender body; long, pointed snout; lower jaw projecting; no spines on head; nasal spines concealed; preopercular spines long and slender; dorsal fins low with deep notch between sections. **SIZE:** Up to 18 in. **COLOR:** Varying shades of gray on back, fading to lighter belly; large, whitish blotches on back; fins tinted a yellowish color tipped with dark gray; caudal fin greenish yellow. **RANGE:** Occurs San Francisco to San Quintin Bay in or near kelp beds in fairly shallow water. Abundant south of Pt. Dume. **BAIT & TACKLE:** Taken on live or fresh-dead anchovies, mussels, shrimp (with shell on), strips of mackerel, or other fish. Hook No. 1 or 1/0.

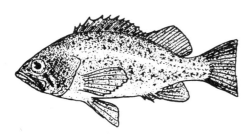

132. Yellowtail rockfish

132. Yellowtail rockfish   *Sebastodes flavidus*

NAME: GIALOTA. **DESCRIPTION:** d. XIII & 14 or 15; a. III & 7 or 8. Caudal fin tipped with bright yellow (more pronounced after death); long, pointed head; large, projecting lower jaw with prominent knob under tip; area between eyes broad, highly convex; eyes large; nasal spines small, sharp; no spines on head. Body usually more robust than in *S. serranoides*. **SIZE:** Up to 2 ft. **COLOR:** Grayish-brown sides and white belly; fins dusky yellow, caudal fin tipped with clear yellow. **RANGE:** Occurs Vancouver Island to San Quintin Bay in moderately deep water. Abundant north of Eureka and believed to be very abundant south of Ensenada. **BAIT & TACKLE:** Taken in same manner as other moderately deep-water rockfish. **COMMENT:** The young appear in moderately shallow water in early summer, remaining until about November.

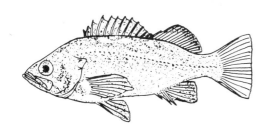

133. Black rockfish

133. Black rockfish   *Sebastodes melanops*

NAMES: BLACK SEA BASS, SEA BASS, BLACK SNAPPER, BLACK ROCK, BLACK BASS, BLACK ROCK COD, PRIESTFISH. Is often mistaken for BASS which it closely resembles. **DESCRIPTION:** d. XIII & 13 to 16; a. III & 7 to 9. Closely resembles *S. mystinus* and *S. flavidus*. Straight profile; area between eyes broad and convex; lower jaw slightly projecting with small knob at tip; absence of spines on top of head; maxillary extending back to rear of eye, or slightly beyond. **SIZE:** Up to 20 in. **COLOR:** Dark gray to dark olive-brown back, fading to lighter sides and whitish belly; dark streak from under eye down across cheek; a series of black spots on lower part of spinous section of dorsal fin (differing in this character from *S. mystinus*); all fins dark gray to blackish; top of head blackish. **RANGE:** Occurs Pt. Conception to Alaska in shallow to moderately deep water. Abundant north of Eureka. **BAIT & TACKLE:** Taken on fresh anchovies, sardine, herring, strips of fresh fish, crustaceans, and flesh of mollusks. Hook No. 2/0. Will readily take lure at slow troll—3 knots. **COMMENT:** A highly desirable game and excellent food fish.

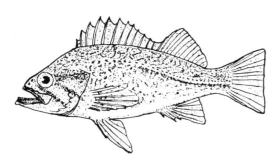

134. Orange rockfish

134. Orange rockfish   *Sebastodes pinniger*

NAMES: BOSCO, BIG RED ROCK COD, FILIONE, CODALARGA, CANARY. **DESCRIPTION:** d. XIII & 14 or 15; a. III & 7 or 8. Smooth, scaly mandible (in *S. miniatus* the scales on mandible rough to touch); lips and inside of mouth blotched with dusky gray; upper profile steep, rounded; snout rounded; lower jaw projecting with pronounced knob; spines above eyes and on upper angle of opercle, sharp, pronounced; other spines about head very small and sharp. Pectoral fin reaching anus. **SIZE:** Up to 30 in. **COLOR:** Light orange to Chinese red with light, greenish-gray mottlings on back, paler sides; belly whitish; fins sometimes with red blotches; three orange stripes across head; a black blotch usually on spinous dorsal of young. In some localities general coloring lighter. **RANGE:** Occurs Vancouver Island to San Quintin Bay. Taken in same manner as other deep-sea ROCKFISHES in moderately deep water. **BAIT & TACKLE:** Live herring, strips of sardine or mackerel best bait. **COMMENT:** Large females give birth to as many as half a million young annually. The young inhabit shallow waters near shore.

135. Rasher
Sebastodes miniatus

NAMES: RED SNAPPER, VERMILION ROCKFISH, RED ROCK COD, BARRACHO. Although often miscalled RED SNAPPER, is not closely related to the very popular RED SNAPPER, *Lutianus blackfordi,* of Atlantic and Gulf of Mexico. DESCRIPTION: d. XIII & 13 to 15; a. III & 7 or 8. Distinguished principally by the vermilion coloration (in larger specimens, the vermilion may fade to an orange color, as in *S. pinniger);* rough, scaly mandible; lower jaw slightly projecting with small knob on tip; spines on snout and head small; notch between first and second sections of dorsal fin deep; pelvic fin large, reaching past anus; pectoral fin not reaching to anus. SIZE: Up to 3 ft. COLOR: Deep vermilion back, fading to lighter sides and belly; pinkish mottlings; clusters of black dots forming blotches on back, sides, and head; lips and lining of mouth red; three orange stripes radiating from eye; some black splotches on membrane of fins; fins tipped with blackish; greenish gray at base of spinous dorsal. RANGE: Occurs Vancouver Island to San Quintin Bay in deep water. Taken same as other deep-water ROCKFISHES. BAIT & TACKLE: Live herring, sardine, strips of fish or squid.

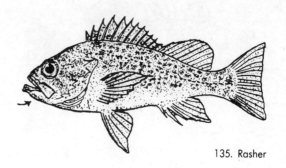
135. Rasher

136. Kelp rockfish
Sebastodes atrovirens

NAME: GOPHER. DESCRIPTION: d. XIII & 14 or 15; a. III & 6 or 7. Second anal spine shorter and stronger than third; spinous-dorsal shorter than soft-rayed section; head and snout short; profile steep; lower jaw slightly projecting with very small knob at tip; eyes moderately large; maxillary reaching past pupil of eye; caudal fin rounded; pelvic and pectoral fins reaching anus; nasal spines small; ridge between eyes and on head, small, followed by small, sharp spines; five spines on preopercle, the two upper slender and sharp; two large spines on opercle. SIZE: Up to 15 in. COLOR: Varying densities of olive and brown, mottled over lighter brown background; throat bright yellow fading to creamy belly; body and head covered with darker specks and spots; upper angle of opercle tipped with black. RANGE: Occurs Pt. Arena to San Quintin Bay. Abundant Pt. Conception south, year round near kelp beds in shallow water. BAIT & TACKLE: Taken on stripbait, mussels, "pinhead" anchovy or squid. Hook No. 2 or 1.

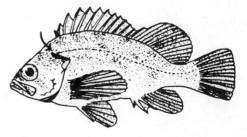
136. Kelp rockfish

137. Speckled rockfish
Sebastodes ovalis

NAMES: VIUVA, ZIPOLA. DESCRIPTION: d. XIII & 14 to 16; a. III & 8 or 9. Body large and oval; head and mouth comparatively small; spinous section of dorsal fin low; second anal spine as long or longer than third (reversed in *S. entomelas*); lower jaw projecting, with short knob at tip; spines on head and between eyes very small; nasal spines sharp; area between eyes wide and convex; small pelvic fins not reaching anus; pectoral fin reaching anus. SIZE: Up to 14 in. COLOR: Greenish tinged with red; blackish spots on back, sides and membrane of dorsal fin; other fins yellowish. RANGE: Occurs San Francisco to San Quintin Bay in moderately deep water. More abundant south of San Diego in fairly shallow water. BAIT & TACKLE: Will take small live bait or stripbait, mollusks, and crustaceans. Hook No. 1/0 in shallow water, No. 4/0 in deep water.

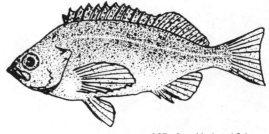
137. Speckled rockfish

138. Redstripe rockfish
Sebastodes proriger

NAMES: RED-STRIPED ROCK COD, LITTLE RED ROCK COD. DESCRIPTION: d. XIII & 13 or 14; a. III & 7. Lower jaw long and projecting with prominent knob on tip; low ridge between eyes; spines about cheeks and head; pectorals long, reaching to anus; pelvic fins reaching anus; second anal spine longer than third and thicker. SIZE: Up to 12 in. COLOR: Light red with olive-green blotches; red stripe along either side of lateral line; olive shades radiating from eye; lips and lower jaw black; caudal fin bright red with greenish specks; first dorsal blackish; other fins of varying shades of bright red. RANGE: San Diego to Alaska.

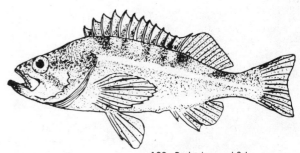
138. Redstripe rockfish

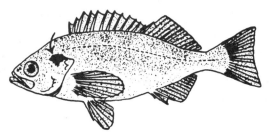

139. Widow rockfish

139. Widow rockfish — *Sebastodes entomelas*

NAMES: WIDOWFISH, BECCAFICO. **DESCRIPTION**: d. XIII & 12; a. III & 7 to 9. Distinguished by the black spot on the upper angle of the opercle. Soft-rayed section of dorsal fin low, not taller than spinous section, not deeply notched between sections; projecting lower jaw; second anal spine a little shorter than the third. (In *S. ovalis* the second spine is longer.) **SIZE**: Up to 14 in. **COLOR**: Dusky with indistinct grayish-green blotches; black spot on opercle. No black spots on back and pectoral fin as in *S. ovalis*. **RANGE**: Occurs Dana Point to San Quintin Bay in shallow water. Believed to be abundant south of Pt. Banda. **BAIT & TACKLE**: Taken in the same manner as other shallow-water members of this family.

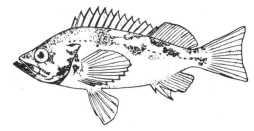

140. Smallmouth rockfish

140. Smallmouth rockfish — *Sebastodes hopkinsi*

NAME: WIDOW ROCK COD. **DESCRIPTION**: d. XIII & 15 or 16; a. III & 6 or 7. Body elongate; pectorals not reaching as far back as anus; very few small spines about head, sometimes absent. **SIZE**: Up to 16 in. **COLOR**: Creamy, with dark blotches on back and sides. **RANGE**: Occurs Pt. Conception to Oregon. Not plentiful. **BAIT & TACKLE**: Taken same as other ROCKFISHES in shallow water on smaller hook, No. 1 or 2. Shrimp or strips of fresh fish best bait.

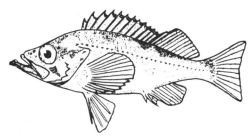

141. Longjaw rockfish

141. Longjaw rockfish — *Sebastodes alutus*

NAME: ROSE FISH. **DESCRIPTION**: d. XIII & 15; a. III & 8. Long, sharp, greatly projecting lower jaw, with very large, pointed knob on tip; large eyes, area between them broad and flat; mouth rather large with maxillary reaching back past the pupil of eye; spines about head small and slender, except on opercle; pectoral and pelvic fins reaching anus; dorsal fin not deeply emarginated. Lower lip black. **SIZE**: Up to 1½ ft. **COLOR**: Sooty-red back fading to lighter belly; greenish-brown blotches at base of both spinous and rayed sections of dorsal fin and on upper surface of caudal peduncle; dusky bars and indistinct blotches about head and opercle; dorsal fin dusky, edged with black. Lining of mouth dusky, never black. **RANGE**: Pt. Loma to Alaska. Not common south of Pt. Conception.

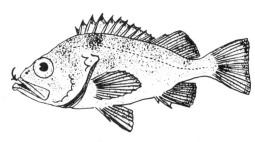

142. Blackmouth rockfish

142. Blackmouth rockfish — *Sebastodes melanostomus*

DESCRIPTION: d. XIII & 14; a. III & 8. Inside of mouth black; eyes very large, area between them concave; body deep and short; head and mouth large; lower jaw projecting; nasal and head spines small, sharp; long spines on opercle and preopercle; spinous section of dorsal fin low, moderately incised; third and fourth spines tallest; second anal spine short, half as long as soft rays. **SIZE**: Up to 2 ft. **COLOR**: Dark red to dusky on back; sides scarlet; belly lighter; indistinct, greenish, dusky blotches on head and back; spinous dorsal fin vermilion tipped with black, other fins bright red tipped with black; a black blotch above opercle; and the black mouth. **RANGE**: Occurs Catalina Island to Pt. Banda. Not common. **BAIT & TACKLE**: Taken same as other deep-water ROCKFISHES.

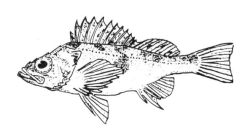

143. Halfbanded rockfish

143. Halfbanded rockfish — *Sebastodes semicinctus*

DESCRIPTION: d. XIII & 13; a. III & 7. Distinguished by the five dark blotches or bands across the back, a wide, saddle-shaped one encircling half the body back of base of pectoral fin, becoming narrower above lateral line—another on caudal fin base; a half-band extending from second section of dorsal fin down to lateral line, one across top of head; and a short one extending down from the fourth and fifth dorsal spines. Slender body; projecting lower jaw with small knob; pronounced spines about snout, head, and opercle; second anal spine strong, longer than third; pelvic and pectoral fins reaching anus. **SIZE**: Up to 12 in. **COLOR**: Brownish back fading to silvery belly flushed with red; blackish spots in front of first dorsal fin extending onto back, one on caudal peduncle; other fins whitish. **RANGE**: Monterey Bay to Cedros Island. Believed abundant south of Pt. Banda.

144. Honeycomb rockfish
Sebastodes umbrosus

NAME: SHADED ROCKFISH. DESCRIPTION: d. XIII & 12; a. III & 6 or 7. Body robust; spinous dorsal low; opercle, preopercle, head, and snout with many sharp spines; area between eyes concave with two prominent ridges; second anal spine large. SIZE: Up to 1½ ft. COLOR: Blackish back with shades of orange, fading to lighter belly; fins dusky orange; five or six pinkish blotches on back and sides. RANGE: Pt. Conception to Ensenada. Not abundant.

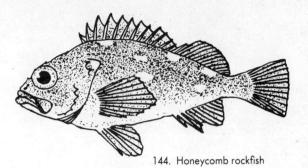

144. Honeycomb rockfish

145. Corsair
Sebastodes rosaceus

NAMES: DUDE, ROSY ROCKFISH. DESCRIPTION: d. XIII & 13; a. III & 6. Body elongate; jaws equal, with small knob on tip of lower; prominent, sharp spines on snout and under eyes; head spines absent; spinous section of dorsal, low, moderately incised; second anal spine strong, much longer than third. SIZE: Up to 12 in. COLOR: Bright orange or Chinese red fading to light belly; three to five pale spots bordered with dark red on body, fins rose, mottled with orange; reddish stripes radiating from eye, an overall brownish or rust tinge on adults. No small light dots as in *S. constellatus*. RANGE: Occurs Puget Sound to Cape San Lucas in moderately deep to deep water. Found in abundance on reefs near Monterey Bay. BAIT & TACKLE: Taken same as other deep-water ROCKFISHES. COMMENT: There are a half dozen or so other species with similar color designs, such as the three to five, pale; round spots on the dorsal surface as occurs in *S. rhodochloris*, *S. chlorostictus*, *S. eos*, and *S. constellatus*. These fishes are often mistakenly considered as being of the same species by anglers. Coloring and other characters must be carefully checked to properly identify them.

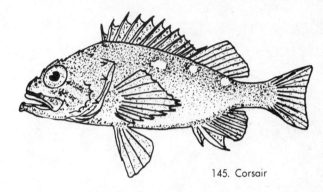

145. Corsair

146. Flyfish
Sebastodes rhodochloris

DESCRIPTION: d. XIII & 13; a. III & 6. Distinguished by the second anal spine being greatly elongated, moderately slender; jaws about equal; caudal fin slightly furcate; long, sharp spines on head, snout, between eyes, on opercle and preopercle; eyes very large, area between them narrow, deeply concave, with thin ridges; mandible partly scaly. SIZE: Up to 12 in. COLOR: Bright rose-red; irregular green streaks on back becoming orange to bright yellow on sides, sometimes mixed with light red, lighter on belly; green streaks radiating from eye; three to five spots on back (as in *S. rosaceus*), pale pink but with greenish borders; fins yellowish or green with red rays. RANGE: Eureka to Cedros Island. Abundant south of Pt. Banda.

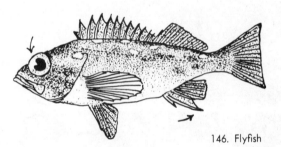

146. Flyfish

147. Greenspotted rockfish
Sebastodes chlorostictus

NAMES: BELINA, CERNIE, RED ROCK COD, CHINA FISH, CHUCKLEHEAD. DESCRIPTION: d. XIII & 12 or 13; a. III & 6. Spinous dorsal very high, deeply incised; second spine of anal fin longer than third; head and shoulders deep and heavy; very strong, high spines on snout, above eyes, on head, opercle, and preopercle; profile steep; head short; jaws equal with knob on tip of lower; high, spinous ridges between eyes; maxillary reaching past eye; pectoral fin extending past anus. SIZE: Up to 16 in. COLOR: Greenish back; lighter belly; the three to five spots on back (as in *S. rosaceus*), pinkish, but surrounded by dark green; fins red, sometimes with yellow rays; base of dorsal fin green. RANGE: Eureka to Cedros Island. Abundant southern California.

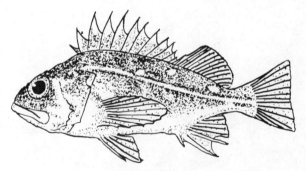

147. Greenspotted rockfish

148. Pink rockfish
Sebastodes eos

DESCRIPTION: d. XIII & 13; a. III & 6 or 7. Body oblong; jaws about equal with large knob on tip of lower; area between eyes deeply concave with narrow ridges; eyes large; spines on snout, head, cheeks, and opercle sharp, strong, some turned outward; spinous dorsal deeply incised. SIZE: Up to 2 ft. COLOR: Back, head, and fins pink to faded rose with pale brownish blotchings; three to five spots on dorsal surface of faded rose surrounded by brownish. RANGE: Occurs Santa Barbara Island to Pt. Banda in rather deep water. Fairly common in southern California. BAIT & TACKLE: Taken same as other deep-sea ROCKFISHES.

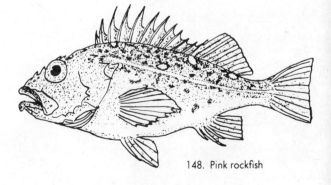

148. Pink rockfish

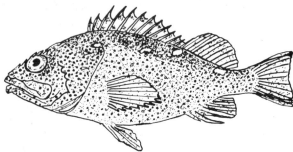

149. Starry rockfish

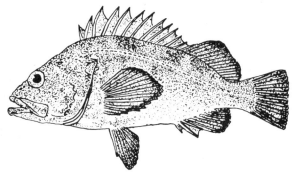

150. Tambor rockfish

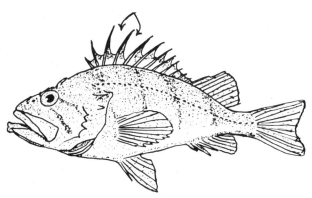

151. Cow rockfish

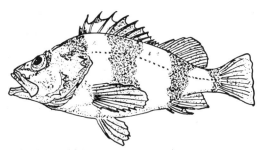

152. Flag rockfish

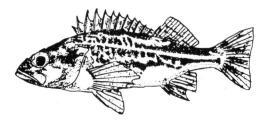

153. Strawberry rockfish

149. Starry rockfish *Sebastodes constellatus*

NAMES: SPOTTED ROCK COD, SCACCIATALE. DESCRIPTION: d. XIII & 13 or 14; a. III & 6. Distinguished by the numerous, small white spots which cover the head and body. Head and shoulders deep, heavy; area between eyes narrow, concave; lower jaw slightly projecting with very small knob at tip; second spine of anal fin very long, longer than third; spines on snout and head moderate; pectoral fin not reaching anus. SIZE: Up to 15 in. COLOR: Orange-red back with greenish mottlings fading to yellowish sides and lighter belly; fins light red; three to five spots on back (as in *S. rosaceus*), but light red to whitish. RANGE: San Francisco to Cedros Island. Common southern California. Abundant south of Pt. Banda.

150. Tambor rockfish *Sebastodes ruberrimus*

NAMES: POTBELLY, RED SNAPPER, COWFISH, TURKEY RED ROCK, TURKEY ROCK. DESCRIPTION: d. XIII & 14 to 16; a. III & 7. Distinguished by the bright red coloration and black-tipped fins. Body very deep; head and mouth large; snout blunt; lower jaw slightly projecting; area between eyes flat and narrow; spines around eyes and on head, small; on upper angle of opercle, large; second anal spine large, equal in length to third; pelvic and pectoral fins not reaching to anus. SIZE: Up to 38 in. COLOR: Head, back, and fins bright vermilion-red fading to lighter belly; indistinct, whitish streak along lateral line, sometimes with dark blotches on back; all fins (except spinous section of dorsal) tipped with black on posterior margins, sometimes faded in older individuals (fins covered with black in young). RANGE: Occurs Alaska to San Quintin Bay. Very abundant north of Pt. Arena. BAIT & TACKLE: Taken same as other moderately shallow or deep-sea ROCKFISHES. COMMENT: Believed to be the largest of the members of the family.

151. Cow rockfish *Sebastodes levis*

NAMES: COWFISH, ROOSTERFISH, GALLO, CHEFRA. DESCRIPTION: d. XIII & 13 or 14; a. III & 7. Spines of dorsal fin very tall and deeply incised, especially between the third and fifth spines; soft rays low; very large head; deep, heavy shoulders tapering rapidly to small caudal peduncle; absence of scales on maxillary; second anal spine thick, shorter than third; spines on snout, above eyes, and on opercle; lower jaw projecting with knob on tip, small. SIZE: Up to 3 ft. COLOR: Light red to pink with indistinct dusky or blackish crossbars or blotches, not always present in older individuals. RANGE: Monterey to Pt. Santo Tomas. Abundant south of La Jolla.

152. Flag rockfish *Sebastodes rubrivinctus*

NAMES: SPANISHFLAG, SHOOFLIES, BARBERPOLE SNAPPER. DESCRIPTION: d. XIII & 13 or 14; a. III & 6 or 7. Distinguished by the four, wide crimson bars. *(S. nigrocinctus* has five crossbars; *S. serriceps* has seven black bars.) Body moderately deep, compressed; lower jaw slightly projecting; high, strong spines above eyes, on head, preopercle, and on upper angle of opercle; head large, pointed; second anal spine much larger than third. SIZE: Up to 20 in. COLOR: Pale rose on back, sometimes faded pink becoming lighter on belly; the distinct crossbars crimson red; one across top of head, second extending from behind pectoral fin across back and middle of spinous dorsal, the third encircling body from base of anal fin, the fourth around caudal fin base. RANGE: British Columbia to Ensenada. Common in California.

153. Strawberry rockfish *Sebastodes elongatus*

NAMES: REINA, GREEN STRIPED ROCKFISH, POINSETTA, SERENA. DESCRIPTION: d. XIII & 12 to 14; a. III & 6 or 7. Distinguished by the irregular stripes running the length of the body. Elongate, slender body; pointed snout; projecting lower jaw; profile straight; eyes large, area between them narrow and concave; small, sharp spines on head, snout, about eyes, preopercle, and upper angle of opercle; second anal spine longer than rays; pectoral fin reaching anus, pelvic not. SIZE: Up to 1 ft. COLOR: Light red or pink with the irregular, broken green stripes on back; a straight, unbroken pink stripe along lateral line; two broken green stripes interspersed with pink below lateral line, joining to become one posteriorly; belly pale or whitish; olive on dorsal, pectoral, and caudal fins; pale red on pelvic and anal fins; black on tip of the chin. RANGE: Straits of Georgia to San Quintin Bay. Abundant in southern California.

154. Bolina
Sebastodes auriculatus

NAME: SAND BASS. DESCRIPTION: d. XIII & 12 to 14; a. III & 7. Distinguished by the brown coloration and the blackish blotch on the upper angle of the opercle. Body very deep; eyes moderate, area between them narrow and convex; jaws about equal; spines on snout and head small and weak; second anal spine slightly larger than third; maxillary extending well past eye. SIZE: Up to 18 in. COLOR: Blackish brown fading to lighter belly, mottled with lighter brown; red streaks radiating from eye; fins greenish to reddish; the blotch on opercle olive to blackish. RANGE: Occurs Puget Sound to Cedros Island. Abundant south of Pt. Conception in very shallow water along rocky shore line or in coves and bays where there is a good growth of sea vegetation. Most common ROCKFISH in backwaters south of Pt. Conception. BAIT & TACKLE: Mussels, clams, shrimp, small rock crabs, sand worms, and small strips of fresh mackerel or sardine. Hook No. 2 or 1.

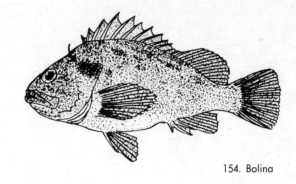

154. Bolina

155. Grass rockfish
Sebastodes rastrelliger

NAMES: LINGCOD, KELP ROCKCOD, SCOMODA, SCHMO. DESCRIPTION: d. XIII & 13; a. III & 6. Body elongate, moderately deep; spinous dorsal lower than soft rays; snout blunt; eyes moderate, area between them wide and convex; strong, low spines about head, snout, opercle, and preopercle; maxillary extending well past eye; second anal spine stouter than third. SIZE: Up to 5 lbs. COLOR: Blackish green, sometimes with light green mottlings; fins olive green; pelvic and pectorals tipped with dusky red. RANGE: Occurs Eureka to San Quintin Bay in moderately shallow water. Abundant near kelp beds south of the border. Occasionally found in backwaters BAIT & TACKLE: Taken on stripbait, fresh-dead, mollusks and crustaceans. Hook No. 1 or 1/0. COMMENT: A favorite of Jewish cooks.

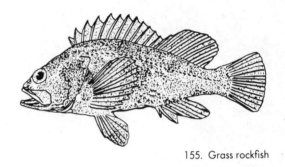

155. Grass rockfish

156. Whitebelly rockfish
Sebastodes vexillaris

NAMES: PALERMOTANA, SAILFIN ROCKCOD. DESCRIPTION: d. XIII & 12 or 13; a. III & 6. Distinguished by the tall, deeply incised spinous, dorsal fin. Deep, compressed body; back elevated; head large; lower jaw projecting, no knob at tip; eyes large; area between them narrow, with two scale-covered ridges; strong spines on snout, head, and upper angle of opercle; preopercle spines branched at tip; second anal spine larger and longer than third. SIZE: Up to 26 in. COLOR: Bright, Chinese red to yellowish or brownish back with large, lighter blotches, fading to red or whitish belly; greenish stripes on snout and cheeks; fins green with rays orange or yellowish. Resembles *S. caurinus* in some respects. RANGE: Cape Mendocino to Cape San Lucas. Abundant south of Pt. Banda in moderately deep water.

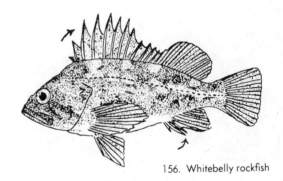

156. Whitebelly rockfish

157. Copper rockfish
Sebastodes caurinus

NAMES: NORTHERN ROCKFISH, BARRIGA, BRANCA, GOPHER. DESCRIPTION: d. XIII & 12 to 14; a. III & 6 or 7. Long, blackish pectoral fin reaching past anus; dorsal fins high, spinous section moderately incised; body elongate; lower jaw slightly projecting with small knob on tip; eyes small, area between them narrow, concave; sharp spines on snout, above eyes, on head, and upper angle of opercle. SIZE: Up to 20 in. COLOR: Dark greenish-brown to blackish back with darker blotches; belly lighter; everywhere tinged with copper; greenish stripes radiating from eye; fins blackish; a pale stripe along rear two-thirds of body. RANGE: Occurs Cape Mendocino to Alaska in moderately shallow water. Abundant in Straits of Georgia. BAIT & TACKLE: Taken on live bait, strip bait, shrimp with shell on, and small crabs. Hook No. 1/0 or 2/0.

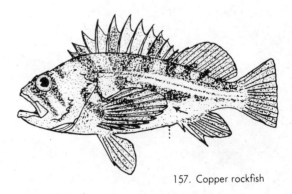

157. Copper rockfish

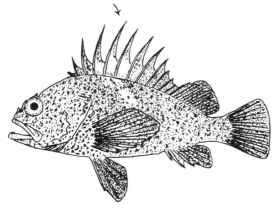

158. Quillback rockfish

158. Quillback rockfish
Sebastodes maliger

NAMES: YELLOW-BACK ROCKCOD, ORANGE SPOTTED ROCKCOD. DESCRIPTION: d. XIII & 12 to 14; a. III & 6 or 7. Distinguished by the very high, spinous section of the dorsal fin, with deeply incised membrane between the eight forward spines. Profile curved, deeply indented above nasal spine; jaws about equal with small knob on tip of lower; high ridge between eyes with high, strong spines; spines about head, pre-opercle, and opercle; body deep; tips of caudal fin rounded. SIZE: Up to 2 ft. COLOR: Yellow to brownish orange on back, fading to lighter belly; body covered with small orange and brownish spots; pale-brownish stripes radiating from eye, sometimes indistinct in larger species; wedge-shaped, light yellow streak on dorsal fin from third to fifth spine, the point extending down to lateral line, sometimes absent in adults; rayed dorsal and other fins black. RANGE: Occurs Monterey to Alaska in moderately shallow to moderately deep water. Abundant northern end of range. BAIT & TACKLE: Many taken by anglers on stripbait or fresh-dead herring or other small fish and crustaceans. Hook No. 1/0 or 2/0. A good scrapper.

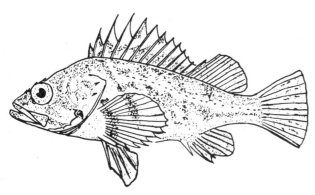

159. Calico rockfish

159. Calico rockfish
Sebastodes dalli

NAMES: BROWN ROCKFISH, PRETTY ROCK COD. DESCRIPTION: d. XIII & 13 or 14; a. III & 6. Short pectoral fin, not reaching anus; profile straight; jaws equal; area between eyes narrow, with high ridges; spines on snout and above eye thick, those on head and opercle slender, sharp; second and third spines of anal fin equal; body moderately elongate; tips of caudal fin pointed. SIZE: Up to 9 in. COLOR: Light brown with darker, dusky streaks on back, some crossing lateral line; belly lighter; dark brown to blackish streaks radiating from eye; fins dusky; two dark bars on pectorals; pale streak with dark border along lateral line. RANGE: Occurs San Diego to Pt. Arena. Not abundant. BAIT & TACKLE: Taken same as other moderately shallow-water ROCKFISH.

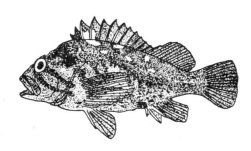

160. Black-and-tan rockfish

160. Black-and-tan rockfish
Sebastodes chrysomelas

NAMES: BLACK AND YELLOW ROCKFISH BASS, SAND BASS, GOPHER. DESCRIPTION: d. XIII & 12 or 13; a. III & 6. Body deep, stout; dorsal spines tall and strong; pectoral fin reaching back to anus; rays of pectoral fin greatly thickened; second anal spine equal in length to third; jaws equal; sharp, strong spines on snout, above eyes, on head, and upper angle of opercle. SIZE: Up to 15 in. COLOR: Predominantly dark brown to blackish; six or seven irregular orange or yellow spots on back, one extending up on spinous dorsal; belly yellowish; streaks radiating from eye blackish, sometimes vague; dorsal and caudal fins brownish to blackish; pelvic and anal fins yellow; pectoral yellow with dark blotch. RANGE: Occurs Eureka to San Quintin Bay in very shallow water. Common in California. Very abundant south of Pt. Banda. BAIT & TACKLE: Taken on mussel, shrimp, clams or stripbait. Hook No. 2 or 1.

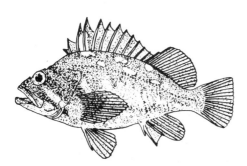

161. Gopher rockfish

161. Gopher rockfish
Sebastodes carnatus

NAMES: GOPHER ROCKCOD, BUTTERBALL, BUTTER BASS. DESCRIPTION: d. XIII & 12 or 13; a. III & 6. Closely resembles *S. chrysomelas*, differing principally in the coloration. Deep, short body; steep profile; short snout; deep head; area between eyes narrow, concave; jaws equal with no knob; absence of scales on snout; second spine of anal fin longer than third; spinous dorsal high, higher than soft rays; spines on head small; rays of pectoral fin less thickened than in *S. chrysomelas*. SIZE: Up to 14 in. COLOR: Pale brown to tan on back extending over sides to lighter belly; six or seven irregular, pinkish or flesh-colored spots on back (similar in pattern to *S. chrysomelas*); indistinct darker rays radiating from eye; dorsal and caudal fins light brown; pelvic and anal fins flesh color; pectoral light brown, sometimes mottled with pink. RANGE: Occurs Pt. Arena to San Quintin Bay. Abundant south of Pt. Dume in moderately shallow water. BAIT & TACKLE: Stripbait, small live bait, clams, and shrimp with shell on. Hook No. 2 or 1.

162. China rockfish
Sebastodes nebulosus

NAMES: YELLOW STRIPED ROCKFISH, BLACK AND YELLOW ROCK COD, CEFALUTANO, CHINA FISH. DESCRIPTION: d. XIII & 13; a. III & 7. Distinguished by the pronounced yellow stripe along back. Head and shoulders heavy, deep; body short; jaws heavy, blunt, about equal; area between eyes deeply concave, narrow, with high ridges; spines on snout, over eyes, and on head high, sharp; on opercle and preopercle, thick and blunt; dorsal spines tall, deeply incised; pectoral fin extending to anus. SIZE: Up to 16 in. COLOR: Bluish black on back and sides becoming lighter on belly; the bright yellow stripe extending from the base of the caudal fin along the lateral line, thence across back and spinous dorsal at the third spine; whitish and light blue speckling over head, fins, and body, becoming pale on belly; fins bluish black. RANGE: Occurs Pt. Conception to Alaska in moderately deep to shallow water. Abundant north of Eureka. BAIT & TACKLE: Taken on strips of fish or squid on No. 4/0 hook in deep water; fresh-dead anchovies, stripbait, shrimp, crabs, squid, on hook No. 2/0 in shallow places.

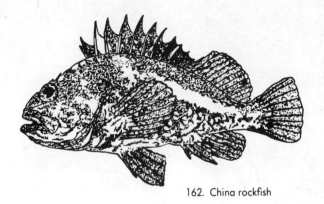

162. China rockfish

163. Treefish
Sebastodes serriceps

NAMES: CONVICT FISH, BARBER POLE. DESCRIPTION: d. XIII & 13 to 15; a. III & 6. Distinguished by the six or seven black bands across body. (In *S. rubrivinctus* there are usually four crimson bars, in *S. nigrocinctus,* usually five black bars with reddish tinge.) Body short and compressed; jaws equal; thick, blunt spines about the snout and head; area between eyes narrow and concave; high, thick ridges on snout and head. SIZE: Up to 14 in. COLOR: Dark olive back; yellowish belly; coppery red mouth and mandible; two blackish bands radiating from eye. RANGE: Occurs Pt. Reyes to Cedros Island. Very abundant in southern California. BAIT & TACKLE: Taken in shallow water among kelp beds and rocks on mussels, flesh of mollusks, crustaceans, and stripbait. Hook No. 1. COMMENT: Makes good bait for large fishes.

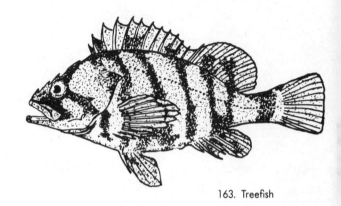

163. Treefish

164. Barred rockfish
Sebastodes nigrocinctus

NAMES: BANDED ROCKFISH, BLACKBANDED ROCK COD. DESCRIPTION: d. XIII or XIV & 14 or 15; a. III & 7. Distinguished by the five, well-defined black bars across back and sides and by the very high, bluntly-spined ridges on snout, between eyes and on forehead; area between ridges very narrow and concave; lower jaw slightly projecting; pelvic fin reaching anus. Pectoral fin of male reaching anus, female not. SIZE: Up to 2 ft. COLOR: Bright red to grayish with the five, jet-black bars across sides, back, and over dorsal fin; two black stripes radiating from eye across cheek; black blotch over eye. Compare with TREEFISH description. RANGE: Pt. Conception to Arctic. Common Oregon and Washington.

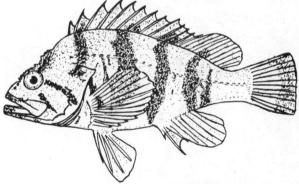

164. Barred rockfish

165. (Slim) thornhead
Sebastolobus alascanus

NAMES: BONEHEAD, CHANNEL ROCKFISH, GURNARD, GURNET, CHANNEL COD, FAGIANO. DESCRIPTION: d. XV to XVII & 9 or 10; a. III & 5. Distinguished by the large head and slender body; large scales; large number of spines in dorsal fin; the sharp, spinous ridge across cheek; prominent spines on snout, head and preopercle, large and sharp; spinous-dorsal deeply incised with deep notch almost separating it from soft-rayed section. SIZE: Up to 2 ft. COLOR: Uniformly bright red with darker to black irregular markings on fins and back. RANGE: Occurs southern California to Alaska in deep water from 50 to 800 fathoms. Abundant north of Pt. Conception. BAIT & TACKLE: Seldom taken by anglers south of Coos Bay because of depth. COMMENT: An excellent food fish.

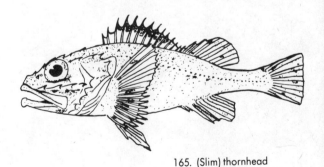

165. (Slim) thornhead

FAMILY: *Anoplopomatidae*—Sablefishes.

166. Sablefish
Anoplopoma fimbria

NAMES: BLACK COD, SKILL, COALFISH, COAL COD, BLUE COD, CANDLEFISH, BUTTER-FISH. Although bearing some resemblance to and often mistakenly called "COD," the SABLEFISH is not closely related to the true COD family, Gadidae. DESCRIPTION: 1st d. XVII to XXI; 2nd d. I & 16 to 21; a. III & 15 to 19. Distinguished by the long, slender cod-like body; long, slender caudal peduncle; two low well-separated dorsal fins; eyes small; head conical; upper jaw projecting; nostrils double; single lateral line; absence of spines or cirri about head; maxillary narrow, barely reaching eye pupil. SIZE: Up to 40 in. COLOR: Dark green to blackish back; lighter on sides below lateral line and light gray on throat and belly; narrow, black edging on spinous dorsal fin; other fins tipped with light gray; lining of gill covers black. RANGE: Occurs Catalina Island to Alaska. Abundant north of Coos Bay. Seldom south of Pt. Conception. Usually taken in deep water, in company with PACIFIC HALIBUT. BAIT & TACKLE: Squid and fresh stripbait. Hook No. 4/0 to 6/0. COMMENT: On occasion follows schools of squid or small fish into shallow water. An enormous, fifteen-day run occurred in Monterey Bay, July, 1947. Vast numbers were taken from pier on sundry lures and bait. North of Eureka such occurrences are common. Excellent food fish if kept damp and cool. SABLEFISH is among the best as smoked fish. Liver is rich in vitamins A and D. Another member of this family, the GIANT SKILFISH, *Erilepis zonifer,* is distinguished by the narrow interspace between the dorsal fins and by its enormous size. Is of negligible interest to anglers. Taken on northern banks on heavy PACIFIC HALIBUT tackle. Range northern California to Alaska in deep water.

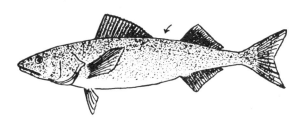

166. Sablefish

FAMILY: *Hexagrammidae*—Greenlings.

Members of this family sometimes called "SEA TROUT" for marketing purposes. The GREENLINGS are a family of fishes in "technicolor" changing rapidly to match the color scheme of the surroundings, from bright green of the seaweeds to reds and grays of rocks. There is also a marked contrast in color and design between the male and female in some species.

The GREENLINGS are especially fine game fishes but over-looked because few have developed a technique for catching them. The most common mistake made is in the use of large hooks, none of which should be above a No. 2.

Few fishes out-rate the GREENLING as a food fish. Stripbait cut from any of them is very effective for other species.

One or the other of the three species can be found in great abundance wherever animal sea life is plentiful among the vegetation or rocks north of Pt. Arena.

167. Kelp greenling
Hexagrammos decagrammus

NAMES: GREENLING SEATROUT, ROCK TROUT, KELP TROUT, KELP COD, KELP, BLUE-FISH. Not closely related to true TROUT family, Salmonidae. DESCRIPTION: d. XXI or XXII & 24; a. I & 23 or 24. Distinguished by the presence of five lateral lines; two pairs of cirri—one pair above each eye, the other on top of head; the long dorsal fin originating above the upper angle of the opercle, moderately notched between the sections; very large pectoral fin (extending back to anus in males, slightly short of anus in females); one small spine in front of anal fin. SIZE: Up to 21 in. COLOR: Males more often brown, at times green, reddish brown to gray, sometimes tinged with blue or copper; light spots on head, cheeks, forepart of dorsal fins and body, more often in blue encircled with small, brown spots or dots; pectoral fin with whitish spots and thin lines in brown to blackish. Females dominantly light brown with very small spots on head, back, and sides in reddish blue and orange; red to orange on dorsal fin, blotched with blue; orange to yellow on pelvic and anal fins. The above colors are the most prevailing, but are not to be taken as specific. RANGE: Occurs Pt. Conception to Aleutian Islands. Very abundant north of Pt. Arena in shallow water among sea vegetation in rocky places. BAIT & TACKLE: Taken on mussels, ghost shrimp, clams, small strips of fish, sea worms, and crustaceans. Hook No. 2. COMMENT: An excellent food fish. Par excellent as stripbait for other fishes. The color and design of the male differs so greatly from the female, fishermen mistake them for separate species, calling the male "SEA TROUT," the female "KELP COD."

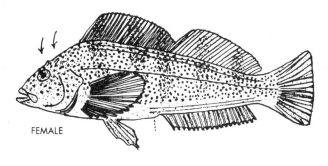

FEMALE

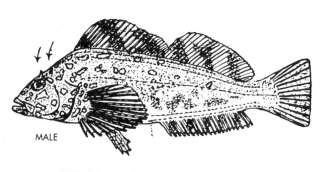

MALE

167. Kelp greenling

168. Whitespotted greenling
Hexagrammos stelleri

NAMES: TOMMY-COD, ATKA MACKEREL, SEA TROUT. DESCRIPTION: d. XXII to XXV & 19 to 24; a. 23 to 25. Distinguished by the many, small white spots over body; the single, small cirrus above each eye and the slender caudal peduncle. Body moderately slender; head conical; first and fourth lateral lines short. SIZE: Up to 2 ft. COLOR: Green predominant, but varying from tan to pale red with dark or dusky bars or irregular spots; dark stripes on pectoral on yellow background; about six dark spots or bars on anal fin, pale yellow background; the numerous white spots more or less evenly scattered over body. RANGE: Occurs San Francisco to Aleutian Islands in shallow water. Very abundant in sounds, straits, and coastal rocky places in Washington and British Columbia. Occasionally appearing in waters off sandy beaches. BAIT & TACKLE: Taken in swift currents and around rocks or near kelp beds on shrimp, small crabs, mussels, clams, and stripbait. Hook No. 2 or 4.

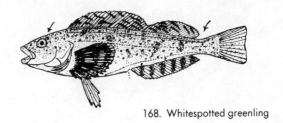

168. Whitespotted greenling

169. Rock greenling
Hexagrammos superciliosus

NAMES: PACIFIC RED ROCK TROUT, FRINGED GREENLING, RED GREENLING, SEA TROUT, KELP COD. DESCRIPTION: d. XX or XXI & 23 or 24; a. 21 or 22. Distinguished by the large, black spot above base of pectoral fin and the very large, fringed cirrus above each eye. Caudal peduncle deep; head short; five lateral lines; single dorsal fin moderately notched between sections. SIZE: Up to 24 in. COLOR: Multicolored and variable from bright red and brown to bright green; sometimes with bright, round spots; alternating, curved, light green and red stripes on pectoral fin; red spots or bars usually on pelvic and anal fins; caudal fin green, tipped with red; black spot above pectoral. RANGE: Occurs Pt. Conception to Alaska. Abundant north of Coos Bay in shallow water along rocky shore lines, especially near shellfish beds. BAIT & TACKLE: Mussels, clams, crustaceans, and stripbait. Hook No. 2.

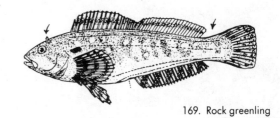

169. Rock greenling

FAMILY: *Ophiodontidae*—Lingcods.

170. Lingcod
Ophiodon elongatus

NAMES: CULTUS, SKILFISH, CULTUS COD, BUFFALO COD, LEOPARD COD, BLUE COD, LING, BOCALAO. Not closely related to true COD family, Gadidae. DESCRIPTION: d. XXIV to XXVII & 21 to 24; a. III & 21 to 24. Distinguished by the large, canine teeth; the very long dorsal fin which originates in advance of the upper angle of the opercle; and the long head and body. Caudal peduncle long, slender; head depressed; mouth large; single lateral line; single large thick cirrus over each eye. SIZE: Up to 5 ft. COLOR: Like the GREENLINGS, the LINGCOD is also a sea-going chameleon of sorts, as likely to appear black on back and sides as brown, blue, or green; belly usually lighter, from whitish to cream or grayish. Spots, blotches, and other designs are not specific. These darker areas are generally larger on sides and dorsal surface with smaller spots below; dorsal and caudal fins with dark spots or bars; pectoral, pelvic, and anal fins usually grayish green. The flesh is sometimes greenish becoming white when cooked. RANGE: Occurs Pt. Banda to Sitka, Alaska, in moderately deep to deep water, appearing in shallow water at spawning time (December through March). BAIT & TACKLE: Taken in shallow, rocky places on strips of greenling, chrome lures, herring, anchovies, sardine, squid, or other whole bait. Hook No. 4/0 to 6/0. Taken in deep water on live bait, fresh or frozen stripbait, shrimp or squid. Usually feeds near bottom. COMMENT: North of Eureka the LINGCOD could be termed a shallow-water species. In this area it frequents shallow places the year round. Because of its ever increasing popularity as a game fish, the commercialization of the LINGCOD should be regulated. The great length of time required for the LING'S growth to maturity makes controls all the more imperative. A highly esteemed food fish. Liver rich in vitamins A and D. The name "LINGCOD" is one of the most far-fetched that popular usage has imposed on any of our fishes. Not only is it not a COD, it is not a LING, *Molva vulgaris*, a species common to north Europe.

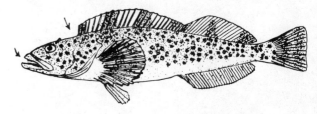

170. Lingcod

171. Convictfish
Oxylebius pictus

NAMES: PAINTED GREENLING, KELP FISH. DESCRIPTION: d. XVI & 14 to 16; a. III or IV & 12 or 13. The long, compressed, pointed head; the six or seven vertical bars across the body and the three or four hard spines in the anal fin distinguish the CONVICTFISH from GREENLINGS which it otherwise resembles. Single lateral line, nearly straight; two pairs of red cirri, one pair above each eye, the other at top of head; single dorsal fin moderately notched between sections; pectoral fin extending past anus; pelvic fin shorter; maxillary not reaching eye. SIZE: Up to 12 in. COLOR: Varying according to habitat from gray to light brown, sometimes blotched with light orange with the six or seven dark crossbars extending onto vertical fins; dark stripes across pectoral and pelvic fins; caudal and pectoral fins sometimes orange; head gray or brown on top, underside orange; dark stripes radiating from eye, sometimes absent. Coloring not specific. RANGE: Occurs Straits of Georgia to San Quintin Bay among sea vegetation and coral beds along rocky shores. BAIT & TACKLE: Angling technique and choice of baits not yet ascertained, at least by the author. All efforts so far with various baits have failed to entice this one. Hook No. 4.

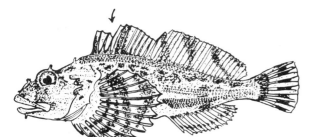

171. Convictfish

FAMILY: *Cottidae*—Sculpins. There are numerous members of this family. Listed below are those of particular interest to anglers. Most of the others are small and inhabit tide pools, or fresh water.

172. (Spotted) Irishlord
Hemilepidotus hemilepidotus

NAMES: RED IRISH LORD, BULLHEAD. DESCRIPTION: d. X to XII & 18 to 20; a. 13 to 16. Distinguished by the lateral stripes of scaleless skin interspersed with rows of coarse scales; spinous section of dorsal fin notched; snout rounded with large, sharp spine; two large, sharp spines on upper edge of preopercle; four short, sharp spines on margin of opercle; anus near anal fin; caudal fin rounded; prominent cirri on head, above eye, and on nose. SIZE: Up to 20 in. COLOR: Various shades of red on back with brownish mottling, fading to greenish or pale red sides and belly; ventral surface covered with dark to black spots. RANGE: Occurs Monterey Bay to Alaska. Abundant north of Newport, Oregon. Taken in moderately deep to very shallow water among rocks and near streams on fresh stripbait, mussels, ghost shrimps, small crabs and crawfish. Hook No. 1 or 1/0.

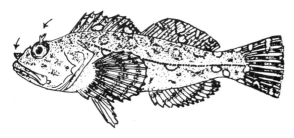

172. (Spotted) Irishlord

173. Cabezon
Scorpaenichthys marmoratus

NAMES: MARBLE SCULPIN, GIANT SCULPIN, BULLHEAD, BLUE COD. DESCRIPTION: d. X to XII & 15 to 18; a. 11 to 13. Distinguished by the smooth, slick skin (scales absent); green or bluish lips and mouth; large cirrus on tip of snout and a tall one above each eye; three broad spines on back margin of preopercle; one strong spine on snout; pectoral fin extending to anus; single dorsal fin deeply notched between sections; head large, moderately broad; no spines in anal fin; caudal fin slightly rounded; single lateral line; eyes large, highly placed. SIZE: Up to 30 in.; 25 lbs. COLOR: Various shades of brown to greens, reds, and yellows; belly bright blue, green to tan; fins and body with lighter blotches or spots; pectoral, pelvic, and anal fins sometimes with dark bars; green or bluish mouth and lips. Flesh, bluish. RANGE: Occurs Alaska to San Quintin Bay near mouth of streams and among rocks year round. Abundant whole range. Feeds on the bottom. BAIT & TACKLE: Mussels, clams, crawfish, ghost shrimp, small live bait, stripbait, and sea worms. Hook No. 1 to 2/0. COMMENT: Considered by many the best food fish of all. Flesh becomes white when cooked. Roe of CABEZON is toxic.

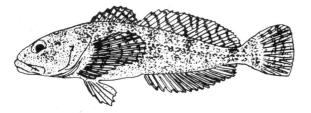

173. Cabezon

174. Prickly sculpin
Cottus asper

NAMES: BULLHEAD, MUDDLER. DESCRIPTION: d. IX or X & 19 to 21; a. 17 or 18. Distinguished by the deep shoulders and the broad, depressed wedge-shaped head, the wide area between the eyes and the many stiff prickles over head and body. SIZE: Up to 14 in. COLOR: Grayish olive with blackish spots and mottlings; dark, wavy stripes across all fins except pelvic and anal. RANGE: Occurs Pt. Conception to Washington in sloughs, backwaters, and for some distances up streams. Abundant San Francisco Bay to British Columbia. BAIT & TACKLE: Will take many kinds of baits, but prefers pieces of shrimp and clams. Hook No. 2.

174. Prickly sculpin

175. Staghorn sculpin
Leptocottus armatus

NAME: BUFFALO SCULPIN. **DESCRIPTION:** d. VI to VIII & 15 to 20; a. 15 to 20. Distinguished by the large, black spot on the spinous dorsal fin and the very strong, antler-like preopercular spine. When disturbed, it expands the gill covers so that the spines are pointed outward giving the fish a formidable appearance. Body elongate; heavy, stout shoulders tapering to small caudal peduncle; pectoral fins large; small eyes; single lateral line; absence of spines (other than preopercular) or cirri about head or above eyes; absence of scales on body. **SIZE:** Up to 14 in. **COLOR:** Dark green to brown on back; silver to yellowish belly; all fins except pelvic and anal with green and black bars. **RANGE:** Occurs San Quintin Bay to Alaska in shallow water. Abundant north of Pt. Arena in bays and backwaters. **BAIT & TACKLE:** Taken on sea worms, clams, mussels, stripbait and crawfish tails. Hook No. 1 or 2.

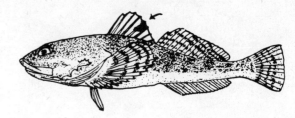

175. Staghorn sculpin

❧ VIVIPAROUS PERCHES ☙

ORDER: *Holconoti.* FAMILY: *Embiotocidae*—Viviparous perches.

In the general confusion in the common names of Pacific Ocean fishes, the so-called "SALT WATER PERCHES" have heretofore presented a very perplexing problem. Classified in a single group, they were variously called MARINE PERCHES, OCEAN PERCHES, SEA PERCHES, SURF PERCHES, SALT WATER PERCHES, PERCH, and PACIFIC PERCHES. Since they are not all marine fishes and are not closely related to the true PERCHES, *Percidae,* it seems proper and timely that the new clarifying arrangement by Hubbs and Follett be speedily adopted.

In this classification those species frequenting the sandy surf will be known as SURFPERCH, while those found in deep water or along rocky shores are named SEAPERCH. The reader will note that the name is one unhyphenated word. One species, *Hysterocarpus traski,* does not appear in either of the two groupings since it occurs only in fresh water (central California). Because of its inclusion in this family, it is obviously an error to call the collective family, OCEAN, SALT WATER, or SEA PERCHES.

The difference between some of the species is not always easily observed. There is considerable similarity in color and design as well as in characters. As a family, they are recognized by a distinct furrow on each side of the base of the dorsal fin. The body is compressed, deep, and elliptical in outline. The lateral line is continuous and high on the body. There is a long, single dorsal fin with two completely connected sections; the first spinous, the second containing soft rays. The caudal fin is deeply notched or forked. There are three spines in the forepart of the anal fin. In most males, the forepart of the anal fin is modified into a thickened, glandular-like structure thought to be associated with the process of breeding which takes place during spring and early summer. The birth of the offspring occurs about a year later. The female has an ovary-uterus in which the eggs are fertilized and develop into embryos between the delicate folds of tissue of this organ. She gives birth to 8 to 45 young of considerable size, perfect miniatures of their parents except that they have comparatively larger fins and brighter colors than the mature fishes.

176. Walleye surfperch
Hyperprosopon argenteum

NAMES: WALLEYED PERCH, SURFFISH, SILVER PERCH, CHINA POMPANO, WHITE PERCH. **DESCRIPTION:** d. IX to XI & 27 to 29; a. III & 31 to 33. Distinguished by the large eyes, very short snout, black-tipped pelvic fins, and the very deep, greatly compressed body. Head small; spinous section of dorsal fin higher than soft-rayed section. **SIZE:** Up to 9 in. **COLOR:** Steel-bluish back fading to silver sides and belly, with indistinct, dusky vertical bars, and the black-tipped pelvic fins. **RANGE:** Occurs Vancouver Island to San Quintin Bay in shallow waters along sandy beaches and around piers. Abundant south of Pt. Arena. Specimens taken north of Pt. Conception seem much larger than those taken south of the Point. **BAIT & TACKLE:** Mussels, bits of fish, marine worms and shrimp. Hook No. 5.

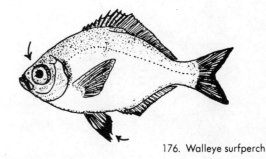

176. Walleye surfperch

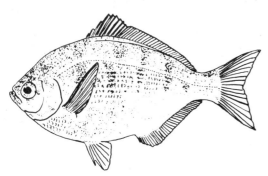

177. Silver surfperch

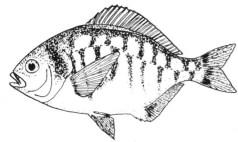

178. Redtail surfperch

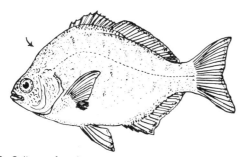

179. Calico surfperch

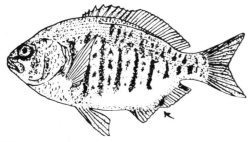

180. Barred surfperch

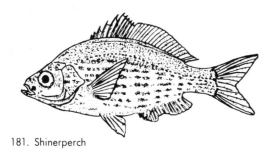

181. Shinerperch

177. Silver surfperch · *Hyperprosopon ellipticus*

NAMES: SHINER, SILVER PERCH. **DESCRIPTION:** d. IX or X & 25 to 29; a. III & 29 to 35. Closely resembles WALLEYE but has a relatively smaller eye and no black on tips of pelvic fins. Small head; body deep, greatly compressed; profile nearly straight. **SIZE:** Up to 9 in. **COLOR:** Dark gray on back with metallic luster; silver sides and belly, with faint, dark crossbands; pelvic fins silvery. **RANGE:** Occurs Dana Point to Vancouver Island in sandy surfs and around old piers or other structures. Common in Washington and Oregon. **BAIT & TACKLE:** Takes many kinds of small baits. Hook No. 5.

178. Redtail surfperch · *Holconotus rhodoterus*

NAMES: PORGY, OREGON POGIE. **DESCRIPTION:** d. IX or X & 26; a. III & 28 to 31. Distinguished by the nine or ten, vertical, orange to brassy bars alternating at the lateral line and the light red pelvic, anal, and caudal fins. Body moderately deep and compressed; scales small; spines of dorsal taller than rays. **SIZE:** Up to 1 ft. **COLOR:** Light green back; silver sides and belly. **RANGE:** Occurs Pt. Conception to British Columbia. Most abundant SURFPERCH in bays and backwaters north of Pt. Arena. **BAIT & TACKLE:** Taken in shallow water over sandy bottoms and around old structures, in same manner as other small SURFPERCHES. Hook No. 6.

179. Calico surfperch · *Amphistichus koelzi*

NAMES: CALIFORNIA POGIE, HUMPBACK PERCH. **DESCRIPTION:** d. XI or XII & 23 to 28; a. III & 25 to 31. Distinguished by the high, steep profile and very deep shoulders. Blunt snout; very small head; deep, short caudal peduncle; spinous dorsal rounded, low; rayed section and anal fin long and symmetrically balanced. **SIZE:** Up to 1 ft. **COLOR:** Olive to silvery with numerous brown or reddish specks sometimes forming irregular crossbars or blotches; sides of head and ventral surface sometimes flushed with copper; all fins except pectorals tipped with dusky. **RANGE:** San Diego to San Francisco. More common north of Pt. Dume. **BAIT & TACKLE:** Taken same as other small SURFPERCHES.

180. Barred surfperch · *Amphistichus argenteus*

NAMES: BARRED PERCH, SURF PERCH, SILVER PERCH. **DESCRIPTION:** d. IX to XI & 23 to 28; a. III & 25 to 32. Distinguished by the pronounced, greenish to brown vertical bars across body alternating with rows of spots of like color and by the nearly divided anal fin. The spinous section of dorsal fin low, three-fourths the height of soft rays; eyes small; head moderately large. **SIZE:** Up to 17 in., 4-3/4 lbs., 9 years old. **COLOR:** Brassy olive to gray or bluish between the vertical bars and spots on back; sides and belly silvery to light gray. **RANGE:** Bodega Bay to south of San Quintin Bay in sandy surfs, bays, and among rocks where bottom is sandy. Abundant in Baja California. **BAIT & TACKLE:** Soft-shell sand crabs, rock worms, mussels, also bits of shrimp and strips of fish. Hook No. 5.

181. Shinerperch · *Cymatogaster aggregata*

NAMES: SHINER PERCH, BAY PERCH, YELLOW SHINER. **DESCRIPTION:** d. IX or X & 18 to 23; a. III & 24 or 25. Short, slender caudal peduncle; large scales; head short, depressed above eyes; spinous section of dorsal fin taller than soft-rayed section; lateral line high on body. **SIZE:** Up to 7 in. **COLOR:** Back dusky; sides and belly silver; three, vertical, light yellow bars on sides below lateral line. Males becoming dark in early spring at mating time. **RANGE:** Occurs San Quintin Bay to Alaska in shallow water. Particularly abundant north of Pt. Arena. Found about old structures, docks, and in bays during summer months. **BAIT & TACKLE:** Taken in same manner as WALLEYE SURFPERCH, on mussels, bits of fish, marine worms, and shrimp. Hook No. 5. **COMMENT:** Another (very slender) species, *Cymatogaster gracilis,* is found around northern Channel Islands.

182. Kelpperch
Brachyistius frenatus

NAMES: KELP SURFPERCH, BROWN SEA PERCH. **DESCRIPTION:** d. VIII or IX & 14 to 16; a. III & 21 to 24. Large scales; very deep, long caudal peduncle; very small head; small snout; base of dorsal fin short; last spines of dorsal fin equal to length of first soft rays; mouth small. **SIZE:** Up to 8 in. **COLOR:** Dark olive, greenish to brown back with small, darker spots under scales; sides and belly coppery red with bluish spots under scales; all fins light red. **RANGE:** Occurs San Quintin Bay to British Columbia in shallow water usually where there is an abundance of sea vegetation. **BAIT & TACKLE:** Taken in same manner as BLACKPERCH.

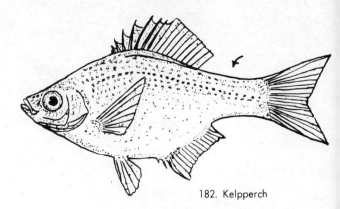

182. Kelpperch

183. Blackperch
Embiotoca jacksoni

NAME: BLACK SURFPERCH. **DESCRIPTION:** d. IX or X & 19 to 21; a. III & 24 to 25. Distinguished by the dark color which more or less evenly covers the whole body. Cluster of large scales between pectoral and pelvic fins; spinous section of dorsal fin very low; caudal peduncle deep, short; lips thick, but not as thick as those of RUBBERLIP. **SIZE:** Up to 14 in. **COLOR:** Dark brown to light tan, tinged by red to yellow, sometimes green or dark bluish; pelvic and anal fins often red to yellow; anal occasionally blotched or striped with blue; lips orange to yellowish. All coloring variable. **RANGE:** Occurs Turtle Bay to Pt. Arena. Chiefly along rocky coast lines, occasionally in bays and around piers. Abundant south of Pt. Conception. **BAIT & TACKLE:** Mussels, sand worms, small sand crabs, and shrimp. Hook No. 5. **COMMENT:** It was Dr. A. C. Jackson who, in 1853, discovered that members of this family were viviparous when he noticed a number of very small fishes about 2 inches long in a pail of water in which he had some mature BLACKPERCH. On further examination, he discovered that more little ones were just being born. It was in his honor that the name *"jacksoni"* was given.

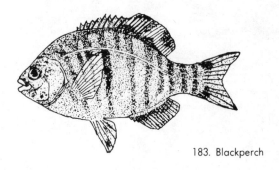

183. Blackperch

184. Striped seaperch
Taeniotoca lateralis

NAMES: STRIPED SURFPERCH, RAINBOW PERCH, BLUE PERCH, SQUAWFISH, CRUGNOLI. **DESCRIPTION:** d. X to XII & 23 or 24; a. III & 28 to 31. Distinguished by the narrow, orange and blue, longitudinal stripes. Caudal peduncle short, deep; spines of dorsal fin low, about half the length of first rays; body moderately deep and compressed; caudal fin lunate. **SIZE:** Up to 14 in. **COLOR:** The lighter stripes on back sometimes overlaid with red to greenish with very fine blackish speckling; dark blue to blackish on dorsal and anal fins, the outer margins tipped with lighter; pelvic fins bluish black; caudal fin dusky; pectoral clear or matching lighter stripes. **RANGE:** Occurs Magdalena Bay to Alaska year round, near old structures and in bays but caught more consistently along rocky shores wherever mussels and seaweed abound. While these fish rarely exceed 12 inches north of Pt. Banda, they are caught up to 14 inches, weighing 3 pounds or more along the coast of Baja California. Abundant along whole range. **BAIT & TACKLE:** Mussels, shrimp and sand worms. Hook No. 3 to 5.

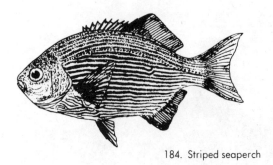

184. Striped seaperch

185. Rainbow seaperch
Hypsurus caryi

NAMES: RAINBOW SURFPERCH, STRIPED PERCH, BUGARA. **DESCRIPTION:** d. X & 23; a. III & 24 or 25. Distinguished by the long, straight belly; the anus situated below the middle of the second section of the dorsal fin, and the pointed snout. Straight profile; small eyes; the last spines of the dorsal about three-fourths the length or shorter than the soft rays; base of anal fin short. **SIZE:** Up to 10 in. **COLOR:** Extremely variegated; longitudinal stripes, bright red or orange alternating with vivid blue on body, irregular on head and throat; ten to thirteen vertical, orange bars across back, some extending down over lateral line; light blue circle around eye; one blackish blotch or spot on second section of dorsal fin, another on forepart of anal fin; caudal fin orange, sometimes with dusky crossbars; anal tipped with blue; other fins orange, sometimes mottled. **RANGE:** Occurs San Diego to Canadian border. More common north of Monterey. **BAIT & TACKLE:** Mussels, clams, bits of squid, and sand worms. Hook No. 5 or 6. **COMMENT:** Among the most beautifully colored fishes of our coastal waters.

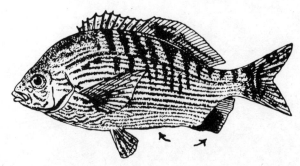

185. Rainbow seaperch

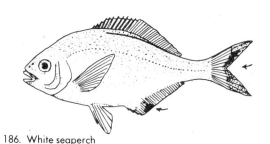

186. White seaperch

186. White seaperch · *Phanerodon furcatus*

NAMES: WHITE SURFPERCH, SPLIT-TAIL PERCH, SHINER, FORKED-TAIL PERCH. DESCRIPTION: d. X or XI & 22 to 26; a. III & 29 to 34. Body elliptical, tapering to a long, slender caudal peduncle; caudal fin deeply forked; first and second sections of dorsal fin of about equal height. SIZE: Up to 1 ft. COLOR: Entire body metallic, graduating from darkish silver back to light grayish-silver belly; fins yellowish, often dusky on margin of caudal fin; no black spot on cheek. RANGE: Occurs Vancouver Island to San Quintin Bay year round. Found near piers and docks, in bays, stream entrances, and occasionally on sandy beaches. BAIT & TACKLE: Mussels, sand worms, shrimp, and small pieces of prepared bait. Hook No. 3. COMMENT: Another closely related species in deep water the BLACKFOOT SEAPERCH, *Phanerodon atripes,* has black pelvic fins.

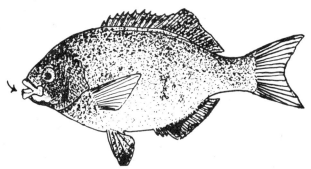

187. Rubberlip seaperch

187. Rubberlip seaperch · *Rhacochilus toxotes*

NAMES: RUBBERLIP SURFPERCH, PORGEE, ALFIONE, LIVERLIP, BUTTERMOUTH. DESCRIPTION: d. X & 23 or 24; a. III & 28 to 30. Distinguished by the very thick, white or light-pinkish lips. Head and body moderately deep, heavy; short interspace between pelvic and anal fins; spines of dorsal fin about half the length of soft rays. SIZE: Up to 18 in. COLOR: Dusky-blue back becoming more silver toward belly; fins dark or tipped dark, except for pectorals which are usually pale orange or yellow. RANGE: Occurs Eureka to San Quintin Bay along rocky shores and in bays, wherever seaweeds and mussels or other mollusks abound. BAIT & TACKLE: Mussels, sand worms, small soft-shell sand crabs. Hook No. 5.

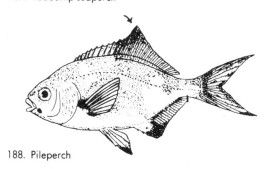

188. Pileperch

188. Pileperch · *Damalichthys vacca*

NAMES: WHITE PERCH, SPLIT-TAIL, PORGEE, FORKTAIL, SILVER PERCH. DESCRIPTION: d. X to XII & 21 to 24; a. III & 25 to 29. Distinguished by the black spot on cheek behind maxillary, the very deeply forked caudal fin, and the tall, first soft rays of the dorsal fin being about twice the height of the last spines. Slender caudal peduncle; very short interspace between the anal and pelvic fins. SIZE: Up to 16 in. COLOR: Varying from brown to dusky gray on back and sides, sometimes mottled; sometimes dusky on dorsal, anal, and caudal fins; pectoral fins clear; pelvic fins light orange to yellowish, tipped with black. RANGE: Occurs San Quintin Bay to Alaska around rocky shore lines and old piers. Common whole range. Abundant north of Pt. Conception and south of Pt. Banda. BAIT & TACKLE: Mussels, soft-shell sand crabs, shrimp, and sand worms. Hook No. 2 to 4. COMMENT: Large, darker specimens taken below Pt. Banda up to 16 inches are believed to be of the same species.

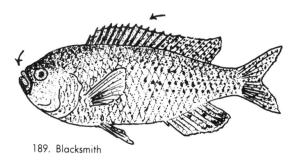

189. Blacksmith

ORDER: *Chromides.* FAMILY: *Pomacentridae*—Damselfishes.

189. Blacksmith · *Chromis punctipinnis*

NAMES: PERCH, BLUE PERCH, KELP PERCH. DESCRIPTION: d. XIII & 11 or 12; a. II & 10. Distinguished by the short, blunt head, the very short, turned up snout and the very large, tightly fixed scales. Body oblong, thick; long continuous dorsal fin; caudal fin notched with pointed lobes; lateral line ending under posterior end of dorsal fin; area between eyes wide, rounded. SIZE: Up to 10 in. COLOR: Dark slate or green back becoming lighter on belly; everywhere flushed with blue; fins dark blue or green to blackish; small, darker spots on soft-rayed section of dorsal and caudal fins. RANGE: Occurs Pt. Conception to Turtle Bay among rank growth of kelp or other marine vegetation. Common south of Dana Point. BAIT & TACKLE: Taken on bits of mussel, soft clam, or shrimp. Hook No. 6. Not easily caught.

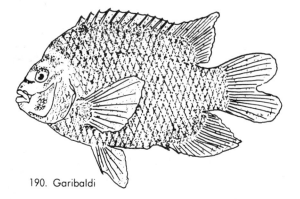

190. Garibaldi

190. Garibaldi · *Hypsypops rubicunda*

NAMES: OCEAN GOLDFISH, GARIBALDI PERCH, GOLDEN PERCH. DESCRIPTION: d. XII & 16 or 17; a. II & 13 to 16. Distinguished from all other fishes along our coast by the brilliant, orange coloring which completely covers the whole body. Body very deep; steep profile; large fins; caudal fin notched and rounded; scales large and tightly fixed. SIZE: Up to 15 in. RANGE: Pt. Conception to Todos Santos Bay, Baja California. Abundant entire range. Seen in marine gardens throughout the year from glass-bottom boats. COMMENT: Illegal to take in any manner.

191. Sheep-head   *Pimelometopon pulchrum*

NAMES: CALIFORNIA REDFISH, FATHEAD, HUMPY. Not closely related to ATLANTIC SHEEPSHEAD, *Archosargus probatocephalus,* or to the fresh-water DRUM, *Aplodinotus grunniens,* called SHEEPSHEAD. **DESCRIPTION:** d. XI or XII & 10 or 11; a. III & 12 or 13. Large, protruding canine-like teeth in heavy jaws; small, high-set eyes; deep, white chin; heavy body; deep, heavy caudal peduncle; lobes of caudal fin pointed; spines of dorsal fin shorter than rays; rayed dorsal and anal fins pointed. A bulging, fatty lump extends forehead of males, more pronounced during mating time. **SIZE:** Up to 3 ft. and to 35 lbs. **COLOR:** In mature males the head and posterior end of the body including soft-rayed section of dorsal fin, caudal, and anal fins, reddish black to jet black; body and fins between black areas red; lower jaw white. Females and immature males light to dull red, sometimes blackish; belly lighter; chin whitish. **RANGE:** Occurs Monterey Bay to Cape San Lucas and in Gulf of California year round among kelp beds and along rocky shores, especially near mussel beds. Common south of Pt. Conception. Very abundant south of Pt. Banda. **BAIT & TACKLE:** Mussels, rock crabs, lobster, shrimp (with shell on), clams, abalone, strips of fish, and live bait. Hook No. 3/0 from shore; No. 5/0 long-shank for deeper water. Enters very shallow water at high tide. **COMMENT:** Note new spelling of SHEEP-HEAD not SHEEPSHEAD.

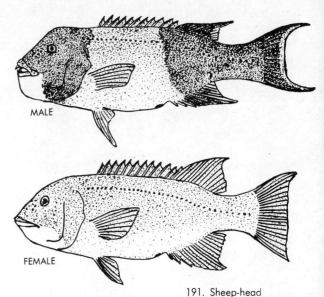

MALE

FEMALE

191. Sheep-head

192. Rock wrasse   *Halichoeres semicinctus*

NAMES: CALIFORNIA WRASSE, PARROT FISH. **DESCRIPTION:** d. IX & 12; a. III & 12. Eyes small and reddish; body rather long and slender; dorsal fin long and continuous; snout pointed; small mouth with protruding teeth; large, thick scales; deep caudal peduncle; caudal fin short; pelvic and pectoral fins small. **SIZE:** Up to 14 in. **COLOR:** Dark brown to greenish back, fading to lighter belly; three or four, narrow, wavy, bright blue stripes running across opercle over bronze background; pelvic fins cream colored, other fins with wavy, red streaks; black spot on upper base of pectoral fin. Males with wide, blue band just back of base of pectoral and pelvic fins; absent in females. **RANGE:** Occurs Pt. Banda to Pt. Conception among rocks. **BAIT & TACKLE:** Taken in same manner as SHEEP-HEAD. Is infrequently caught because of its habit of snatching the bait and scooting back to its habitat, a hole under a rock. Hook No. 2 or 1.

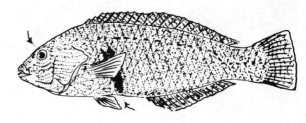

192. (Rock) wrasse

193. Señorita   *Oxyjulis californica*

NAMES: KELP WRASSE, KELP FISH, BUTTERFISH. **DESCRIPTION:** d. IX & 12 or 13; a. III & 12 or 13. Very long, slender body; sharp-pointed snout; very small teeth, sharp and protruding; dorsal fin long and continuous, spines flexible; scales large. **SIZE:** Up to 8 in. **COLOR:** Kelp-brown back fading to light belly; brown and bluish streaks on sides of head; black blotch at base of caudal fin. **RANGE:** Occurs Monterey Bay to Cape San Lucas among rank growth of ocean vegetation. Over-abundant whole range. **BAIT & TACKLE:** Rock worms, mussels, shrimp, strips of fish, or almost any bait offered. Hook No. 4 to 6. **COMMENT:** Disliked by anglers, swarms attack baits intended for other fish, quickly robbing the hook. Strange flavor but good food fish.

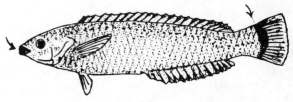

193. Senorita

194. (Longjaw) mudsucker   *Gillichthys mirabilis*

NAME: LONGJAW GOBY. **DESCRIPTION:** 1st d. VI or VII; 2nd d. 12 or 13; a. 10 or 11. Differs from other GOBIES by having a very large head, mouth, and maxillary which extends back almost to the base of the pectoral fin. Two separate dorsal fins; united pelvic fins; body long and slender; eyes highly placed. **SIZE:** Up to 8 in. **COLOR:** Dark greenish back with darker mottlings; belly yellowish; fins olive green. **RANGE:** Occurs Puget Sound to Cape San Lucas in back-bays and sloughs. An excellent bait, will live out of water for six to eight days if kept in damp seaweed. A number of other small species of this family are found in like localities, almost all of which are good as live bait. Are located in mixture of mud and sand by the two spurts of water discharged from gills, or by their habit of rising to the surface. **COMMENT:** The MUDSUCKER should be propagated commercially as it is a superior bait and will soon be in great demand by rock anglers and private boat owners. Already being used extensively for fresh-water fishing. Now numerous in Salton Sea.

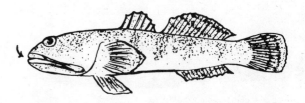

194. (Longjaw) mudsucker

195. Kelpfish

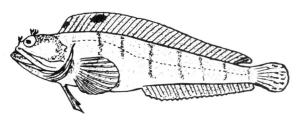

196. (Sarcastic) fringehead

197. Wolf-eel

198. Monkeyface-eel

ORDER: *Jugulares*. SERIES: *Blenniformes*. FAMILY: *Clinidae*—Klipfishes.

195. Kelpfish   *Heterostichus rostratus*

NAMES: KELP BLENNY, BUTTERFISH. **DESCRIPTION**: d. XXXIII to XXXVI & 11 to 13; a. II & 32 to 35. Distinguished by the very sharp, pointed head and snout; very small eyes; sharp, projecting lower jaw; slender caudal peduncle; caudal fin forked; small pelvic fin containing one spine and three soft rays situated in advance of the pectoral fin; dorsal fin long, continuous; a deep notch following fifth spine; base of anal fin extending half the length of body; dorsal fin originating in advance of upper gill opening. **SIZE**: Up to 16 in. **COLOR**: Variable, brown most prevailing but ranging from blackish brown, purple to green with large, lighter blotches (sometimes absent) over body and fins; transparent areas on fins. **RANGE**: Occurs British Columbia to San Quintin Bay. Common south of Pt. Conception in kelp beds and along rocky shore lines, especially near coral beds. **BAIT & TACKLE**: Takes mussels, live bait, clams, shrimp, or strips of fish. Hook No. 5 or 6. **COMMENT**: Very good, firm flesh, unusual flavor.

FAMILY: *Blennidae*—Blennies.

196. (Sarcastic) fringehead   *Neoclinus blanchardi*

NAME: KELP FISH. **DESCRIPTION**: d. XXIV & 15 to 17; a. 29 or 30. Distinguished by the large head and mouth, gape enormous; maxillary extending past opercle; very blunt snout; jaws about equal, capable of great expansion; cirri; one pair on snout branching, one over center of eye, three or more above eye. Males with a very tall, branched cirrus over front of eye. Body long, becoming very slender posteriorly; caudal peduncle slender; caudal fin rounded; pelvic fins small and slender, situated in advance of base of pectoral; dorsal fin long, continuous, originating in advance of the upper angle of the opercle; slightly notched between spinous and soft-rayed sections of dorsal fin; spines and rays running fairly equal in height. **SIZE**: Up to 10 in. **COLOR**: Varies greatly through the many shades of red and brown to a number of green hues, sometimes mottled with darker shades; dorsal fin dark with one or two darker spots between first few spines; one to three white spots on opercle; light bars across body; pectoral and anal fins dusky in males with longitudinal, reddish stripes, the outer margin whitish; in females all fins whitish. (Designs not specific.) **RANGE**: Occurs Monterey Bay to San Quintin Bay among kelp beds and other sea vegetation. Not common. **BAIT & TACKLE**: Taken same as KELPFISH. Hook No. 5 or 6.

FAMILY: *Anarhichadidae*—Wolffishes.

197. Wolf-eel   *Anarrhichthys ocellatus*

Not closely related to the true EEL family, Anguillidae. **DESCRIPTION**: d. CCXXX to CCL; a. 200 to 233. Body long and eel-like; both dorsal and anal fins separated from pointed caudal fin by small, narrow notches; dorsal fin composed of flexible spines running full length of body; the similarly shaped anal fin of soft rays beginning a head-length back of pectoral fin and running to caudal fin; absence of pelvic fins; large, pugnacious mouth with strong, canine and molar teeth; absence of lateral line. **SIZE**: Up to 8 ft.. **COLOR**: Dark green or grayish green; large, round darker spots on dorsal fin and body; smaller ones on pectoral fins and about head; anal fin pale. **RANGE**: Occurs Alaska to Turtle Bay in very shallow water. **BAIT & TACKLE**: Because of its odd appetite (feeds on such shellfish as sea urchins and sand dollars), the WOLF-EEL is not often caught on regular fishing tackle, but is taken by probing under rocks with a 10-foot stick with two large, long-shank hooks attached to the end curving inward. A few are caught incidentally on regular bait and tackle.

FAMILY: *Ptilichthyidae*—Monkeyface-eels.

198. Monkeyface-eel   *Cebidichthys violaceus*

NAME: BLENNY-EEL. Not closely related to the true EEL family, Anguillidae, or the MORAY EEL family, Muraenidae. **DESCRIPTION**: d. XXIII to XXV & 41 to 43; a. I or II & 41 or 42. Distinguished by the single lateral line and the three stripes on head and cheeks. Long, slender, eel-like body; head small, sometimes with fleshy lumps on crest; snout blunt; pectoral fin small, dorsal fin originating above base of pectoral fin and extending full length of body; caudal fin small, rounded, connecting with dorsal and anal fins; anal fin extending more than half the length of body; absence of pelvic fins. **SIZE**: Up to 45 in. **COLOR**: Brownish, dull green back with lighter mottlings, paler on belly, sometimes with irregular, light spots, sometimes tinged with red or orange; vertical fins tipped with red; the three, dark stripes on head edged with whitish. **RANGE**: Occurs Pt. Conception to Eureka in inter-tidal zones.

199. Rock-eel
Xiphister mucosus

NAMES: BLENNY-EEL, ROCK BLENNY, SLICK EEL. DESCRIPTION: Body long, slender, and slippery; four lateral lines with numerous, short branches on each side of body; very small pectoral fin about size of or slightly longer than the eye; absence of spine in anal fin; absence of soft rays in dorsal fin; eyes very small; small, imbedded scales; head small; snout blunt; absence of pelvic fin. SIZE: Up to 24 in. COLOR: Greenish black with many light bars becoming more pronounced posteriorly; stripes radiating from eye with very narrow, black border. RANGE: Occurs Santa Barbara to Alaska in inter-tidal zones. BAIT & TACKLE: Taken from submerged ledges and rocks with eel hook (on end of stick) or with regular fishing tackle on mussels and other small baits. Hook No. 4.

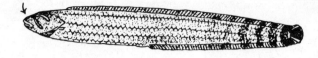

199. Rock-eel

200. (Giant) wrymouth
Delolepis gigantea

NAMES: WRY-MOUTH, CONGO EEL. DESCRIPTION: d. LXXIII to LXXVII; a. II & 43 to 49. Both dorsal and anal attached to rounded caudal fin; pelvic fins absent; body long, slender, eel-shaped; head long, flattened on top; eyes small; pectoral fin comparatively large, length three times diameter of eye; maxillary extending well back of eye; eyes small; lower jaw projecting; small scales on posterior half of body and along lateral line. SIZE: Up to 4 ft. COLOR: Tan to light brown with yellowish or bluish tinge; dark stripes sometimes along lateral line and near dorsal fin, at times with mottlings and dark spots. RANGE: Occurs Coos Bay, Oregon, to Alaska in rocky places, kelp beds and in bays. BAIT & TACKLE: Taken with eel hook on end of pole or with regular tackle from very shallow to moderately deep water (80 fathoms). More common north of Columbia River. COMMENT: A good food fish.

200. (Giant) wrymouth

---

201. Northern midshipman
Porichthys notatus

NAMES: MIDSHIPMAN, SINGING FISH, BULLHEAD, TOADFISH. DESCRIPTION: 1st d. II; 2nd d. 33 to 37; a. 30 to 34. Distinguished by the extended and protruding eyes; the numerous rows of photophores (small, shiny, button-like lens) on head and along body, and the small first dorsal fin, with two short spines set in depression. Head broad; mouth large; lower jaw projecting; area between eyes wide; teeth large; caudal fin rounded; four lateral lines; absence of scales; large maxillary extending to edge of opercle. SIZE: Up to 15 in. COLOR: Dark blue to grayish brown back fading to lighter sides; yellowish belly; white directly under eye followed by blackish crescent below; anal fin dusky without dark margin. RANGE: Occurs Pt. Banda to Alaska on deep-water banks, entering shallow water during spring spawning period. Common north of Columbia River. BAIT & TACKLE: Taken on strips of herring, sardine, or mackerel, small live bait, shrimp, or squid. Hook No. 1. COMMENT: Eggs are deposited on rocks. An edible species. The photophores must have reminded the discoverer of the buttons on the uniform of an old time midshipman, hence the name.

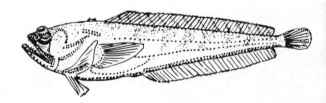

201. Northern midshipman

202. Slim midshipman
Porichthys myriaster

NAMES: MIDSHIPMAN, SINGING FISH, BULLHEAD, TOADFISH. DESCRIPTION: 1st d. I or II; 2nd d. 37 or 38; a. 33 to 37. Differing from *P. notatus* principally by having blackish outer margins on dorsal, anal, and caudal fins; a more slender body and darker coloration. Many rows of photophores about head and along body; head broad; mouth large; lower jaw projecting; teeth large; eyes extended, projecting, area between them wide. SIZE: Up to 15 in. COLOR: Deep purple to bronze back; sides sometimes lighter; belly yellow, orange or tan; dark blotches on sides; vertical fins tipped blackish as described above. RANGE: Occurs Pt. Conception to Turtle Bay in bays and shallow water hiding under rocks. BAIT & TACKLE: Caught incidentally by rock and bay fishermen in same manner as *P. notatus*. Of additional interest to anglers in that it makes good bait for BLACK SEA BASS, GROUPERS, and other large game fishes. COMMENT: Edible.

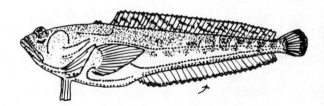

202. Slim midshipman

When the ocean angler becomes seriously interested in his sport, he will find that the following chart will simplify his study. At a glance he will be able to ascertain the family to which a certain species belongs as well as the overall grouping, and whether or not two different species are closely related.

Scientific names are subject to certain rules established by the International Commission on Zoological Nomenclature. A name that conforms to these rules is known throughout the world and is the same in all languages.

Each species has two names, usually in Greek or Latin. The first is that of the genus or group of fishes to which the particular species is most closely related. The second is that of the particular species. The name of the person who first described the fish is then added. When the describer's name appears in parentheses, it indicates that he placed the species in a genus different from that to which it is currently ascribed. When parentheses are omitted, it signifies that the person who named the species placed it in the same genus to which it is currently ascribed.

Members of a species are fertile with each other; but individuals of two separate species are frequently infertile, even though they are of the same genus.

When a number of genera have similar characters, the aggregation is known as a family. The WHITE SEABASS and the QUEENFISH are not enough alike to belong to the same genus. They do, however, have enough similar features, internally as well as externally, to be considered members of the same family.

If the branches of the animal world as a whole are visualized as the limbs of a tree, this work would be seen as dealing with two branches of that tree. They are both branches of the marine vertebrates, and are temed "classes." The first class, Elasmobranchii, includes the SHARKS and RAYS; the second class, Osteichthyes, the BONY FISHES.

Classes are divided into branches called superorders, which have more structural resemblances in common. As the resembling characters increase, the fishes are arranged into separated branches—orders, suborders, families, genera, and finally, species, the members of which have the identical resembling characters. For instance, the scientific name of the ALBACORE of the Pacific is *Germo alalunga*. The first name, *Germo,* is that of the genus; the second, *alalunga,* indicates the species. The ALBACORE is a member of the TUNA family, Thunnidae, which is included in the suborder, Scombroidea, MACKEREL-LIKE FISHES; this again is assembled with others into the order, Percomorphi, which is a division of the superorder, Acanthopterygii, the SPINY-RAYED FISHES.

Since the work of Hubbs and Follett has been accepted as the most up-to-date and authentic listing, it seems imperative that it should be followed, especially by writers making use of the scientific names of the salt-water fishes. A comparison with the old listings would reveal that a great many changes have been made.

The arrangement of the fishes in this check list is in proper continuity, that is in accordance with evolution. The SHARKS are first because of their being the most primitive forms dealt with in this volume. Of the Osteichthyes, the LADYFISH is the most primitive game fish treated.

This chart, showing the relationship of those marine fishes of the Northeastern Pacific that are of interest to anglers, is a section taken from the Manuscript List of the Fishes of California by Dr. Carl L. Hubbs and W. I. Follett.

COMMON NAME	GENUS	SPECIES	DESCRIBER

Class: ELASMOBRANCHII
  Subclass: SELACHII—**Sharks**
    Order: CESTRACIONTES
      Suborder: PROARTHRI
        Family: HETERODONTIDAE—**Horn Sharks**

1. **(California) horn shark,** *Heterodontus francisci* . . . . (Girard)
    Order: NOTIDANI
      Suborder: OPISTHARTHRI
        Family: HEXANCHIDAE—**Cowsharks**
2. **Sevengill cowshark,** *Notorynchus maculatum* . . . . Ayres
3. **Sixgill cowshark,** *Hexanchus corinum* . . . . Jordan and Gilbert
    Order: EUSELACHII
      Suborder: GALEI—**True Sharks**
        Family: ALOPIIDAE—**Threshers**
4. **(Common) thresher,** *Alopias vulpinus* . . . . (Bonnaterre)
        Family: LAMNIDAE—**Mackerel Sharks**
5. **Salmon shark,** *Lamna ditropis* . . . . Hubbs and Follett
6. **Bonito shark,** *Isurus glaucus* . . . . (Müller and Henle)
7. **White shark,** *Carcharodon carcharias* . . . . (Linnaeus)
        Family: CETORHINIDAE—**Basking Sharks**
8. **Basking shark,** *Cetorhinus maximus* . . . . (Gunner)
        Family: SCYLIORHINIDAE—**Catsharks**
9. **(California) swell shark,** *Cephaloscyllium uter* . . . . (Jordan and Gilbert)
        Family: TRIAKIDIDAE—**Smoothhounds**
10. **Leopard shark,** *Triakis semifasciata* . . . . Girard
11. **Brown smoothhound,** *Rhinotriacis henlei* . . . . Gill
12. **Gray smoothhound,** *Mustelus californicus* . . . . Gill
13. **Sicklefin smoothhound,** *Mustelus lunulatus* . . . . Jordan and Gilbert
        Family: CARCHARHINIDAE—**Requiem Sharks**
14. **Bay grayshark,** *Carcharhinus lamiella* . . . . (Jordan and Gilbert)
15. **Blue shark,** *Prionace glauca* . . . . (Linnaeus)
16. **Tiger shark,** *Galeocerdo cuvieri* . . . . (Peron and LeSueur)
17. **Soupfin,** *Galeorhinus zyopterus* . . . . Jordan and Gilbert
        Family: SPHYRNIDAE—**Hammerheads**
18. **(Common) hammerhead,** *Sphyrna zygaena* . . . . (Linnaeus)

    Order: TECTOSPONDYLI
      Suborder: SQUALOIDEI
        Family: SQUALIDAE—**Dogfishes**
19. **(Pacific) dogfish,** *Squalus suckleyi* . . . . (Girard)
      Suborder: SQUATINOIDEI
        Family: SQUATINIDAE—**Angel Sharks**
20. **(California) angel shark,** *Squatina californica* . . . . Ayres

    Order: BATOIDEI—**Rays**
      Suborder: SARCURA
        Family: RHINOBATIDAE—**Guitarfishes**
21. **Shovelnose guitarfish,** *Rhinobatos productus* . . . . (Ayres)
22. **Mottled guitarfish,** *Zapteryx exasperata* . . . . (Jordan and Gilbert)

Family: PLATYRHINIDAE—**Thornbacks**
23. **(California) thornback,** *Platyrhinoides triseriata* . . . . (Jordan and Gilbert)

Family: RAJIDAE—**Skates**
24. **California skate,** *Raja inornata* . . . . Jordan and Gilbert
25. **Big skate,** *Raja binoculata* . . . . Girard
26. **Longnose skate,** *Raja rhina* . . . . Jordan and Gilbert
27. **Starry skate,** *Raja stellulata* . . . . Jordan and Gilbert

Suborder: MASTICURA—**Whiptailed Rays**
Family: DASYATIDIDAE—**Stingrays**
28. **Diamond stingray,** *Dasyatis dipterurus* . . . . (Jordan and Gilbert)
29. **Round stingray,** *Urolophus halleri* . . . . (Cooper)
30. **(California) butterfly ray,** *Gymnura marmorata* . . . . (Cooper)

Family: MYLIOBATIDIDAE—**Eagle Rays**
31. **Bat Ray,** *Myliobatis californicus* . . . . (Gill)

Suborder: NARCACIONTES
Family: TORPEDINIDAE—**Electric rays**
32. **Electric ray,** *Torpedo californica* . . . . Ayres

Subclass: HOLOCEPHALI
Order: CHIMAEROIDEI
Family: CHIMAERIDAE—**Chimaeras**
33. **Ratfish,** *Hydrolagus colliei* . . . . (Lay and Bennett)

Class: OSTEICHTHYES—**Bony Fishes**
Subclass: TELEOSTOMI—**Ray-finned Fishes**
Superorder: TELEOSTEI
Order: ISOSPONDYLI—**Soft-rayed Fishes**
Suborder: ELOPOIDEA—**Herring-like Fishes**
Family: ELOPIDAE—**Tenpounders**

34. **(Pacific) ladyfish,** *Elops affinis* . . . . Regan

Suborder: ALBULOIDEI
Family: ALBULIDAE—**Bonefishes**

35. **Bonefish,** *Albula vulpes* . . . . (Linnaeus)

Suborder: CLUPEOIDEI
Family: DUSSUMIERIIDAE—**Round herrings**
36. **(California) round herring,** *Etrumeus acuminatus* . . . . Eigenmann

Family: CLUPEIDAE—**Herrings**
37. **(Pacific) herring,** *Clupea pallasi* . . . . Valenciennes
38. **(Pacific) sardine,** *Sardinops caerulea* . . . . (Girard)
39. **(American) shad,** *Alosa sapidissima* . . . . (Wilson)

Family: ENGRAULIDIDAE—**Anchovies**
40. **Deepbody anchovy,** *Anchoa compressa* . . . . (Girard)
41. **Slough anchovy,** *Anchoa delicatissima* . . . . (Girard)
42. **Northern anchovy,** *Engraulis mordax* . . . . (Girard)

Suborder: SALMONOIDEI
Family: OSMERIDAE—**Smelts**
43. **Candlefish,** *Thaleichthys pacificus* . . . . (Richardson)
44. **Night smelt,** *Spirinchus starksi* . . . . (Fisk)
45. **Surf smelt,** *Hypomesus pretiosus* . . . . (Girard)
46. **(Pacific) capelin,** *Mallotus catervarius* . . . . (Steller)

Family: SALMONIDAE—**Trouts**
47. **Brown trout,** *Salmo trutta* . . . . Linnaeus
48. **Cutthroat trout,** *Salmo clarki* . . . . Richardson
49. **Rainbow (steelhead) trout,** *Salmo gairdneri* . . . . Richardson
50. **Pink salmon,** *Oncorhynchus gorbuscha* . . . . (Walbaum)
51. **Chum salmon,** *Oncorhynchus keta* . . . . (Walbaum)
52. **Chinook salmon,** *Oncorhynchus tshawytscha* . . . . (Walbaum)

53. **Silver salmon,** *Oncorhynchus kisutch* . . . . (Walbaum)
54. **Sockeye salmon,** *Oncorhynchus nerka* . . . . (Walbaum)
55. **Dolly Varden,** *Salvelinus malma* . . . . (Walbaum)

Order: SYNENTOGNATHI
Family: SCOMBERESOCIDAE—**Sauries**
56. **(Pacific) saury,** *Cololabis saira* . . . . (Brevoort)

Family: BELONIDAE—**Needlefishes**
57. **(California) needlefish,** *Strongylura exilis* . . . . (Girard)

Family: EXOCOETIDAE—**Flyingfishes**
58. **(California) flyingfish,** *Cypselurus californicus* . . . . (Cooper)

Order: INIOMI
Family: SYNODIDAE—**Lizardfishes**
59. **(California) lizardfish,** *Synodus lucioceps* . . . . (Ayres)

Order: APODES
Suborder: COLOCEPHALI
Family: MURAENIDAE: **Morays**
60. **(California) moray,** *Gymnothorax mordax* . . . . (Ayres)

Order: CYPRINODONTES
Family: CYPRINODONTIDAE—**Killifishes**
61. **(California) killifish,** *Fundulus parvipinnis* . . . . Girard

Order: ANACANTHINI
Family: MERLUCCIIDAE—**Hakes**
62. **(Pacific) hake,** *Merluccius productus* . . . . (Ayres)

Family: GADIDAE—**Codfishes**
63. **(Walleye) pollack,** *Theragra chalcogramma* . . . . (Pallas)
64. **(Pacific) tom cod,** *Microgadus proximus* . . . . (Girard)
65. **Pacific cod,** *Gadus macrocephalus* . . . . Tilesius

Order: HETEROSOMATA—**Flatfishes**
Family: BOTHIDAE—**Left-eyed Flounders**
66. **Bigmouth sole,** *Hippoglossina stomata* . . . . Eigenmann and Eigenmann
67. **California halibut,** *Paralichthys californicus* . . . . (Ayres)
68. **Fantail sole,** *Xystreurys liolepis* . . . . Jordan and Gilbert
69. **Pacific sanddab,** *Citharichthys sordidus* . . . . (Girard)
70. **Longfin sanddab,** *Citharichthys xanthostigma* . . . . Gilbert
71. **Speckled sanddab,** *Citharichthys stigmaeus* . . . . Jordan and Gilbert

Family: PLEURONECTIDAE—**Right-eyed Flounders**
72. **Arrowtooth halibut,** *Atheresthes stomias* . . . . (Jordan and Gilbert)
73. **Pacific halibut,** *Hippoglossus stenolepis* . . . . Schmidt
74. **Slender sole,** *Lyopsetta exilis* . . . . (Jordan and Gilbert)
75. **Petrale sole,** *Eopsetta jordani* . . . . (Lockington)
76. **Sand sole,** *Psettichthys melanostictus* . . . . Girard
77. **Diamond turbot,** *Hypsopsetta guttulata* . . . . (Girard)
78. **Curlfin turbot,** *Pleuronichthys decurrens* . . . . Jordan and Gilbert
79. **Hornyhead turbot,** *Pleuronichthys verticalis* . . . . Jordan and Gilbert
80. **C-O turbot,** *Pleuronichthys coenosus* . . . . Girard
81. **Spotted turbot,** *Pleuronichthys ritteri* . . . . Starks and Morris
82. **Butter sole,** *Isopsetta isolepis* . . . . (Lockington)
83. **English sole,** *Parophrys vetulus* . . . . Girard
84. **Rock sole,** *Lepidopsetta bilineata* . . . . (Ayres)
85. **Dover sole,** *Microstomus pacificus* . . . . (Lockington)
86. **Rex sole,** *Glyptocephalus zachirus* . . . . Lockington
87. **Starry flounder,** *Platichthys stellatus* . . . . (Pallas)

Suborder: ACANTHOPTERYGII—**Spiny-rayed Fishes**
Order: PERCOMORPHI
Suborder: PERCESOCES

Family: ATHERINIDAE—**Silversides**
88. **(California) grunion,** *Leuresthes tenuis* . . . . (Ayres)
89. **Jacksmelt,** *Atherinopsis californiensis* . . . . Girard
90. **Topsmelt,** *Atherinops affinis* . . . . (Ayres)

Family: MUGILIDAE—**Mullets**
91. **(Striped) mullet,** *Mugil cephalus* . . . . Linnaeus

Family: SPHYRAENIDAE—**Barracudas**
92. **(California) barracuda,** *Sphyraena argentea* . . . . Girard

Suborder: SCOMBROIDEA—**Mackerel-like Fishes**
Family: CYBIIDAE—**Spanish Mackerels**
93. **Sierra grande ,** *Scomberomorus sierra* . . . . Jordan and Starks
94. **Monterey Sierra ,** *Scomberomorus concolor* . . . . (Lockington)
95. **(California) bonito,** *Sarda lineolata* . . . . (Girard)

Family: SCOMBRIDAE—**Mackerels**
96. **(Pacific) mackerel,** *Pneumatophorus japonicus* . . . . (Houttuyn)

Family: KATSUWONIDAE—**Skipjacks**
97. **(Oceanic) skipjack,** *Katsuwonus pelamis* . . . . (Linnaeus)

Family: THUNNIDAE—**Tunas**
98. **Albacore,** *Thunnus alalunga* . . . . (Gmelin)
99. **Yellowfin tuna,** *Neothunnus macropterus* . . . . (Temminck and Schlegel)
100. **(California) bluefin tuna,** *Thunnus saliens* . . . . Jordan and Evermann

Family: ISTIOPHORIDAE—**Billfishes**
101. **Striped marlin,** *Makaira audax* . . . . (Phillipi)

Family: XIPHIIDAE—**Swordfishes**
102. **Swordfish,** *Xiphias gladius* . . . . Linnaeus

Series: CORYPHAENIFORMES
Family: CORYPHAENIDAE—**Dolphinfishes**
103. **(Common) dolphinfish,** *Coryphaena hippurus* . . . . Linnaeus

Series: STROMATEIFORMES
Family: STROMATEIDAE—**Butterfishes**
104. **(California) butterfish,** *Palometa simillima* . . . . (Ayres)
    (Market name **pompano**)

Series: CARANGIFORMES
Family: CARANGIDAE—**Jacks**
105. **(California) yellowtail,** *Seriola dorsalis* . . . . (Gill)
106. **Mackerel jack,** *Trachurus symmetricus* . . . . (Ayres)
    (Market name **jack mackerel**)

Series: PERCIFORMES—**Perch-like Fishes**
Family: SERRANIDAE—**Basses**
107. **Striped bass,** *Roccus saxatilis* . . . . (Walbaum)
108. **(California) black sea bass,** *Stereolepis gigas* . . . . Ayres
109. **Broomtail grouper,** *Mycteroperca xenarchus* . . . . Jordan
110. **Baya grouper,** *Mycteroperca jordani* . . . . (Jenkins and Evermann)
111. **Kelp bass,** *Paralabrax clathratus* . . . . (Girard)
112. **Sand bass,** *Paralabrax nebulifer* . . . . (Girard)
113. **Spotted bass,** *Paralabrax maculatofasciatus* . . . . (Steindachner)

Family: XENICHTHYIDAE—**Salemas**
114. **(California) salema,** *Xenistius californiensis* . . . . (Steindachner)

Family: HAEMULIDAE—**Grunts**
115. **(California) sargo,** *Anisotremus davidsoni* . . . . (Steindachner)

Family: SCIAENIDAE—**Croakers**
116. **Black croaker,** *Cheilotrema saturnum* . . . . (Girard)
117. **Spotfin croaker,** *Roncador stearnsi* . . . . (Steindachner)

118. **Tommy croaker,** *Genyonemus lineatus* . . . . (Ayres)
119. **Yellowfin croaker,** *Umbrina roncador* . . . . Jordan and Gilbert
120. **(California) corbina,** *Menticirrhus undulatus* . . . . (Girard)
121. **Queenfish,** *Seriphus politus* . . . . Ayres
122. **White seabass,** *Cynoscion nobilis* . . . . (Ayres)

Family: BRANCHIOSTEGIDAE—**Blanquillos**

123. **Ocean-whitefish,** *Caulolatilus princeps* . . . . (Jenyns)

Family: GIRELLIDAE—**Nibblers**

124. **Opaleye,** *Girella nigricans* . . . . (Ayres)

Family: KYPHOSIDAE—**Rudderfishes**

125. **Zebraperch,** *Hermosilla azurea* . . . . Jenkins and Evermann

Family: SCORPIDIDAE—**Halfmoons**

126. **(California) halfmoon,** *Medialuna californiensis* . . . . (Steindachner)

Order: CATAPHRACTI—**Mail-cheeked Fishes**
Family: SCORPAENIDAE—**Scorpionfishes** (Rockfishes)

127. **(California) scorpionfish,** *Scorpaena guttata* . . . . Girard
(Market name **sculpin**)
128. **Bocaccio,** *Sebastodes paucispinis* . . . . (Ayres)
129. **Chilipepper,** *Sebastodes goodei* . . . . Eigenmann and Eigenmann
130. **Blue rockfish,** *Sebastodes mystinus* . . . . Jordan and Gilbert
131. **Bass rockfish,** *Sebastodes serranoides* . . . . Eigenmann and Eigenmann
132. **Yellowtail rockfish,** *Sebastodes flavidus* . . . . Ayres
133. **Black rockfish,** *Sebastodes melanops* . . . . (Girard)
134. **Orange rockfish,** *Sebastodes pinniger* . . . . Gill
135. **Rasher,** *Sebastodes miniatus* . . . . (Jordan and Gilbert)
136. **Kelp rockfish,** *Sebastodes atrovirens* . . . . (Jordan and Gilbert)
137. **Speckled rockfish,** *Sebastodes ovalis* . . . . Ayres
138. **Redstripe rockfish,** *Sebastodes proriger* . . . . (Jordan and Gilbert)
139. **Widow rockfish,** *Sebastodes entomelas* . . . . (Jordan and Gilbert)
140. **Smallmouth rockfish,** *Sebastodes hopkinsi* . . . . Cramer
141. **Longjaw rockfish,** *Sebastodes alutus* . . . . Gilbert
142. **Blackmouth rockfish,** *Sebastodes melanostomus* . . . . Eigenmann and Eigenmann
143. **Halfbanded rockfish,** *Sebastodes semicinctus* . . . . (Gilbert)
144. **Honeycomb rockfish,** *Sebastodes umbrosus* . . . . (Jordan and Gilbert)
145. **Corsair,** *Sebastodes rosaceus* . . . . (Girard)
146. **Flyfish,** *Sebastodes rhodochloris* . . . . (Jordan and Gilbert)
147. **Greenspotted rockfish,** *Sebastodes chlorostictus* . . . . (Jordan and Gilbert)
148. **Pink rockfish,** *Sebastodes eos* . . . . Eigenmann and Eigenmann
149. **Starry rockfish,** *Sebastodes constellatus* . . . . (Jordan and Gilbert)
150. **Tambor,** *Sebastodes ruberrimus* . . . . Cramer
151. **Cow rockfish,** *Sebastodes levis* . . . . (Eigenmann and Eigenmann)
152. **Flag rockfish,** *Sebastodes rubrivinctus* . . . . (Jordan and Gilbert)
153. **Strawberry rockfish,** *Sebastodes elongatus* . . . . (Ayres)
154. **Bolina,** *Sebastodes auriculatus* . . . . (Girard)
155. **Grass rockfish,** *Sebastodes rastrelliger* . . . . (Jordan and Gilbert)
156. **Whitebelly rockfish,** *Sebastodes vexillaris* . . . . (Jordan and Gilbert)
157. **Copper rockfish,** *Sebastodes caurinus* . . . . (Richardson)
158. **Quillback rockfish,** *Sebastodes maliger* . . . . (Jordan and Gilbert)
159. **Calico rockfish,** *Sebastodes dalli* . . . . (Eigenmann and Beeson)
160. **Black-and-tan rockfish,** *Sebastodes chrysomelas* . . . . (Jordan and Gilbert)
161. **Gopher rockfish,** *Sebastodes carnatus* . . . . (Jordan and Gilbert)
162. **China rockfish,** *Sebastodes nebulosus* . . . . (Ayres)
163. **Treefish,** *Sebastodes serriceps* . . . . (Jordan and Gilbert)
164. **Barred rockfish,** *Sebastodes nigrocinctus* . . . . (Ayres)
165. **(Slim) thornhead,** *Sebastolobus alascanus* . . . . Bean

Family: ANOPLOPOMATIDAE—**Sablefishes**

166. **Sablefish,** *Anoplopoma fimbria* . . . . (Pallas)

Family: HEXAGRAMMIDAE—**Greenlings**

167. **Kelp greenling,** *Hexagrammos decagrammus* . . . . (Pallas)
168. **Whitespotted greenling,** *Hexagrammos stelleri* . . . . Tilesius
169. **Rock greenling,** *Hexagrammos superciliosus* . . . . (Pallas)

Glossary of Terms

Abdominal ridge: The ridge extending from the throat to the forepart of the abdomen, as in FLATFISHES.

Adipose fin: A fleshy fin without rays situated between the dorsal and caudal fins, as in the SALMON, TROUT, and SMELTS.

Air bladder: An air-filled sac situated at top of and running almost the full length of the intestinal cavity, giving buoyance to the fish.

Anadromous: Ascending rivers to spawn.

Anal fin: The fin situated between anus and caudal fin.

Anus: The opening at the end of the digestive tract, sometimes referred to as the vent.

Barbel: A fleshy appendage projecting down from lower jaw, as in the CODS and CROAKERS.

Blind side: The light-colored underside of the FLATFISHES.

Caudal fin: The tail fin.

Caudal peduncle: The posterior end of the body, extending from the anal fin to the base of the tail fin.

Cirrus (plural Cirri): A fleshy or limp skin flap projecting upward or outward from the head and body, as in the SCULPINS, BLENNIES, and LINGCOD.

Claspers: Paired extensions from the pelvic fins, sex organs of the male SHARKS and SKATES.

Compressed: Flattened from side to side.

Contiguous: Close together; adjoining.

Corselet: A patch of scales just back of and above the pectoral fin occuring in members of the MACKEREL group.

Crustaceans: A branch of annulose animals having a rigid crusty covering of the body instead of skin or hard shells, in which crabs, shrimps, crawfish, lobsters, sand crabs, sand fleas, are included.

Depth: The greatest vertical distance through the body, not including the fins.

Dextral: Right-sided, denoting eyes are on the right, not left side, as in some of the FLATFISHES.

Disk: The flat, somewhat circular shape of the forepart of SKATES and RAYS—formed by the spreading pectoral and pelvic fins.

Dorsal: the back.

Dorsal fin: The fin situated on top of the back in most fishes, or on the outer margin of the dorsal surface, as in the FLATFISHES.

Eye side: Opposite to blind side—the rounded, colored side on which both eyes are situated, as in the FLATFISHES.

Eye spots: Circular color designs near the base of the pectoral fins of the SKATES, not associated with eyes or spiracles.

Finlets: Series of small fins following the dorsal and anal fins.

Furcate: Curved inwardly. Somewhat forked but not enough to form a notch.

Genus (plural Genera): A group of species with resembling characters, very closely related yet not fertile between separate species. The genus is classified as ranking next above the species and next below the family, which is a group of genera.

Gill arch: The bony structure to which the gill filament and gill rakers are attached.

Gill cover: Opercle. The door which opens to allow water and gasses to pass out between gills, after the necessary oxygen has been trapped by the gills.

Gill rakers: Protuberances attached to the gill arch opposite gill filaments.

Gill slits: Openings serving SHARKS, SKATES, etc., as doors in place of gill covers.

Herbiverous: Vegetarian, subsisting on vegetable matter.

Incised: Angular, as if cut, as in membrane between spines.

Isthmus: The narrow triangular portion of the body beneath the head and between the gill chambers.

Keel: A ridge projecting out from sides of caudal peduncle.

Larva: An immature form, frequently different in appearance from the adult.

Lateral line: A sensory organ composed of a canal which connects with a series of openings or pores along the sides of the body, sometimes with branches on head and back.

Lobe: Points of the forked caudal fin.

Lobule: Additional point or flap projecting from the lobe.

Lunate: Between crescent and halfmoon in shape. Used in describing the caudal or tail fin.

Mandible: The bone forming the lower jaw.

Maxillary: The bone forming the upper jaw.

Mollusks: Invertebrate animals with soft bodies, usually covered with one or two hard shells, as in the squid, octopus, (soft) clams, mussels, abalone, etc.

Notched: Indented.

Opercle: Gill cover.

Oviparous: Producing eggs which are developed after exclusion from body.

Pectoral fins: The paired fins attached to the pectoral girdle (bony structure), usually situated just back of the gill openings.

Peduncle: See caudal peduncle.

Pelagic: Living in open waters.

Pelvic fins: The paired fins attached to the pelvic girdle (a structure of bone or cartilage) usually situated in underside of forepart of body.

Photophores: A specialized organ on the body and head capable of producing light.

Placoid scales: Bony plate-like scales.

Plankton: Minute marine plants and animals.

Predatory: Living by preying on others.

Preopercle: Cheek—bony structure situated in advance of the opercle or gill cover.

Pyloric caeca: Internal organ composed of a number of sacs, attached to the intestine.

Rays: Flexible or cartilaginous supports of the fins; can be seen when fin is backlighted.

Reticulations: Markings in the form of a network of lines.

Serrated: Saw-tooth notches.

Shagreen: The rough, hard-scaled skin of some sharks. (Often used for polishing.)

Sinistral: Left side, i.e., eyes on left side of the head.

Snout: The area between point of upper jaw to the eyes.

Species: A scientific grouping into a single category of individuals of the animal or vegetable kingdom which bear close anatomical resemblances and which are fertile with each other.

Specific: Unbreakable rule—exact.

Spinous: Composed of spines.

Spiracle: The opening behind the eye through which water passes to be expelled through the gills, as in the SHARKS and RAYS.

Striae: Small ridges or lines, as on the opercle of the SARDINE, and EULACHON.

Symmetrical: Forming a balanced pattern.

Tubercle: A small rounded lump; a modified scale, hard or soft.

Ventral: The lower surface of the body and head; belly side.

Viviparous: Producing young alive.

Vomer: The bony structure in roof of mouth, sometimes bearing teeth.

Index of Common Names

Index of Scientific Names